MW00800257

AMERICAN MEMORIES

AMERICAN MEMORIES

ATROCITIES AND THE LAW

JOACHIM J. SAVELSBERG AND RYAN D. KING

A Volume in the American Sociological Association's
Rose Series in Sociology

Russell Sage Foundation • New York

Library of Congress Cataloging-in-Publication Data

Savelsberg, Joachim J., 1951–
American memories : atrocities and the law / by Joachim J. Savelsberg and Ryan D. King.
  p. cm. — (Rose series in sociology)
Includes bibliographical references and index.
ISBN 978-0-87154-736-1 (hardcover : alk. paper)—ISBN 978-1-61044-749-2 (ebook) 1. Collective memory—United States. 2. Atrocities—United States. 3. War crimes—United States. I. King, Ryan D. II. Title.
HM1027.U6S38 2011
909—dc23
                                                          2011022368

Copyright © 2011 by the American Sociological Assocation. All rights reserved. Printed in the United States of America. No part of this publication may be reproduced, stored in a retrieval system, or transmitted in any form or by any means, electronic, mechanical, photocopying, recording, or otherwise, without the prior written permission of the publisher.

Reproduction by the United States Government in whole or in part is permitted for any purpose.

The paper used in this publication meets the minimum requirements of American National Standard for Information Sciences—Permanence of Paper for Printed Library Materials. ANSI Z39.48-1992.

Text design by Suzanne Nichols.

RUSSELL SAGE FOUNDATION
112 East 64th Street, New York, New York 10065
10 9 8 7 6 5 4 3 2 1

The Russell Sage Foundation

The Russell Sage Foundation, one of the oldest of America's general purpose foundations, was established in 1907 by Mrs. Margaret Olivia Sage for "the improvement of social and living conditions in the United States." The Foundation seeks to fulfill this mandate by fostering the development and dissemination of knowledge about the country's political, social, and economic problems. While the Foundation endeavors to assure the accuracy and objectivity of each book it publishes, the conclusions and interpretations in Russell Sage Foundation publications are those of the authors and not of the Foundation, its Trustees, or its staff. Publication by Russell Sage, therefore, does not imply Foundation endorsement.

BOARD OF TRUSTEES
Mary C. Waters, Chair

Kenneth D. Brody	Kathleen Hall Jamieson	Shelley E. Taylor
W. Bowman Cutter III	Lawrence F. Katz	Richard H. Thaler
Robert E. Denham, Esq.	Sara S. McLanahan	Eric Wanner
John A. Ferejohn	Nancy L. Rosenblum	
Larry V. Hedges	Claude M. Steele	

EDITORS OF THE ROSE SERIES IN SOCIOLOGY

Diane Barthel-Bouchier	Daniel Levy	Michael Schwartz
Cynthia J. Bogard	Timothy P. Moran	Gilda Zwerman
Michael Kimmel	Naomi Rosenthal	

THE ROSE SERIES IN SOCIOLOGY EDITORIAL BOARD

Margaret Abraham	Kathleen Gerson	Mary Clare Lennon
Javier Auyero	Naomi Gerstel	Kelly Moore
David Brady	Jack A. Goldstone	Pamela E. Oliver
Lisa D. Brush	Jeremy Hein	Patricia A. Roos
Lynn Sharon Chancer	Michael Hout	Beth E. Schneider
Mary Ann Clawson	David Jacobson	Gay W. Seidman
Yinon Cohen	Jeffrey D. Kentor	Hwa-Ji Shin
Cynthia Fuchs Epstein	Rebecca E. Klatch	Verta A. Taylor
Kathryn Feltey	Laura Kramer	Amy Elizabeth
Abby L. Ferber	Rachel V. Kutz-Flamenbaum	Traver
Joshua Gamson	Richard Lachmann	Reeve Vanneman
Judith Gerson	David E. Lavin	Richard Williams

Previous Volumes in the Series

Forthcoming Titles

Exceptional Children, Challenged Families:
Raising Children with Disabilities
Dennis Hogan

Family Relationships Across the Generations
Judith A. Seltzer and Suzanne M. Bianchi

Global Order and the Historical Structures of Daral-Islam
Mohammed A. Bamyeh

The Logic of Terrorism: A Comparative Study
Jeff Goodwin

The Long Shadow: Family Background, Disadvantaged Urban Youth,
and the Transition to Adulthood
Karl Alexander, Doris Entwisle, and Linda Olson

Nurturing Dads: Fatherhood Initiatives Beyond the Wallet
William Marsiglio and Kevin Roy

Repressive Injustice: Political and Social Processes
in the Massive Incarceration of African Americans
Pamela E. Oliver and James E. Yocum

Social Movements in the World System: The Politics of Crisis
and Transformation
Dawn Wiest and Jackie Smith

"They Say Cut Back; We Say Fight Back!" Welfare Activism
in an Era of Retrenchment
Ellen Reese

The Rose Series in Sociology

THE AMERICAN Sociological Association's Rose Series in Sociology publishes books that integrate knowledge and address controversies from a sociological perspective. Books in the Rose Series are at the forefront of sociological knowledge. They are lively and often involve timely and fundamental issues on significant social concerns. The series is intended for broad dissemination throughout sociology, across social science and other professional communities, and to policy audiences. The series was established in 1967 by a bequest to ASA from Arnold and Caroline Rose to support innovations in scholarly publishing.

DIANE BARTHEL-BOUCHIER
CYNTHIA J. BOGARD
MICHAEL KIMMEL
DANIEL LEVY
TIMOTHY P. MORAN
NAOMI ROSENTHAL
MICHAEL SCHWARTZ
GILDA ZWERMAN

EDITORS

For Jana (from RDK) and Pamela (from JJS)

"We must establish incredible events by credible evidence."
Justice Robert Jackson, U.S. Chief Prosecutor at the International
Military Tribunal at Nuremberg,
on June 7, 1945

"Collective frameworks are . . . precisely the instruments used by the collective memory to reconstruct an image of the past which is in accord, in each epoch, with the predominant thoughts of the society."
Maurice Halbwachs
in *On Collective Memory*

"Judges . . . enclose their thought within forms that . . . bear the imprint of a remote period. This indicates how deeply legal thought is pervaded by history."
Maurice Halbwachs
in *On Collective Memory*

"Beliefs express . . . life in terms of representations; rites organize it and regulate its functioning."
Emile Durkheim
in *The Elementary Forms of Religious Life*

Contents

About the Authors

Joachim J. Savelsberg is professor of sociology at the University of Minnesota.

Ryan D. King is associate professor of sociology at the University at Albany, State University of New York.

Yu-Ju Chien is Ph.D. candidate in sociology at the University of Minnesota and received her master's degree in sociology from National Taiwan University.

Courtney Faue received her bachelor's degrees in sociology and psychology from the University of Minnesota and recently graduated from the John W. Draper Interdisciplinary Master's Program in Humanities and Social Thought at New York University.

Jeremy Minyard is instructor at Saint Paul College and holds a J.D. from Vanderbilt University and a master's degree in sociology from the University of Minnesota.

Lacy Mitchell is graduate student in sociology at the University at Albany, State University of New York, and earned her bachelor's degree in sociology from the University of Houston–Downtown.

Rajiv Evan Rajan is pursuing graduate work in sociology and received his bachelor's degree in sociology from the University of Minnesota.

═══ Acknowledgments ═══

W E ACKNOWLEDGE the contributions of several institutions that funded and hosted us and of many individuals, including collaborating students and colleagues who engaged us in critical exchanges.

First, work toward this book was supported by several institutions at the University of Minnesota. Joachim Savelsberg received the 2006 David Cooperman Summer Institute grant from the Department of Sociology, a fall 2007 fellowship at the Institute for Advanced Study, and a fall 2008 single-semester leave provided by the College of Liberal Arts. Ryan King acknowledges support through the Graduate Research Partnership Program, College of Liberal Arts, University of Minnesota (with Savelsberg), and a University of Minnesota Doctoral Dissertation Research Grant. Further support was provided by another Graduate Research Partnership Program grant (Jeremy Minyard with Savelsberg) and the Undergraduate Research Opportunity Program (Rajiv Evan Rajan with Savelsberg). Some of the final revision was helped by Savelsberg's 2010 to 2011 Visiting Research Professorship at Humboldt University in Berlin, where Hans Bertram and Klaus Eder offered generous hospitality and Astrid Schaal perfect secretarial help. Finally, the American Sociological Association, through its Rose Monograph Series, provided resources for the unusually thorough process of critical discussion and review that inspired us.

Second, we are most grateful to several current and former students at the University of Minnesota and the University at Albany, State University of New York, who contributed to the work on three of the chapters over the past decade. Rajiv Evan Rajan and Lacy Mitchell worked diligently and with great determination on the My Lai and *New York Times* analyses (chapter 3). Jeremy Minyard did valuable data collection on the Haditha killings and contributed substantially to the writing of chapter 4. Courtney Faue industriously and with great dedication collected data on the Milosevic case (chapter 5), and Yu-Ju Chien skillfully contributed data work for that chapter. We acknowledge all of these young scholars as co-authors of the respective chapters. Our work on collecting history textbooks was helped by Benjamin Jacobs, College of Education and Human Development at the University of Minnesota; Nancy Heather and Laurel Haycock from Wilson Library at the University of Minnesota; and Peter Bae at the University at Albany, who provided access to the lion's share of books. Colin Gruner and Chris Rees at the University at Albany provided excellent research assistance; Tianyue Ma, also at Albany, contributed careful editorial assistance; and Karl Krohn at the University of Minnesota gave welcome computer advice. Prosecutors in Minnesota, Wisconsin, and the German state of Lower Saxony generously agreed to be interviewed, and Christian Pfeiffer, then justice minister of Lower Saxony, Stefan Suhling, and the *Kriminologisches Forschungsinstitut Niedersachsen* supported work on chapter 8. We are grateful to all.

Third, we jointly presented themes from this book at the 2003 and 2010 annual meetings of the American Sociological Association. Savelsberg presented other parts at the Law and Society Program of New York University; the Center for the Study of Violence of the University of Sao Paulo (Brazil); Northwestern and Yale Universities' sociology departments; Humboldt and Free Universities in Berlin; and the Universities of Washington and Erlangen-Nuremberg and at meetings of the American Sociological Association (2007), the American Society of Criminology (2007), the Law and Society Association (2006), and the Social Science History Association (2007). On these and other occasions we received valuable feedback from many, including Martin Abraham, Julia Adams, Jeff Alexander, Ron Aminzade, Hans Bertram, Liz Boyle, Wendy Espeland, Ron Eyerman, Pamela Feldman-Savelsberg, Gary Fine, David Garland, Jürgen Gerhards, Philip Gorski, David Greenberg, John Hagan, Terence Halliday, Kathy Hull, Valerie Jenness, Monika Jungbauer-Gans, Stephen Kalberg, Ross Matsueda, Karl-Ulrich Mayer, Jens Meierhenrich, Sally Merry, Elizabeth Mertz, Phyllis Moen, Thomas Scheffer, Barry Schwartz, Philip Smith, Chris Uggen, and Robin Wagner-Pacifici.

Fourth, we jointly presented the first draft of the book manuscript at the Russell Sage Foundation on December 11, 2009. We received precious feedback from guests who had undertaken the labor of reading the entire first draft, or significant parts of it, including Dana Adams, Lynn Chancer, Elizabeth Cole, Jo Dixon, Wolf Heydebrand, Guillermina Jasso, Philip Smith, and Robin Wagner-Pacifici, and from members of the board of the Rose Monograph Series and its supporting staff, specifically Diana Baldermann, Diane Barthel-Bouchier, Cynthia Bogard, Louis Edgar Esparza, Michael Kimmel, Daniel Levy, Timothy Moran, Naomi Rosenthal, Michael Schwartz, and Gilda Zwerman. Coming out of this meeting, we were both impressed with the generosity of our critics and healthily shaken. Crucial critique and advice on the next-to-final draft of September 2010 came from two anonymous reviewers for the Russell Sage Foundation, who read and commented in great detail on the entire manuscript. We benefited greatly from comments and support that Suzanne Nichols at the Russell Sage Foundation straightforwardly provided throughout the process. April Rondeau, production editor, and Katherine Kimball, copy editor, paid careful attention to details, and their exertions improved our manuscript. Notably, this book project might not have been realized without Daniel Levy's initiative.

We thank all institutions and individuals for their contributions. Only we, of course, are responsible for any errors and flaws. Parts of chapters 6 and 8 are revised versions of an article that was previously published in volume 111 (2005) of the *American Journal of Sociology*. We were honored when this article was awarded the 2006 Best Article Award of the Law and Society Association and the 2007 Best Article Award of the Section on Culture of the American Sociological Association. We thank the publisher for permission to reprint this segment, albeit with revisions. We finally, and especially, thank our respective spouses, Jana Hrdinová and Pamela Feldman-Savelsberg. The encounters of the different social worlds that created us and that meet in our marriages—nation-states, religions, and ethnicities—never allow our minds to stray too far from issues of collective memory. This book is dedicated to Jana and Pamela.

Introduction

How Maurice Halbwachs Died—and How We Remember Him

E NTERING one of the exhibition halls of the memorial site of the former German Buchenwald concentration camp, just outside the
picturesque town of Weimar with its history of humanist thought,
visitors encounter a small exhibit commemorating Maurice Halbwachs,
the late French sociologist and student of Emile Durkheim. It is at this
site where, as inmate 17,161, Halbwachs suffered pain and humiliation
and finally, in mid-March of 1945, shortly before the liberation of the
camp and the end of World War II, death. In 1944 he had dared to demand
information and justice from the authorities after the brutal murder of
his Jewish in-laws either by the Gestapo or by henchmen of the collaborative Vichy regime of his native France. His suffering and death, like
that of millions of others in the Nazi concentration and extermination
camps, was most certainly real.

Yet our memory of this suffering is constructed. We learn about it
through the Buchenwald display, a dedication in René König's renowned
Handbuch der empirischen Sozialforschung (König 1967), or in Lewis Coser's
introductory chapter to Halbwachs's texts on collective memory. Coser, a
former president of the American Sociological Association, was himself a
refugee from Nazi Germany and a victim of Vichy France's internment
camps (Coser 1992, 6–7). Narratives and memorials provided by later and
present-day actors, including scholars and government agencies, are
based on such accounts, and we will never know what shape the stories
might have taken under Halbwachs's own authorship. It is through the
former that Halbwachs emerges as a ghostly, haunting figure in today's
world—a theme to which we return in chapter 4. We engage Maurice
Halbwachs's scholarship on collective memory in greater detail in chapters 1 and 2.

The Nazi atrocities that victimized Maurice Halbwachs were also
processed in courts of law, most famously in the International Military

Tribunal at Nuremberg, and these legal proceedings played a crucial role in documenting and memorializing the horrors of the Nazi past. Justice Robert Jackson, the American chief prosecutor at the tribunal, had hoped that they would do so, and he expressed his hope with often cited words: "Unless we write the record of this movement with clarity and precision, we cannot blame the future if in days of peace it finds incredible the accusatory generalities uttered during the war. *We must establish incredible events by credible evidence*" (quoted in Landsman 2005, 6–7; our emphasis).

Justice Jackson was not alone in this hope, of course. President Franklin Delano Roosevelt clearly thought along similar lines. As his confidant, Judge Samuel Rosenman, noted, Roosevelt "was determined that the question of Hitler's guilt—and the guilt of his gangsters—must not be left open to future debate. The whole nauseating matter should be spread out on a permanent record under oath by witnesses and with all the written documents" (quoted in Landsman 2005, 6). Roosevelt had come to believe that revisionist interpretations of World War I, which challenged the doctrine of Germany's primary guilt, had contributed to isolationist tendencies in the United States that Roosevelt despised. His interest in documenting the Nazi regime's aggression and atrocities through court proceedings, and thus preserving them for posterity, was thus not just an effort to seek accountability and to write history but also a political strategy that was shared by his World War II allies.[1]

Today, Jackson's and Roosevelt's convictions, at least overlapping with Emile Durkheim's classical sociological ideas about the effects of legal proceedings, find renewed relevance in light of recent atrocities such as those in Rwanda, East Timor, Sudan's South and its Darfur region, the former Yugoslavia, and Iraq and also following the end of dictatorial or autocratic regimes in East Central Europe, Asia, Africa, and Latin America. Simultaneously, and unavoidably after the rewriting of history in the post–civil rights movement era, attention has also been directed inward: How do Americans remember atrocities, not just those committed by foreign powers but also those perpetrated in the course of American history? What role did foreign and domestic trials play in establishing such memories? What are the consequences for today's responses to grave human rights violations at home and abroad?

We wrote this book as the twentieth century had recently drawn to a close. The period's political history is in many respects Janus faced. The century witnessed multiple genocides, brutal dictators, and countless mass atrocities. The occurrence of mass killings and abuses of uncounted human beings, unfortunately, does not distinguish the last century from many previous ones—even if the context of modern states caused a qualitative change. However, as the Harvard legal scholar Martha Minow

(1998) keenly notes, a truly exceptional facet of the twentieth century has been the invention of legal institutions to seek some form of accountability, redress, or perhaps even reconciliation in the wake of collective violence and atrocity.

During the past century democracy expanded across much of the globe, and a new vocabulary emerged around the idea of human rights. Some have even diagnosed the late twentieth and early twenty-first centuries as a "justice cascade" (Sikkink 2011). For instance, World War II and the Holocaust were followed by the Nuremberg tribunals and eventually by reparations—albeit never adequate—for some victims; the atrocities in the former Yugoslavia led to the International Criminal Tribunal for the former Yugoslavia (the ICTY); an International Criminal Tribunal was established after the Rwandan genocide; and the end of apartheid in South Africa gave way to a novel Truth and Reconciliation Commission. The decades preceding World War II witnessed the emergence of humanitarian law, codified in the Hague and Geneva Conventions. These cases, of course, represent but a sampling of injustices and legal responses in their aftermath. But they provide inspiration and material for our thoughts.

Maurice Halbwachs's suffering and that of the tens of millions of other victims of atrocities, law's contribution to the collective memory of such suffering, and the consequences of collective memories for the control of future hate-inspired violence are the subjects of this book. Halbwachs's ideas on collective memory, richly developed in a growing body of scholarship, guide us in the project. Our empirical examples focus primarily on American memories of atrocities committed by Americans and by others; on ways law contributed to these memories; and on paths along which memories, in turn, inspired later lawmaking and enforcement aimed at the establishment of a more peaceful world.

The first two chapters of this book establish some basic principles, lessons provided by many decades of inspiring scholarship. Insights concern the nature of collective memory, the role law plays in establishing such memory, and the effects of collective memory on later stages of conflict, especially as they entail the making and enforcement of new laws. They also address the role of emergent global scripts and norms regarding human rights and, simultaneously, the role social actors play in generating and enacting such scripts. Chapter 1 especially links these discussions with ideas developed by Martha Minow about cycles of violence and the Minnesota political scientist Kathryn Sikkink on the justice cascade.[2] These ideas motivate our scholarly and practical interest in ways in which cycles of violence, accelerated too often in human history, can be slowed or even brought to a halt. While our empirical analysis will have to stop at the moment at which control mechanisms are enacted and implemented, our theorizing reaches toward the potential consequences of such control mechanisms.

The subsequent three chapters offer a set of case studies that shed empirical light on the question of how legal interventions color our memories of evil. Throughout these chapters we ask whether Jackson's and Roosevelt's trust in the history-writing power of law is indeed justified. Or do the limitations and the particular logic of legal proceedings distort history in ways that fail to teach us the desired lessons?

Specifically, chapter 3 considers the infamous My Lai massacre committed by American soldiers during the Vietnam War. This atrocity was narrated early on by three independent sources: an Army commission, a famous journalistic account, and also—and especially important here—criminal court proceedings. A comparison of these early accounts is followed by an empirical exploration. We ask whether and how these partially competing narratives are reflected in American history textbooks and in media reporting throughout subsequent decades. How, for instance, do our history lessons teach us to remember My Lai, if at all? What do journalists have to add? What role do political interests of later days play in the memorization of My Lai? Is the presumed ritual force of law confirmed? And what might the patterns we identify say about American culture more broadly? Our findings provoke questions regarding the consequences of a resurgence in American pride in the military and American soldiers' attitudes regarding torture and war crimes.

Chapter 4 builds on arguments regarding the path dependency of collective memory. It thus asks how previous commemorations color later memories. It also examines the use of "bridging metaphors" that link My Lai to later events. Here we focus on one empirical case, the killing of many civilians in the town of Haditha during the Iraq War by U.S. military. How do different news media compare My Lai and Haditha; that is to say, how do they build bridges that connect them? Do they stress their likeness (mimetic bridging) or similarities of context (contextual bridging)? Do they use consequences of My Lai to predict the impact of the Haditha killings (prognostic bridging)? Or do they highlight differences between the old and the new (bridging challenges)? Using websites of pro-soldier movements we also ask how the legal process channels emotional energy against the killers. Did law intensify emotions, or did it restrain them by undermining critical coverage? We finally introduce the concept of "haunting" and explore the role of trials in promoting or putting an end to haunting.

Chapter 5 takes us outside the United States, into the former Yugoslavia. Here, too, we seek to understand how legal narratives interact with competing accounts to reach a broader public through mediators such as news reports. At the center of this story is the late Slobodan

Milosevic, the former Serbian and Yugoslav president and defendant before the ICTY until his March 2006 death in custody shortly before the court could reach a verdict. Again, we analyze American media reports, beginning shortly before the outbreak of the Balkan wars until several years beyond its ending (from 1989 to 2006). We ask how journalists report about Milosevic at different stages of war and how their reporting is affected by legal proceedings. How did the ritual potency of trials work out in this case? Again, are Jackson's old hopes that trials may document incredible events through credible evidence confirmed? Or does law distort the story of Milosevic and the Balkans? How do its narratives interact with accounts from other fields such as foreign policy and diplomacy?

In chapter 6 we ask what image emerges when many processes of memory formation, like those we studied for My Lai, Haditha, and the Balkans, aggregate to form the structure of American memories of atrocities. What is the impact on the composite picture of domestic legal responses in which only low-level perpetrators are found guilty, combined with cases that did not evoke any legal response and with foreign cases in which high-ranked leaders of state crime are prosecuted? How do American memories differ from those of a country like Germany, in which atrocities, albeit of a most different—in fact, unique—quality, were processed in criminal trials, including trials against high-level perpetrators?

Having used such case studies to shed light on the question of how legal proceedings affect the representations and memories of past atrocities, we then set out to ask, Why care? Why do such memories matter anyway? In chapter 7 we provide a preliminary answer. We draw on a range of the extant literature to show that collective memories have considerable consequences. Collective memories motivate social actors to take a stand in the face of grave atrocities, they inspire social movements, and—crucial for our purposes—they may mobilize the use of law as a weapon against hate and violence. Carrier groups, the use of bridging metaphors, and historical consciousness play important roles. Chapter 7 then progresses to two examinations of the effect of collective memory on law, specifically hate crime law, and its enforcement in cross-national and, within the United States, cross-jurisdictional comparisons.

Chapter 8 explores how American and German differences in memory translate into distinct laws on the books and law in action. We use hate crime law as an example, a type of law that seeks to forestall hate-inspired violence. How do differences in collective memory act in combination with particularities of the institutional context in which carrier groups form and operate, of state organization, and of differential exposure to international scripts?

While such comparison yields important insights, countries are clearly not monolithic. We thus take the core ideas from chapters 6 through 8 and, in chapter 9, apply them to a singular case in the United States. Is variation in the memory of atrocities and injustice within the United States associated with legal responses to hate-inspired crime? Here a much larger number of units allows for a statistical test of our theoretical expectations. The reader will learn what differences we found in the distribution of collective memory markers across the country, especially Holocaust memorials and streets named after Martin Luther King Jr. Such patterns open the door to several questions to which we were able to find at least preliminary answers: Do law enforcement agencies implement hate crime policies more vigorously where past episodes of bigotry and hatred are commemorated? What is the effect on practices such as police compliance with federal hate crime law and the creation of formal departments on hate crime enforcement? Do we find differences between the effect of the commemoration of foreign atrocities and that of domestic injustice? Chapter 9 provides answers to these questions.

Finally, a concluding chapter 10 links our empirical findings with those of previous research on related themes. This discussion yields comparative insights, reaching far beyond the case of American collective memories and law. It indeed tells us that we must take into account the reciprocal relationship between law and collective memory of hate and atrocities when we seek to interrupt cycles of violence. With regard to American history, it speaks to the problematic effects of focusing on low-level actors alone in cases of perpetration committed by the government and the military of the United States.

= Chapter 1 =

From Law to Collective Memory: Breaking Cycles of Violence?

THIS BOOK deals with American memories of atrocities, the role law plays in their construction, and the way law itself is affected by them. We begin, however, with two stories that help situate our work and show its contemporary relevance. The first story takes us back to Europe more than two centuries ago. It illustrates some central ideas on how law, and the collective memory to which it contributes, affects cycles of violence. This reference is temporally and geographically distant, but as the great playwright Bertolt Brecht understood, insight is sometimes more easily gained from a distance. The second story involves a contemporary American debate among scholars and the public alike on the relative costs and benefits of transitional justice. This debate illustrates that our concerns should indeed be shared by all who have an interest in ending cycles of violence. It also shows that our central questions, while speaking to academic themes, are simultaneously of the highest relevance for policymaking. Interwoven with these two accounts is a brief exploration of the central theses we explore in this book, followed by a short methodological excursus.

A European Story of Law, Memory, and Cycles of Violence

In 1806 Napoleon Bonaparte and his army invaded and easily defeated Prussia. The French Army subsequently attacked Russia and marched on all the way to Moscow. The outcome is well known: Napoleon and his troops were eventually defeated by the Russian military, which used innovative strategies, partly reminiscent of guerilla warfare. It drove back the Napoleonic aggression in a devastating campaign. Much of this is masterfully portrayed in Leo Tolstoy's classic *War and Peace*. Prussia recovered slowly and initiated reforms, inspired by H. F. Karl vom Stein and

1

Karl August von Hardenberg, meant to strengthen the kingdom and prevent future conquest. In fact, the 1813 battle of Leipzig brought the final victory over the French armies. Yet memories of the French occupation never faded, and indeed they had consequences.[1] By the 1860s Prussia had gained substantial strength, and fifty-eight years after Napoleon's final expulsion from its land, Prussian leaders revived memories of French aggression and declared war on France. Victory in the Franco-Prussian War of 1871 culminated in the crowning of the Prussian king as German emperor in the magnificent chateau of Versailles just outside of Paris, a moment of great humiliation for the French nation.

The next period of peace lasted even fewer decades than the previous one: The year 1914, forty-four years after the Franco-Prussian War, witnessed the outbreak of World War I. The gruesome trench warfare along the French-German border is remembered as among the fiercest, deadliest, and most futile fights in the modern history of war. This outcome, too, is well known: after intervention by the American military, the Axis powers, including the German Empire, were defeated. The Kaiser fled Germany, and the empire was replaced by the Weimar Republic. The end of the war was sealed in a demeaning signing of the Versailles peace treaty by the German delegation. Its members had to pass through a phalanx of horribly wounded and disfigured French soldiers to reach the railroad car in which the ceremony took place. Not accidentally, the location was in the immediate vicinity of the Versailles palace, where the crowning of the German Emperor a good four decades earlier had deeply humiliated the French nation. In addition, the Versailles Treaty obliged the German nation to massive reparation payments, the burden of which caused great pain throughout German society.

We know that the Weimar Republic was to last only fourteen years. In 1933 the Nazis took over the country and changed its political system into a fascist dictatorship. When Nazi Germany unleashed World War II with its invasion of Poland in September of 1939, the renewed warfare against France was just a short one year away. This time, as in 1871, France was thoroughly defeated, and major parts of it were occupied. On June 21, 1940, the French were forced to surrender to Adolf Hitler in the same railroad car in which the German generals had signed the Versailles Treaty just twenty-two years earlier. German engineers, in fact, demolished the walls of the museum in which the car was kept so it could be moved to the exact location where the previous surrender had occurred.[2] Thus are the ways in which states work with symbols that store collective memories to humiliate, to recover, and even to rewrite history.

We all know the outcome of this cruel chapter of history, which included the Holocaust and the loss of 40 million lives in the course of World War II. We also know that the war ended, like World War I, with the defeat of the Axis powers. Only this time the reaction of the victors differed. As opposed to penalizing the entire nation with massive economic sanctions, the victors chose individuals to face criminal trials.[3] The surviving leaders of the Nazi regime and of the German military were brought before a court of law, the International Military Tribunal in Nuremberg. Many of their helpers from the worlds of law, medicine, and elsewhere were tried in the subsequent Nuremberg trials. In addition, at least some of those responsible for the mass carnage as members of execution squads and staff of extermination camps were tried by German courts in the late 1950s and 1960s. Even at the time of this writing, John Demjanjuk is standing trial in Munich, accused of brutal treatment and killing in the camps. In Jerusalem, Adolf Eichmann, one of the chief organizers of the Holocaust, was tried, sentenced, and executed in 1961. Paralleling such penal action against individuals immediately after the war, massive aid was delivered through the Marshall Plan to help the German economy recover. A new constitution was created, superior to its Weimar predecessor as it promised a more stable democracy. First steps toward the building of the European Union were undertaken shortly after the end of the war.

Yet the horrors of the war remained ingrained in German collective memory, retold again and again in stories, literature, art, films, commemorative speeches, and scholarship. Concurrently, the images produced by trials against perpetrators of the Holocaust and initiators of aggressive warfare began to settle in the public mind, albeit with delay. Since the end of World War II, sixty-six years of peaceful coexistence between France and Germany have become accepted as the rule rather than the exception. A long cycle of violence had been brought to an end. To be sure, many factors helped establish the current, comparatively enduring era of stability, prosperity, and peaceful coexistence. Yet it is entirely plausible that the collective memories produced by the post–World War II trials were a contributing factor. As Gary Bass notes in his acclaimed work on war crimes tribunals, "The rehabilitation of Germany after World War II is one of the great political successes of the century, turning a fascist enemy into a democratic ally; *Nuremberg gains prestige as part of that terrific success* [our emphasis]."[4]

Elsewhere, too, criminal trials against perpetrators of mass atrocities have engraved the images of horror in collective memories, impeding denial.[5] Consider Argentina and the trials against the generals of the so-called Dirty War of 1976 to 1983, Chile and its trial against General Augusto Pinochet, Iraq and the trial of Saddam Hussein and his coterie. In some of these places, truth commissions supplemented trials or set the stage for them, as in Argentina.[6] In yet other countries truth commissions were conducted instead of trials, as in South Africa after apartheid.

In each of these cases, however, judicial or quasi-judicial institutions likely played central roles in the formation of collective memories of past atrocities and in reducing the likelihood of them being repeated.

Yet the precise causal role that trials play in the construction of collective memory, not to mention their purported role in ending cycles of violence, remains conjecture more than undisputed conclusion. Indeed, the examples cited here are only suggestive. We can easily think of occasions in which collective memory of past atrocities, especially those committed by previous and new enemies, inflamed emotions and contributed to future violence. The recent history of the conflict in the Balkans provides but one example. In yet other cases, histories of atrocities were successfully glossed over, even after trials. These cases appear to be more common in situations of regime continuity, which typically are associated with the pursuit of low-level actors by the law while the leaders are left untouched. Consider, for instance, the United States. Prosecuting only low-level actors in response to atrocities has often created a public perception that frontline agents were selected as scapegoats, as our chapters on My Lai (Vietnam) and Haditha (Iraq) show. This perception has cast legitimatory doubt over those trials. Simultaneously, higher ranks and entire organizations that might have borne responsibility remained untouched by American trials, and their reputations and the memories of their deeds untainted. This may be one explanation for the fact that—according to the International Social Survey Programme—Americans' pride in the military, always high, is today far more pronounced than that in any other institution in the United States. It is also higher than the pride any other nation invests in its military.[7]

In short, the effect of trials, and the memories they create, on cycles of violence warrants thorough investigation. We engage in such investigation here for a selection of cases involving the United States, although the ideas put forth in this book are of much broader historical and global relevance.

Debating Transitional Justice and the Underexplored Role of Collective Memories

The function of law in slowing or ending violence, especially enduring cycles of violence, has been hotly debated in recent scholarly and public exchanges.[8] One remarkable debate concerns the role of criminal justice intervention, especially but not exclusively at the international level, against perpetrators of massive human rights violations, war crimes, crimes against humanity, and genocide. Opponents of such intervention argue that the threat of sanctions by criminal courts may extend periods of atrocities. From this perspective, dictators and warlords are reluctant to support transitions to democracy or sign peace agreements when the threat of sanctions is looming in the background. Why hand the hangman the rope? Proponents of this critical position include scholars such as the Harvard law professor Jack Goldsmith, previously on the staff of the Justice Department during the George W. Bush administration.[9] Such writers often rely on case studies, impressively at times, to make their point. They argue, for example, that some of the worst atrocities of the Balkan wars occurred after the International Criminal Tribunal for the former Yugoslavia (ICTY) had been instituted. Their assertions are often supported by conservative media. Consider reactions by the *Wall Street Journal* to the arrest warrant issued by the International Criminal Court (ICC) against President Omar al-Bashir of Sudan for war crimes and crimes against humanity committed in the Darfur region, as expressed in a July 16, 2008, editorial:

> The International Criminal Court's decision to seek an arrest warrant for Sudanese president Omar Bashir is being hailed in the usual places as a landmark in the effort to stop the bloodshed in Darfur. In fact, the indictment is of a piece with the same toothless moral posturing that has already prolonged Darfur's misery for more than four years. . . . The U.N. Security Council referred Darfur to the International Criminal Court in 2005, both to appear to be doing something and as a way to embarrass the Bush Administration. . . . Three years and 200,000 deaths later, the ICC prosecutor now claims to have solid evidence that Mr. Bashir has always been in full control of the genocidal apparatus in Darfur. To whom, outside the U.N. itself, can this possibly come as news? (A16)

This attack on the ICC is specified in another op-ed piece that appeared in the same paper just one week later, on July 23, written by David B. Rivkin Jr. and Lee A. Casey, both Washington attorneys who had served in the Justice Department under Presidents Ronald Reagan and George H. W. Bush:

> Luis Moreno-Ocampo, the prosecutor for the International Criminal Court . . . , has just made a mistake that will make it harder to help people suffering in Darfur. Last week, he filed charges against Sudanese President Omar al-Bashir. There is no doubt that terrible crimes have been committed in Darfur. But the international community has been unwilling to use military force to stop the atrocities, and this indictment takes Darfur's second-best hope for peace—a diplomatic settlement—off of the table. . . . By acting while Mr. Bashir was still in office, with no prospect of forcing him out, the ICC prosecutor has just made Darfur's tragedy harder to resolve. (A15)

Critics of transitional justice, including international courts, however, face considerable opposition. Their case histories may be challenged by counterexamples. Consider the case of trials against the Argentinean generals after the Dirty War of the 1970s. These trials were followed by considerable stabilization of democracy in Argentina. Critics of legal intervention also cannot say for certain how the war in the Balkans would have unfolded had there not been an ICTY. Nor are they prepared to account for the democratization and nascent integration into the European Union by most of Yugoslavia's successor countries, steps that would have been much more difficult had these countries not faced considerable pressure to rid themselves of (or at least to hide) leading perpetrators. Even during the war, the Bosnian-Serb military felt it had to take precautions in its communications, indicating at least some concern about later prosecutions by the ICTY. This was well illustrated by military intercepts in which officers' references to "3500 parcels that I have to distribute" actually meant men and boys from the town of Srebrenica who were to be slaughtered by the thousands.[10]

Those same critics are now also being confronted with additional empirical evidence that goes far beyond the anecdotal case study approach commonly used to support their claims. Based on a systematic and innovative study of some two hundred transitions from dictatorship to democracy and from civil war to peace, the Minnesota political scientist Kathryn Sikkink and her collaborators demonstrate that legal intervention is most commonly associated with improved human rights and democracy records.[11] Their analyses show clear statistical associations between the holding of trials, especially in combination with truth commissions, and posttransition indicators for democracy and human rights.[12] These, of course, are probabilistic relationships. What typically holds may well fail in some specific cases. Wherever warmongers and those involved in grave human rights violations hold on to power, transitional justice mechanisms—especially external interventions—are at least at risk of failing. Further challenges derive from the lack of effective law enforcement by the international community. Yet Sikkink and her colleagues argue convincingly that the potential benefits of legal intervention in the international realm today are strong in part because such intervention fills a total void. It moderates a situation in which complete impunity was the rule.

While Sikkink and her collaborators offer the strongest statistical evidence to date in support of criminal trials against perpetrators of humanitarian and human rights crimes, we are concerned with two crucial questions and specifications left unanswered by this new body of work. First, where leaders are successfully prosecuted, and where the probabilistic relationship between transitional justice and improved human rights and democracy records holds, what is the nature of the causal mechanism? Why do trials keep successor regimes from following in the bloody footsteps of their predecessors? We briefly put this latter question in context, as it motivates a principal objective of this book: to assess when and how law affects collective memory and whether memory, in turn, is implicated in fomenting legal changes that might further reduce violence.

Assuming that tribunals indeed minimize violence after atrocities, we recognize that multiple factors may account for this association. The Princeton University professor of politics and international affairs Gary Bass, for instance, identifies five "benefits" of tribunals after massive human rights violations.[13] The first is rather straightforward: guilty parties are purged from leadership positions. The second and third— deterrence of future war criminals and the rehabilitation of former enemy countries (for example, Germany after Nuremberg)—align with traditional goals of criminal law, albeit on a much grander scale in this case. Fourth, Bass notes, trials have the capacity to place blame on individuals rather than entire ethnic groups, thereby quelling intergroup conflict. The final benefit is the establishment of "the truth about wartime atrocities" (Bass 2000, 286).

This last benefit speaks to the mechanism that is at the heart of this book. This is a cultural process, the delegitimizing function of trials. Bass (2000, 302) indeed emphasizes the importance of "debunking" and of getting the historical record on paper.[14] Thus, and much in line with the quotations by President Roosevelt and Justice Jackson presented in the introduction to this book, criminal proceedings may engrave in a group's collective memory the horrors of the past and thereby reduce the chances of their being repeated.[15] Even rational actors, who are ostensibly receptive to the threat of sanctions, would base their reasoning on their knowledge of past horrors and on the memory of trials and resulting punishments. In other words, the collective memory function of criminal law is crucial when making rational choice assumptions. Political scientists often imagine rational actors, including political and military leaders and their frontline agents, as facing decision trees, each of whose branches represents a possible strategy or course of action. By delegitimizing grave human rights violations as one option, court trials have at least the potential of severing the atrocities-based branch of decision trees.

Second, however, and here we must return to the situation in which regime change does not occur, how effective can penal law be at forestalling future human rights and humanitarian crimes when the law is only enforced against the lowest ranks in the state or military hierarchy? Again, consider America's situation and its wars in Korea and Vietnam, which involved massive humanitarian law and human rights violations, as did the more recent wars and occupations in Iraq and Afghanistan.

Those punished tended to be low-level soldiers such as Private Lynndie England, the daughter of a working-class family from an impoverished region of West Virginia. Arguments that members of the U.S. administration under President George W. Bush should be prosecuted for crimes committed through the conduct of the most recent wars, for which they bore final responsibility, did not lead anywhere.[16] The Barack Obama administration has shown no interest in pursuing such cases—just like the Gerald Ford administration, following the Lyndon Johnson and Richard Nixon eras, showed no willingness to unleash the Justice Department against potentially criminal conduct perpetrated during the Vietnam War. We address this issue more explicitly in chapter 3.

Atrocities, Law, and Collective Memory: Questions and Theses

Here, then, are some lessons suggested by the introductory stories and associated observations, condensed for the moment into a couple of simple theses. While we work from the assumption that legal institutions can and often do play powerful roles in ending cycles of mass violence, we are concerned here with empirical specifications of this broad thesis and with the mechanisms through which law works. And while we acknowledge the potential role that deterrence and the rearrangement of leadership following guilty verdicts play, we propose that alongside these factors sits an important but heretofore underemphasized cultural mechanism, collective memory, serving as a crucial mediating force when legal intervention forestalls atrocity or interrupts cycles of violence. To state it more formally we advance Thesis 1: Once established, through trials or other mechanisms, collective memory may counteract violence directly, by delegitimizing grave human rights violations, or indirectly, by evoking new control responses. Figure 1.1 illustrates this causal path.

In other words, we argue that collective memory is likely to be a central mechanism in the black box between judicial intervention and improved democracy and human rights records. Where legal proceedings succeed in producing such collective memories, reductions of violence are likely. Where they fail, more violence is to be expected. While the empirical chapters of this book do not directly test the first part of this thesis on the association between collective memory and violence, we make use of novel data to examine whether collective memories, once established, contribute to new laws and law enforcement efforts that seek to combat atrocities and intergroup violence.

Our Thesis 1, of course, implies and assumes much, and before proceeding we explicate these assumptions and add further specifications. One basic assumption is that legal proceedings, including criminal trials,

Figure 1.1   Collective Memory as an Intervening Factor Between Law and Violence

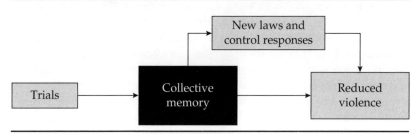

Source: Authors' figure.

are well suited to shape collective memory of past atrocities. As Hannah Arendt wrote after the Eichmann trial, "Eighteen years after the war, our knowledge of the immense archival material of the Nazi regime rests to a large extent on the selection made for prosecution" (Arendt 1963, 201). To wit, but for the trial, knowledge of events that underlie and substantiate Jewish memory of the Holocaust may have been quite different, with clear implications for collective memory. Yet we expect trials to affect collective memory in particular ways. This leads us to Thesis 2: The narrative history produced by trials is unique in that it reflects the institutional logic of the legal sphere. For example, criminal trials focus on individual perpetrators rather than on larger social forces. Moreover, evidentiary rules of trials are quite specific: evidence that may well be fair play in historical investigations is often excluded from legal proceedings. The claim of a specific institutional logic, on its own, should merit much investigation. Previous research on "accepted memory" of atrocity in the wake of selected legal and quasi-legal proceedings speaks to this issue, but many questions remain unanswered.[17] We make use of innovative data in this book to examine more thoroughly whether and how trials become not only venues for determining justice but contributors to historical memory as well.

The reader will have realized by now that our argument rests on the notion of collective memory, by which we mean the ways in which collectivities share and mutually acknowledge memories of the past (a more precise definition is to follow soon). Much classic and contemporary research has explored properties of collective memory. Here we highlight (and explore in greater depth in chapter 2) a few key features from that literature, as they inform our theses. First, collective memories are socially constructed. This does not mean, of course, that the past did not happen. People did suffer pain, they cried, screamed, resigned, and many died. All of this is all too real. Yet the way we know about their suffering is never direct. It is always mediated and filtered.

This premise, which is a staple of collective memory scholarship, comes with a few corollaries, established by a rich and growing body of literature. For one, the construction of collective memory is motivated by material and ideal interests of present-day actors. This argument has become known as "the presentist approach." Furthermore, attempts at shaping and redrafting collective memory must take previous memories into account. We refer to this phenomenon as the path dependency of collective memory. Adding to this, multiple actors always offer competing versions of the past, and hence another feature of collective memory worth emphasizing is that the construction of collective memory is beset by conflict. Finally, as social groups always reconstitute themselves and as their ideal and material interests shift over time, we have to acknowledge a simple fact: collective memory, and by extension its consequence, is always in flux.[18]

To reiterate, historical experience and public and academic debate suggest or imply that law and collective memory matter for cycles of violence. History may well be written through trials, and the collective memory this historical record documents can motivate and shape whether and how states respond to intergroup violence and atrocities. Yet much more empirical work is needed if we want to more safely answer the two questions at hand: First, do trials in fact affect historical narratives? And, second, does memory indeed influence state responses to conflict?

Excursus: A Note on Cases, Method, and Logic of Inquiry

As we consider the world of atrocities and grave human rights violations, the role of judicial intervention, and the way atrocities are remembered, we face a universe of cases that is daunting in both size and scope. Cases from relatively recent history include the slave trade and the slavery system in the United States, atrocities committed against Native Americans, the German genocide against the Herero in today's Namibia in the early twentieth century, the Armenian genocide in the early stages of World War I, and the Stalinist purges in the Soviet Union.[19] Historically, most atrocities never resulted in any legal response. In fact, for much of human history perpetrators of atrocities were celebrated as heroes.[20] Where courts responded, and they have done so with increasing frequency in recent history, we encounter cases in which domestic courts acted and other cases in which foreign or international courts and tribunals responded to atrocities.[21] Cases of domestic legal responses are exemplified by My Lai, Haditha, and Abu Ghraib (all covered in this volume) but also by the Auschwitz trial in Frankfurt, Germany; the Iraqi trials against Saddam Hussein and his henchmen; and the trials in Argentina and Chile against these countries' former military rulers.

Then there are foreign trials like the famous proceedings before the Jerusalem court against Adolf Eichmann, the organizer of the transports into the Nazi extermination camps, and finally international trials such as the International Military Tribunal at Nuremberg and the ICTY. Each of these types of cases may have specific consequences for the formation of collective memory and for altering risks of subsequent violence. The range of possible outcomes is further multiplied as the context of cases also varies. Some trials are held under conditions of regime continuity and others in the context of regime change. Among the latter we may distinguish between trials after an internal overthrow of regimes (Argentina) and others after defeat and occupation by foreign powers (Germany). Trials under conditions of regime continuity are most likely to be limited to proceedings against actors of relatively low rank. All of these specifics of cases and context are likely to create different outcomes.

In selecting cases for analysis in this book we had to make a number of decisions. First, we decided to focus on cases in which trials occurred. Disregarding atrocities that did not lead to trials means that we cannot speak to the likelihood that legal responses will occur. Second, we focus on American memories of atrocities. We cover American trials that were held under conditions of regime continuity and, as we would expect, involved proceedings that were directed against relatively low-ranking frontline agents alone. Yet we expand the analytic range by also considering the case of American memories of foreign perpetrators of the highest levels. The latter were tried after regime change, as exemplified by the case of former president Slobodan Milosevic and his prosecution by the ICTY. In addition, in chapter 6 we take a look at German memories in comparison with those in America.

We think there are good reasons to focus on American cases. First, the United States is a large country, and American collective memories shape the minds and fates of some 300 million people inside its borders. Second, the United States plays a particularly powerful role in world affairs. Hence, how the United States conducts its business has ramifications far beyond its national borders. Third, collective memories that affect America's foreign, military, and economic policies have massive consequences for many others around the globe. Finally, memories are not isolated, nor is the invocation of law in cases of human rights violations just a national affair. Daniel Levy from the State University of New York at Stony Brook, in his recent and most innovative work, discusses "recursive cosmopolitanism." He illustrates, for the case of Argentina, how in the late stages of the military dictatorship local situations were addressed with recourse to global prescriptions, while local practices simultaneously inspired international institutions. Might what applies to a country at the global periphery not also be valid for a powerful country like the United States, with its considerable political, legal, and cultural reach?[22]

Yet we are mindful that lessons learned from the U.S. experience cannot necessarily be generalized. Here we deal with a long-established democracy as opposed to many autocracies around the globe. Information can be produced and disseminated relatively freely. Furthermore, as a very powerful country in the world of international relations, the United States is less susceptible than others to outside influences. This includes potential pressures to hold high-level perpetrators legally responsible and to subscribe and respond to global collective memories that may involve critical notes on America. The United States simply does not depend on such legitimatory exercises, including the advancement of criminal justice proceedings against violators of human rights. Chapter 6, which compares the United States with Germany, a country much more dependent on world opinion for a number of reasons, shows that this factor matters greatly for the formation of collective memory. At the same time, the United States is capable of launching trials, including international trials, where it sees fit. Its recent central role in the building and operation of international criminal tribunals for the former Yugoslavia and for Rwanda illustrates this point. The United States thereby plays a central role in the formation of collective memories in distant lands.

The analytic space within which we locate the United States is thus demarked by several dimensions. First, with regard to types of trials, we distinguish between no trials and domestic trials, on one hand, and international tribunals, on the other. Our case studies address American memories of domestic perpetrations processed in American courts and of foreign perpetrations processed in international tribunals. A second important dimension relates to conditions of regime continuity, under which only low-level perpetrators are typically prosecuted, versus cases of regime change, in which high-level offenders are more apt to face criminal charges. Table 1.1 lays out these dimensions, indicates where the cases in this book fit in, and presents other examples of cases not discussed here. The concluding chapter (chapter 10) places these cases in a broader universe along the dimensions spelled out in this chapter. In chapter 10 we also consider how lessons learned in the ensuing chapters have implications beyond the American experience.

Finally, what is the nature of our evidence as we analyze these selected cases? Each empirical chapter is guided by the extended case method.[23] This method uses specific cases to investigate how broader

Table 1.1   Dimensions and Examples of Cases

| | | Type of Trial or Court and Regime Status | | | |
| | | Domestic | | Foreign and International | |
Locus of Collective Memory	None	Regime Continuity	Regime Change	Regime Continuity	Regime Change
In the United States	*Slavery*	**My Lai, Haditha**	Saddam Hussein	ICC (Sudan/Darfur)	*IMT*, **ICTY (late)**
In other countries	*Herero*	French collaborator trials	*Frankfurt Auschwitz trial*	*ICTY (early)*	*IMT*

Source: Authors' compilation.

Note: Entries in bold = cases for explicit study in this book; entries in italics = cases addressed in this book. "Herero" refers to the German genocide against the Herero and Namaqua peoples in today's Namibia from 1904 to 1907. "Frankfurt Auschwitz trial" refers to the trials from 1963 to 1965 of staff of the Auschwitz concentration and extermination camp. "ICC (Sudan/Darfur)" refers to prosecutions of President Omar al-Bashir of Sudan and others before the International Criminal Court. ICC = International Criminal Court; IMT = International Military Tribunal; ICTY = International Criminal Tribunal for the former Yugoslavia.

theoretical assumptions, in this instance ideas concerning links between law and collective memory, are supported by those specific cases. Each case study may find that its patterns support initial theoretical expectations or, alternatively, that some of the expectations are challenged by the empirical particularities identified. Such challenges then lead to suggestions on how the theory has to be modified or specified to cover the particular case under examination. In this volume we make use of multiple case studies, thus enabling us to examine the links between law and collective memory of atrocities from multiple angles. After each case study we summarize what we have learned with regard to general theoretical ideas about law and collective memory while simultaneously linking new insights to previously discussed cases. Given the number and selection of cases, we obviously cannot provide absolute proof of our theoretical argument. Yet we point to important patterns and commonalities that move us toward a broader and more differentiated theory of atrocities, law, and collective memory. We use our concluding chapter to place the lessons learned from our empirical cases in a larger universe. This allows us to accumulate our insights and provide a platform for future research on this crucial area of inquiry.

= Chapter 2 =

What the Literature Tells Us, and Uncharted Terrain

A S THE preceding pages have shown, collective memory plays a large part in, and is in turn shaped by, the legal response to atrocities. But what exactly do we mean by collective memory? How is it created, and what are its features? How do legal proceedings contribute to shaping collective memory? Through what mechanisms may collective memory, at least under some circumstances, stall future violence? We first answer these questions based on ideas put forth in extant work. This paves the way for us to add our own insights into law's contributions to collective memory and its potential relevance for cycles of violence in the subsequent chapters.

Collective Memory and Cultural Trauma: The Concepts

Collective memory is a term coined in Maurice Halbwachs's classic work (1992). It refers to knowledge about the past that is shared, mutually acknowledged, and reinforced by a collectivity—from small informal groups to formal organizations to nation-states and global communities.[1] Tools include rituals such as Memorial Day or Martin Luther King Day commemorations in the United States and their equivalents elsewhere, as well as symbols such as flags, plaques, and medals in all countries. It is these mechanisms on which the Durkheimian school focused when its followers, most noteworthy Halbwachs, addressed the issue of collective memory. Other tools through which collective memory is stored and communicated include biography and historiography, of central concern to Halbwachs's Hungarian-German colleague Karl Mannheim.[2]

Here we are primarily concerned with a specific kind of collective memory, that of horrific pasts and calamitous events. Their recollection is best captured in the more recent concept of cultural trauma.[3] The Berkeley sociologist and psychoanalyst Neil Smelser (2004, 44) defines *cultural trauma* as "a memory accepted and publicly given credence by a relevant membership group and evoking an event or situation that is (a) laden with negative affect, (b) represented as indelible, and (c) regarded as threatening a society's existence or violating one or more of its cultural presuppositions." The first part of this definition closely resembles that of collective memory, while the following two specifications describe the kinds of collective memories that constitute cultural trauma.

Jeffrey Alexander (2004b, 9), the head of Yale's Center for Cultural Sociology, adds that cultural trauma is anchored in Durkheim's classical idea of "religious imagination."[4] Such imagination, he notes, forms "inchoate experiences, through association, condensation, and aesthetic creation, into some specific shape." In other words, what once was diffuse and chaotic in the minds of those who were exposed to horrific events begins to take shape, to become focused and organized. It is only after such transformation that groups are in the position to communicate effectively about terrifying experiences, potentially sharing them with others who were not directly involved. In line with Smelser's definition, one of the defining qualities of cultural trauma, in contrast to individual trauma, is its communicability.

The contours of collective memory, and by implication cultural trauma, sharpen when juxtaposed against neighboring concepts, notably individual memory and history, and when the distinction is made, within collective memory, between autobiographical and historical memory. Our effort is not to try the reader's patience with this exercise in terminological clarification; rather, we see it as instructive and beneficial for following our arguments in subsequent chapters.

The study of individual memory pays significant attention to the cognitive aspects of retention and recollection. Psychologists, for instance, sometimes study how information is processed, where it is stored, and how accurately we recall events that we observed in the past, such as witnessing a crime.[5] This conceptualization views memory as the property of individuals. Collective memory, by contrast, belongs to groups in that "it is supra-individual, and individual memory is conceived in relation to a group, be this geographical, positional, ideological, political or generationally based" (Eyerman 2001, 6). Moreover, the study of collective memory examines not simply what people might recall of a nation's or community's past; it also entails the subjective meaning attributed to past events.[6] Commemorations and monuments, for instance, are often windows into a society's collective memory. Commemorations, as tangible representations of collective memory, might indeed be thought of as "the lifting from the historical record of events that best symbolize society's ideals" (Schwartz 2009, 132).

Within collective memory we distinguish between autobiographical and historical memory. *Autobiographical memory* refers to events that actors personally experienced in the past and to which they often assign significant meaning.[7] Those of us alive on September 11, 2001, will undoubtedly recall the terrorist attacks on New York City and Washington, D.C. Few of us were on site, and our knowledge of the event is thus mediated, but we will remember, commemorate, and share stories of where we were at the time and how we heard about the attacks.

Over time, as we process our specific recollection and interpretation collectively, autobiographical memory may even change. Yet it is arguably the most personally meaningful memory, especially if it refers to events that occurred during our adolescence.[8] Collective memory is broader in that it incorporates *historical memory*—the recollection of events that we did not experience directly. We learn of these events and assign meaning to them only through historical records (for example, high school textbooks covering the Vietnam War, for those born after the 1970s), media accounts (the "Eyes on the Prize" TV series on the civil rights movement, for post-1960s cohorts), commemorative occasions (Independence Day in the United States, for all Americans), or stories told by elders (the Emmett Till murder, for many African Americans).[9] Halbwachs stressed that historical memory is particularly prone to social construction. Events it evokes are especially filtered through social institutions such as the media, political bodies, and, as we argue in this book, law.

Finally, we distinguish between collective memory and *history*. As Ron Eyerman (2001, 7–8) notes, "History, especially as a profession and academic discipline, aims at something wider, more objective and universal than group memory." According to Barry Schwartz, who may well be thought of as the father of American collective memory research, history tends to be inclusive of events and all aspects of past events; it involves the chronicling of the past. Collective memories of the past, by contrast, are more selective and arguably more malleable. They generally refer to key symbolic events that tell us something about society's consciousness and ideals. Quoting Schwartz (2009, 132) again, "History informs; commemoration inspires and motivates." We are cautious, though, not to overstretch this distinction. History also provides reconstructions of the past through particular disciplinary tools that aim at objective and universal information about the past, but tools that nevertheless select and cast the past in the specific vocabulary of the present.

To be sure, different types and levels of memory are not independent of one another. After contrasting "collected memories," as measured by survey researchers who aggregate memories of individual respondents, and "collective memories," entailed in mythology, tradition, heritage, and all symbolic systems, language most prominent among them, the University of Virginia sociologist Jeffrey Olick (1999a, 346), a leading theorist of collective memory, concludes that "the real point is to open our thinking about the variety of mnemonic processes, practices, and outcomes and about their interrelations. . . . There is no individual memory without social experience nor is there any collective memory without individuals participating in social life."[10]

Fundamental Features of Collective Memory: Halbwachs's Presentist Starting Point

Despite such complexities, Halbwachs's conceptualization of collective memory was novel in that it established a unique area of inquiry in which sociologists could contribute to the study of memory in a manner that clearly differed from psychology and history. We have already noted that his ideas built on the innovative thoughts of his teacher, Emile Durkheim.[11] Yet Halbwachs also distanced himself from his teacher. He maintained and sought to show that our understanding of the past is influenced by present-day interest. Barry Schwartz has famously labeled this perspective "presentist," a concept to which we have already referred.[12] This approach is well demonstrated in fascinating work by the Northwestern sociologist Gary Fine on reputations, the memory of famous or infamous individuals.[13] In a particularly impressive illustration, Fine shows for the case of the former U.S. president Warren Harding that the memory of past presidents is not (just) a reflection of these actors' successes and failures. Instead, it is affected by the position and interest of later, and often competing, reputational entrepreneurs. Specifically, Fine judges Harding's record to be respectable in many ways. Yet, different from John F. Kennedy or Ronald Reagan, for example, Harding lacked influential followers who survived him and would have had an interest in preserving, and in fact celebrating, his memory.

Halbwachs's scholarship, without doubt, set the tone for a growing and fascinating collective memory literature, and scholarly engagement of this theme has intensified in recent years. For instance, a 2009 online search in the quite comprehensive search index *Sociological Abstracts* shows 255 hits with both the terms *collective* and *memory* in the title, 143 of which appeared during the past decade (2000 to 2009). Scholarship that traces its roots back to Halbwachs touches on a variety of themes such as World War II and the Holocaust (Olick and Levy 1997; Olick 2005; Alexander 2004a; Giesen 2004a, 2004b), the Vietnam War (Wagner-Pacifici and Schwartz 1991), the civil rights movement (Griffin and Bollen 2009), threats to human reproduction (Feldman-Savelsberg, Ndonko, and Yang 2005), the repression of gay people and their resistance (Armstrong and Crage 2006), and the assassination of Yitzhak Rabin (Vinitzky-Seroussi

2002). Nearly all of this research cites Halbwachs, and some of it indeed supports Halbwachs's presentist claim.

Path Dependency of Collective Memory

Despite such support for his presentist ideas, Halbwachs is sometimes accused of having been an excessive presentist. He viewed, it is argued, depictions and accounts of the past as largely, if not entirely, reflecting the interests of present-day actors and institutions. Current circumstances then determine both what we as a collectivity choose to remember and the meaning attributed to past events. To wit, the present determines the past. As a trite but perhaps illustrative hypothetical, we might envision Halbwachs frowning at George Santayana's famous words, "Those who cannot remember the past are condemned to repeat it." Halbwachs might have chimed in by adding, "Actually, those who repeated the past simply chose not to remember it." Yet recent empirical scholarship partially challenges this extreme presentist orientation. It suggests that collective memory must involve some measure of continuity with earlier memories, as Barry Schwartz has made clear in his work on commemorations in the U.S. Capitol and the memory of Abraham Lincoln.[14] We might then say that collective memory is also dependent on previous ways of remembering history.

Particularly acute illustrations of this point are provided by Jeffrey Olick and his collaborators.[15] For example, examining the history of German May 8 commemorations (the day Germany capitulated at the end of World War II in 1945) between the 1950s and the 1990s, they demonstrate that the speeches always referred back to commemorative contents of the preceding decade. Political discourse about past events, such as World War II or the Holocaust, thus reflects not only present-day interests and powerful constituencies, as Halbwachs might have suggested, but also previous memories and sensitivities associated with them. Such constraints even affect foreign leaders. President Ronald Reagan, for example, visiting Germany on the occasion of the fortieth anniversary of Victory in Europe Day, had decided not to visit a concentration camp. Simultaneously, he was set to attend a ceremony at a military cemetery where members of Nazi units were buried alongside soldiers of the general German military (a fact Reagan may not have been aware of). President Reagan claimed that it was time to release young Germans from their feelings of guilt and let them move on with their lives. Yet outraged reactions forced Reagan to compromise by laying a wreath at a concentration camp site. In short, the U.S. president had to yield to the established definition of the historical past. He, like politicians generally, was tied to preceding memories. He had to accept that the commemoration of the past is not plain presentist but path dependent.[16]

We explicitly make note of this point, and Olick's work in particular, because it directly informs an idea introduced in this book. In chapter 4, for instance, we discuss the concept of *applied commemorations*— commemorations not for the declared purpose of addressing historical events but commemorations in the context of decisionmaking debates that implicate historic events. Examples include legislative sessions on hate crime and restrictions on free speech. Such debates will involve legal issues such as due process or chances of enforcement. But they will also refer to and recount the history of Nazi crimes to justify restrictions of rights in light of that history.

At times, actors with presentist orientations not only are caught up by past memories and commemorations but also actively refer to them, often using the past as a metaphor for the present. Alexander calls such references "bridging metaphors."[17] Thus establishing the likeness of past events that carry moral or legal obligations to present ones, they invoke those commitments for the present. A most famous example is the depiction on the front pages of almost all major newspapers of an emaciated prisoner from the Trnopolje camp in Bosnia after its liberation. The photograph so clearly evoked iconic images of the Holocaust taken by Soviet or American military when they liberated the Nazi camps that the pressure to intervene increased massively. Chapters 4 and 7 make reference to such bridging metaphors and explore some conditions under which they are more or less likely to succeed.[18]

Again, past memories and commemorations call on later carriers and mnemonic activists, no matter their present interests, to be heard. This is the path dependency of collective memory. And, at times new speakers actively recall earlier images of the past in order to build a bridge from them to the present.

Struggles over Collective Memory

In addition to his presentism argument, Halbwachs also distances himself from his teacher Emile Durkheim in that he more clearly recognizes the separate lives of distinct, often conflicting, groups within societies, each with its own collective memory. In his "Social Frameworks of Memory" (Halbwachs 1992, 35–189), for example, he addresses the specific memories of families, religious groups, social classes, and occupational groups.[19]

This insight is taken for granted today and specified in manifold studies. An astute example for the case of American memories is provided by Howard Schuman and Jacqueline Scott, who find, through a large-scale survey, that Americans differ from one another in their memories of important historical events.[20] Older cohorts tend more to think of the Great Depression than younger ones. African Americans are more likely than whites to include the civil rights movement as one of the most important events; women, more often than men, think of the women's movement. Even where different cohorts remember the same event, they remember it in different ways. Americans of earlier cohorts, when thinking of World War II, remember comrades they may have lost or the lines they had to endure at home to buy groceries; younger Americans, instead, might think of the war as America's great contribution to democracy. Furthermore, more recent research shows that young Americans are more likely than older ones to liken the Iraq War to World War II rather than to the Vietnam War. The same applies to Republicans compared with Democrats.[21]

Where groups do not just differ but are in conflict with one another, they may also debate the memories that legitimize and back up their claims; they engage in mnemonic struggles.[22] In Germany, for example, the 1990s witnessed the so-called Historikerstreit, a massive dispute between opposing camps of historians about the Nazi past. While neither side denied the horrors committed under the Nazi regime, conservative historians sought to interpret some of the mass killings as inventions of the Stalinist regime, seemingly to relativize Germany's guilt. Mnemonic struggles are also not alien to Americans, of course. Here efforts of the heritage movement of the past two decades have begun to challenge a sanitized view of American history that may repress the history of slavery and Jim Crow.[23] At the same time, African American history museums in many cities with influential black communities challenge the depiction of blacks presented on the Washington Mall, which provides little if any room for memories of the terror experienced by the ancestors of today's African Americans.[24] When finally, in 2004, a museum was opened to honor the history of Native Americans, the museum was heavily criticized for neglecting the story of the near annihilation the indigenous American peoples had suffered.

Consider also the controversy of 1993 to 1995 around the exhibit of the Enola Gay, the World War II B-29 bomber that dropped the atomic bomb over Hiroshima. Smithsonian curators at the National Air and Space Museum sought a critical display, but they were confronted by veterans and members of Congress who argued that the Smithsonian should use this exhibit to celebrate the end of the war.[25] One final example will suffice: the massive debate about the 1992 Christopher Columbus exhibit, commemorating the five hundredth anniversary of his "discovery" of America, at the National Museum of American History.[26] The following paragraph from an article in the *Los Angeles Times* provides a fine illustration.

> The first salvo in the war of cultural symbolism was fired in 1986 with the establishment of the Christopher Columbus Quincentenary Jubilee Commission, the official U.S. body commemorating the explorer's landing on the continent. The U.S. and Spanish governments, along with national and international corporations, joined forces in a grand-scale marketing push. But if you talk to the formidable forces allied in challenging the traditional take on Columbus—including an array of artistic, cultural and activist groups, individuals and newly ascendant ethnic and sexual-orientation communities—the trouble really started 500 years ago. While the pro-Columbus camp (and the overwhelming bulk of Western curricular thought) sees Columbus as a hero, the anti-Columbus forces consider him an invading slave trader and mass murderer. The mainstreamers may have been first out of the gate, but in light of the flurry of arts activity over the past year, it is the multicultural arts community and the counter-quincentenarists who can make the stronger claim to victory. (Jan Breslauer, "Happy Quincentennial, Christopher Columbus!" *Los Angeles Times*, October 11, 1992, 5)

The outcome of mnemonic struggles often leads to shifts in collective memories, as many debates about the shape of American history textbooks have shown. Schwartz and Schuman recently demonstrated this impressively for the case of changing collective memories of President Lincoln in the wake of the civil rights movement, memories that increasingly define him as the abolitionist alone, at the expense of competing images of Lincoln as a pioneer, a common man of the people, and as the president who held the Union together.[27]

This is a crucial point familiar to anyone working in this field: Collective memory is not only divided across societal groups and subject to mnemonic struggles, it is also always in flux. Today's collective memories differ distinctly from yesterday's.[28]

Law's Production of Collective Memory— and Its Limits

The central concern of this book, of course, is one particular mechanism through which collective memory may be established or shaped: the proceedings of law. This area of study is badly wanting, as a brief look at different search indexes shows. Only four entries can be found when we enter *collective, memory,* and *law* as combined search terms for article titles in the comprehensive *Sociological Abstracts* search index (as of late 2009). The number increases to twenty entries when we search article abstracts.

A 2006 search in *CAS Worldwide Political Science Abstracts,* using the same three terms as combined search terms, resulted in zero hits for titles and eleven for abstracts. A search of *Criminal Justice Abstracts* yielded zero entries for titles and two for abstracts.[29]

Yet legal scholars provide inspiration, especially in work on cycles of violence and transitional justice. Harvard's Martha Minow (1998, 1), for example, notes in her treatise on the choices facing societies in the aftermath of mass violence, "A most appalling goal of the genocides, the massacres, systematic rapes, and tortures has been the destruction of the remembrance of individuals as well as their lives and dignity." Minow adds that some survivors have turned to legal institutions not only to seek justice but also to tell the story of "what happened," to chronicle horrific events for the annals of history and ultimately to shape the collective memory of a society's past. Law, however, may be used not only by survivors to make sure that their suffering will not be forgotten. It has also been used by rulers for quite different purposes, as Mark Osiel (1997, 6) argues in an influential jurisprudential book on links between law and collective memory: "In the last half century, criminal law has increasingly been used in several societies with a view of teaching a particular interpretation of the country's history, one expected to have a salubrious impact on its solidarity." Here, obviously, we sense a critical note: that law may produce not just memories that serve the interests of victims but other memories, too, in the service of "wider society." Nevertheless, Minow and Osiel agree that the study of atrocities and law has become deeply entwined with the issue of memory.

Despite the shortage of current sociological literature on links between law and collective memory, Minow's and Osiel's themes reflect crucial sociological discussions. From the perspective of classical Durkheimian ideas, for example, law involves highly effective rituals that are suited, at least in principle, to evoke collective effervescence and to lift the court's decision to a level of awareness that helps consolidate the collective conscience and heighten the awareness of social and legal norms.[30] Trials can indeed be considered rituals. They share central features of other social practices that we are more accustomed to recognize as rituals, such as religious services; they direct the attention of collectivities toward the same object; and they further ensure that all participants are mutually aware of this common focus, while simultaneously creating a common mood or emotion.

Randall Collins, the president of the American Sociological Association at the time of this writing, has previously applied this notion to scholarship, where rituals, such as major lectures, seek to sanctify the truth.[31] In the case of trials, the sacred good at stake is justice, and distinctions must be achieved between what is legally right and wrong, lawful and lawless, or law abiding and law breaking. Trials may thereby contribute to the production of what Jeffrey Alexander, in his discussion of cultural trauma, calls "sacred evil," the recognition of social facts as a specific kind of evil.[32] This is an evil that is surrounded by prohibitions, and it can be challenged only at great cost. Denial of the Holocaust, for example, will lead to social exclusion and in fact to criminal punishment in many countries. The Holocaust obviously is an example, maybe the most prominent example, of a sacred evil.

The writing of history is thus added as a potentially important function to criminal trials, in addition to more established functions such as the determination of guilt, retribution, or deterrence. Some have advocated criminal trials in transitional situations in part for this reason, for example, for the cases of post-Communist Eastern Europe and for post-military dictatorship in Argentina.[33] Such proponents of trials recognize that the construction of memories of the repressive past is instrumental in the management of transitions from authoritarian regimes to democracy and from civil war to peace.[34] The ritual power of law is, of course, supplemented by the fact that law is backed by the legitimizing potential of procedure, as highlighted by the great theorist Niklas Luhmann and, in line with Max Weber's classical thought, by the coercive apparatus of the state—even if the latter applies only in more tangential ways in the international realm.[35]

At the same time, legal proceedings face limits when they contribute to the construction of the memory of atrocities. These limits are not just of theoretical interest: practitioners must be mindful of them when they seek to use law in ways envisioned by Justice Jackson or President Roosevelt. Law is subject to a particular set of institutional rules that, for example, restrict access to some information and allow only some evidence to be presented in court. Because of such rules, collective memory produced through legal processes will always differ from memories generated by historians or in the worlds of politics, art, and religion.[36] Wise jurists are aware of such limits of law as a place for the reconstruction of history, as reflected in the words of the judges of the Jerusalem court in its 1961 proceedings against Adolf Eichmann, the organizer of central aspects of the Nazi extermination machine:

> The Court does not possess the facilities required for investigating general questions. . . . For example, to describe the historical background of the catastrophe, a great mass of documents and evidence has been submitted to us, collected most painstakingly and certainly out of a genuine desire to delineate as complete a picture as possible. Even so, all the material is but a tiny fraction of the existent sources on the subject. . . . As for questions of principle which are outside the realm of law, no one has made us

judges of them and therefore our opinion on them carries no greater weight than that of any other person who has devoted study and thought to these questions. (Quoted in Osiel 1997, 80–81)[37]

Additional selectivities of law become obvious in Jeffrey Alexander's discussion on how cultural trauma is created. As noted, cultural trauma is a specific type of collective memory that involves horrific events.[38] The construction of cultural trauma, Alexander argues, is a process that consists of many factors: claims making by agents; carrier groups of the trauma process; speech acts, in which carrier groups address an audience in a specific situation, seeking to project the trauma claim to the audience; cultural classifications regarding the nature of the pain, the nature of the victim, the relation of the trauma victim to the wider audience, and the attribution of responsibility. Alexander observes that linguistic action, through which the master narrative of social suffering is created, is mediated by the nature of institutional arenas that contribute to it. Law certainly is a specific arena that interacts with all of the factors contributing to the construction of collective memory. Clearly, some claims can be better expressed in legal proceedings than others that will forever remain, in Franz Kafka's famous words, before the law. Some carrier groups have easier access to law, classically illustrated for the privileged position of "repeat players," as the sociolegal scholar Marc Galanter calls those who routinely use the law.[39] Furthermore, some classifications of suffering and victims are more in line with those of the law than others. Law's construction of the past, the kind of truth it speaks (vere dicere), the knowledge it produces, and the collective memory to which it contributes is thus always selective.[40]

In short, law faces noteworthy limits when actors use it to write history. These limits result from its institutional logic: a focus on the behavior of individuals; consideration of only a limited set of behaviors; constraints imposed by rules of evidence; and, for criminal law, its binary logic and exclusionary intent. Each of these features has consequences for the narratives that result from legal procedures and, through them, for collective memory.[41]

Today, as indicated in chapter 1, nation-states cannot be considered in isolation. International law has been developed by international organizations, with the involvement of nongovernmental organizations, and by international tribunals and courts, beginning with Nuremberg and later by the International Criminal Tribunal for the former Yugoslavia (ICTY) and the International Criminal Tribunal for Rwanda (ICTR) to the first permanent institution at this level, the International Criminal Court (ICC). The stories these courts tell are reported in news media, documentaries, and films across the globe. Collective memory to some degree is thus global memory, as impressively documented by Daniel Levy and Natan Sznaider in their work on the memory of the Holocaust.[42] It involves global scripts—recipes and moral imperatives for action—that many researchers have found to affect policymaking and implementation at the national level in a variety of areas, from environmental issues to human rights.[43]

While the global thus very much matters in the national and local spheres, the reverse is also true. Global law and global memories cannot be understood in isolation from local and national norms and memories.[44] Actors articulate their local concerns within global settings. For example, American lawyers played a major role in building the ICTY by introducing American case law into the legal standards developed by that court.[45] Furthermore, the global does not exist outside its incarnation into local practices: Global messages about individual human rights are interpreted differently in societies with highly collectivist and societies with individualist cultures and institutions.[46] Finally, concrete local experiences and institutions color memories of events that may be retained globally. An excellent, albeit extreme, example is the memories in the United States and Vietnam of the Vietnam War and of specific events such as the My Lai massacre.[47] The memory of those who were victims and ended up as victors is clearly distinct from that of the perpetrators who left the war defeated.

Competitors and Mediators of Law: Truth Commissions, News Media, Scholarship

Collective memory is obviously not just a product of legal proceedings. Other mechanisms such as truth commissions, art, historiography, the movie industry, museums, mass media, and civil society generally contribute to its formation. These institutions and processes may serve as competitors to legal constructions of the past; but they may also communicate a court's message, even amplify it so that the message is widely received. At any rate, interactions between law and other institutions are likely to mitigate the impact law has on collective memory, and they complicate the empirical examination of this link. In this book, we seek to contribute to efforts at overcoming such challenges, which obviously are not unique to our topic.[48]

Truth Commissions and the Role of Law

This book does not investigate truth commissions (TCs), but a brief discussion sheds additional light on the particular ways in which law writes history, some of law's limits in doing so, and ways in which truth commissions may supplement law's role. Both trials (implicitly) and truth commissions (by their very definition) tell a story about the cruelties committed by perpetrators. Together, they may in fact be especially effective. As the political scientist Kathryn Sikkink's work shows, human rights records and democratic functioning improve most remarkably where both trials and truth commissions address offenses against grave human rights abuses. What, then, is the added value of truth commissions if courts already tell the history of atrocities?

Truth commissions focus on the past, investigate enduring patterns of abuses, work for limited periods of time, and conclude their work with a report. They are officially sanctioned and authorized by the state. This definition underlies the most comprehensive comparative study of truth commissions to date, including those of Argentina, Chile, El Salvador, Guatemala, Germany, Uganda, and South Africa.[49] Most truth commissions share additional characteristics in that they focus on the recent past, were established during a political transition, and investigated politically motivated repression. Most also have the same set of basic goals, even if the specific focuses vary: to bring to light and officially acknowledge past abuses, to respond to victims' needs, to set the stage for justice and accountability, to recommend institutional changes, and to promote reconciliation. The name *truth commission* is often misleading, as the truth is frequently well known; it is its acknowledgement that is at stake. Some two to three dozen truth commissions or truth and reconciliation commissions have been at work since 1974, used primarily as alternatives or complements to criminal trials. They are often perceived as advantageous in light of the limits and selectivities of trials, as noted earlier in this chapter, especially when perpetrators and victims represent two distinct groups in society that must coexist in the postatrocity era.[50]

Truth commissions—working under a different institutional logic from criminal courts—may contribute to accountability in ways not available to criminal courts. Rather than attributing responsibility to particular individuals alone, they are better suited to examining broad patterns of abuses, thereby encouraging institutional reforms. In addition, they can also challenge entire sectors of society and segments of the population that carry some degree of responsibility, from bureaucrats to torturers and profiteers to bystanders who refused to speak up. They are more likely than courts to allow evidence about sick cultural patterns and national shame. In other words, truth commissions establish collective guilt, or at least responsibility, while criminal courts attribute guilt to a relatively small number of individuals, thereby "decoupling" (Giesen 2004a; 2004b, 120) larger segments of the population from the attribution of guilt.

Another difference between truth commissions and courts is the use of distinct emotional registers. While the former often engage in sorrow, hope, and forgiving, the latter aim at condemnation and the buffering of anger. Emile Durkheim (1984), in his famous book on the division of labor in society, wrote about ways in which law, through its formal rules and procedures, mitigates unhampered emotions. Exceptions notwithstanding, as illustrated by the race riots evoked by the not-guilty verdict against several Los Angeles police officers whose brutal beating of the African American motorist Rodney King was caught on camera, this argument seems to have some validity, especially for actors inside the court. Consider findings from a recent Australian study of magistrates: "Magistrates must often regulate their own emotions and those of some court users, many of whom are not legally represented and who express a variety of emotions, including anger and distress, and experience social problems that may elicit emotions or emotional responses from the magistrate" (Anleu and Mack 2005, 590). Different from courts, truth commissions open the trauma outward so that many, including perpetrators, are caught up in the reconstruction of the horrific past.[51]

In short, criminal courts and truth commissions differ along two basic dimensions. First, while truth commissions amplify emotions, courts seek to reduce them even as they highlight and direct public attention at the crimes. Second, while courts engage in "othering," that is, they seek to hold responsible a select few and to exclude them from the community, truth commissions are concerned with integrating. Truth commissions, different from criminal courts, are thus in line with what the Australian criminologist John Braithwaite has referred to as reintegrative shaming.[52] In the words of Desmond Tutu, the leader of the South African Truth and Reconciliation Commission, "Social harmony is for us . . . the greatest good" (quoted in Wilson 2003, 370).[53] It is quite plausible that such complementary advantages of trials and truth commissions contribute to the better outcomes Sikkink identifies when both are jointly at work.

While truth commissions obviously bring surplus value to the construction of collective memories, it must also be noted that their contributions, like those of courts, are selective. Critics stress that truth and reconciliation commissions are more concerned with collective well-being than with the fate of individuals and that the commission's primary interest is the well-being of the state.[54] In his critique of the South African Truth and Reconciliation Commission, the anthropologist Richard Wilson (2003, 369) argues that "a culture of human rights was constructed upon the quicksand of a culture of impunity."[55] Yet other studies are more sanguine in their assessments of truth commissions for the effective construction of collective memory and, through it, for ending long-standing cycles of violence. Consider, for instance, Priscilla Hayner's in-depth analysis of the Argentinian truth commission, the National Commission on the Disappearance of Persons, created in 1983 by decree by President Raúl Alfonsin after seven years of military dictatorship. An estimated ten thousand to thirty thousand citizens endured arrest and torture and were "disappeared." While commission hearings were not held in public, the work nevertheless produced much publicity as exiles returned home to testify and commission staff visited former torture centers and secret cemeteries. Taking more than seven thousand statements, including at least fifteen hundred from survivors of detention camps, the commission documented camp conditions, torture practices, and lists of 365 former torture centers and of 8,960 disappeared persons.

The commission delivered a report after nine months of work that became a best seller in Argentina. The commission turned its files over to the prosecutor's office and thus provided critical evidence for the cases against senior members of the military junta. This example illustrates how truth commissions may create an evidentiary basis for later trials, thereby producing the synergy that joint trials and truth commissions can achieve. In line with this assessment, James Gibson's (2004a, 2004b, 2006) work on South Africa suggests that those who largely accepted the truth about the nation's apartheid past were more likely to hold remedial attitudes, for instance, in the realm of race relations.

News Media and Historical Scholarship

While truth commissions thus illustrate how law's effect may be supplemented, cognitively and affectively, by that of other institutions, news media obviously play an essential role in disseminating the court's message. Criminal courts in modern societies are incapable of reaching large audiences directly.[56] John Hagan, the former president of the American Society of Criminology, in his dual account of the atrocities committed in the Balkan wars and the building of the ICTY, addresses how the charisma of the head prosecutors must work in tandem with mass media: "Even at Nuremberg, Justice Jackson needed . . . the cultivation of an initially unengaged press corps to play his charismatic role in the prosecution of Hermann Goering and his colleagues. . . . By the time of Ted Turner and CNN's globalization of the news, the creation and consequences of charisma were even more important parts of international criminal practice" (Hagan 2003, 7).

Yet to further complicate the story, news media do not simply disseminate the court's accounts of history. At times they reinforce selectivities of the court. The focus on individuals, for example, is a prominent feature of both criminal law and media reporting. At other times, news media apply their own selectivities in the coverage of trials.[57] A recent account of a Holocaust denial case in Canada illustrates this point.[58] Using a "rebuttal" strategy, prosecutors tried to disprove the defendant's statements by calling experts and survivors to the stand. This strategy caused considerable public attention, just as supporters of trials would prefer. Yet publicity also allowed for controversies and misleading newspaper headlines, some of which focused on any element of doubt about selective pieces of evidence. Defense attorneys capitalized on memory slips on the part of elderly survivor-witnesses, for example, who sought to remember terrifying experiences from many decades ago, and news media reported such doubts. After a conviction was overturned on procedural grounds, a second set of prosecutors used an alternative "unmasking" strategy, seeking to show that the defendant, as a Nazi, had an interest in denying the Holocaust.

This strategy sought to discredit the defendant and his motives while avoiding a detailed engagement of past records. In doing so, the prosecution cleverly obviated the need to discredit the defendant's claims.[59] This second trial, void of the presentation of historical evidence, provoked neither public controversy nor problematic publicity for Holocaust deniers. Clearly, prosecutorial strategies, in concert with media responses, can affect what narratives of history come out of court proceedings and the way they are communicated to a broader public. Our analyses of media reporting on the My Lai massacre, the Haditha killings, and the late president Slobodan Milosevic's role in the Balkan atrocities sheds further light on this media-trial nexus (see chapters 3 to 5).

Like news media, historians also examine legal proceedings against high-caliber perpetrators. In doing so they not only tell the history of the trials but also provide accounts of the atrocities to which trials respond. Furthermore, like journalists, historians do not just tell the history of atrocities revealed in trials; they also work with evidence that may result from court orders that were not admitted during the trial proceedings. In addition, as the rules of scholarship—again, like those of journalism—differ from the rules of criminal procedure, scholarly accounts often challenge the narratives that unfold during the court proceedings. Patricia Heberer and Jürgen Matthäus's *Atrocities on Trial* deals with post-Holocaust cases and provides excellent examples.[60] Its historical analyses engage in a profound critique of the legal proceedings, the history post–World War II trials produced, and the judgments at which the courts arrived. The authors also identify conditions of shortcomings, conditions that are attributable not simply to legal logic but also to political context. Insufficiencies in punishment, for example, are attributed to the Allies' postwar policy goals, especially the delegitimization of the Nazi regime and the democratization of the German public (hence the focus on a relatively small number of Nazi leaders) and first signs of the pending Cold War.

In short, evidence produced through trials is often filtered by other mechanisms such as media reporting and scholarship. This evidence is thereby disseminated to a much broader audience than the court proceedings themselves could reach. Yet these "middlemen" (journalists, historians) draw on evidence selectively and in line with the logics of the institutions in which they work. Middlemen may also reflect critically on the historical record produced by the courts and point to factors that have contributed to the distortion of such history—distortion at least in light of the respective rules of evidence under which journalists and historians work. That said, at present we do not know whether historical narratives produced by trials have staying power in the face of critical or alternative accounts from other institutions. This issue is taken up in the next chapter.

From Collective Memory to the End of Violence? Signs of Hope—and Resignation

The construction of collective memory, through legal or other means, may indeed have serious consequences. A line of argument has been developed in recent years that the collective memory of past atrocities is a key mechanism determining whether cycles of violence and hatred will persist or cease. The law professor Martha Minow, for example, claims that the nature of responses to mass violence and the historical narrative that unfolds through these responses can stymie or propel violence in large part because of the resulting collective memory.[61] Minow's reasoning cuts across disciplines, as the political scientist Jens Meierhenrich (2006b, 319–20) makes a similar argument. He states that "the representation of the past is of immediate relevance for the problem of social order. For the representation of the past affects the strategy of conflict, determining legal and other responses to collective violence. . . . The menu of choices available to victims and survivors—from reconciliation to revenge—is filtered through representations of the past."

The argument hints at complexities: Collective memory may have very diverse consequences, depending on the shape it takes. Ethnic leaders in the former Yugoslavia, preceding the decade before the break-up of the country, frequently cultivated collective memory, reminding their followers of past defeats and atrocities committed against their ancestors. They obviously did not do so to put an end to violence. Their purpose was quite the opposite—to marshal support for their cause, which eventually resulted in rape campaigns, the deaths of tens of thousands, and the displacement of millions. In other contexts, however, different memories of past violence may have pacifying consequences. The cultivation of memories of war in Germany, for example, created a culture that has been intensely opposed to the idea of war and military ventures. Nonetheless, we emphasize that cases do not easily fall into one or the other category, owing to mnemonic struggles and changes in collective memory. A spirit of skepticism toward war in the wake of the Vietnam War in the United States, for example, gave way to a much greater willingness to use the military to resolve international conflicts after the quick and decisive victory in the first war with Iraq. This shift in trust in the military was almost certainly affected by changes in collective memory and the commemoration of war, including Vietnam (see chapters 3 and 4 for details).[62]

Collective memory, of course, does not matter only in the unfolding and prevention of violence following periods of transitional justice and international conflict. Collective memory also plays manifold, but frequently overlooked, roles within stable democracies. Liberal democracies, too, are no strangers to hate-inspired violence, and we argue in later chapters that distinct collective memories influence nation- and region-specific legal responses to hatred and intergroup conflict. Chapters 7 through 9 of this volume, while further contributing to an understanding of the making of collective memory, focus on this heretofore underexplored theme—the impact of collective memory on the institutionalization of control mechanisms against hate-inspired violence in stable democracies. In particular, we identify diverse mechanisms through which collective memory motivates and shapes control responses. We pay particular attention to the prominent roles of carrier groups and interest groups, the use of bridging metaphors and analogical connections with the Holocaust, and the importance of historical consciousness. We further argue and demonstrate empirically in these chapters that whatever its source, collective memory contributes to the content and enforcement of law generally and hate crime law specifically. To wit, by considering collective memory we can more fully understand and explain law on the books, law in action, and variation in each at both the national and regional levels.

In short, collective memories of past violence and atrocities can, under particular circumstances, lead to control responses that at least have the potential of reducing or even ending the risk of future violence. Much depends on the way memory is formed, and the way it is formed is inspired by the institutions through which it is created. We think these processes have been underexplored to date. This volume seeks to make a contribution by theoretically and empirically addressing this apparent deficit in existing literature.

Summation

At this juncture we have covered considerable ground and established some basic understanding of collective memory, especially the memory of atrocities, its features, and the conditions under which it emerges, is maintained, and is diffused. We have specifically addressed ways in which court proceedings contribute to the formation of collective memory, the symbolic power trials may have, and the selectivities of legal narratives. We have also looked at other institutions, such as truth commissions, news media, and scholarship, that may supplement courts in the shaping of collective memory. These institutions may at times compete with courts and at other times serve as a megaphone for disseminating the message courts produce to a wider public. We have, finally, taken a brief look at the conditions under which such collective memories, once constructed, may more or less successfully contribute to ending episodes of violence and preventing future occurrences.

This discussion should prepare the reader for the following chapters. Each chapter contains new specifics that are clarified as we move along, including the role of textbooks and media reports as indicators and transmitters of collective memory, the role of carrier groups, historical consciousness, haunting, and the local organization of law and law enforcement. Our discussion so far delineates the common conceptual and theoretical frame for all the following chapters. We have laid a foundation on which to build an understanding of American memories of atrocities and the way law has shaped them and, in turn, been affected by them.

Chapter 3

Constructing and Remembering the My Lai Massacre

WITH RAJIV EVAN RAJAN AND LACY MITCHELL

I F A HIGH school student asked, "What was My Lai?" how would you answer? Could you correctly pronounce *My Lai*? When did it happen? Would you describe it as a watershed event in American history? Who were the key people or institutions involved? Did anyone die, and if so, who, how many, and at whose hands?

Some of these questions are matters of historical fact. My Lai (pronounced "me lie") is a hamlet in the village of Son My on the coast of central Vietnam. It is also accepted that several hundred innocent Vietnamese civilians, mostly women, children, and old men, were killed by members of an American infantry brigade on March 16, 1968, during the peak of the Vietnam War. The historian Kendrick Oliver (2006, 1) provides the following concise description in the introduction to his book, *The My Lai Massacre in American History and Memory*:

> On the morning of 16 March 1968, the men of Charlie Company, 11th Light Infantry Brigade, Americal Division, US Army, entered the hamlet of Tu Cung [which includes the subhamlet of My Lai 4], in the village of Son My. . . . The Company was assigned to a temporary battalion-sized unit named Task Force Barker, and it was led by Captain Ernest Medina. In charge of the company's 1st Platoon was Lieutenant William Calley. Inside Tu Cung, the company encountered no enemy forces, no opposing fire of any kind. Its only casualty was self-inflicted. Nevertheless, by early afternoon, well over 300 residents of the hamlet lay dead. Those killed were, predominantly, either women, old men or small children. For a number of the women, rape had preceded death.

The "when" and "where" questions about My Lai can be answered with little controversy. However, answers given to some of the other

34

questions vary considerably depending on the source of information. For instance, consider the issue of civilian deaths. Oliver makes reference to around 300. A military commission (the Peers Commission; we return to this shortly) investigating the affair estimated a death count of between 175 and 400, and a book by the journalist Seymour Hersh (1970, 75) puts the number killed at 450 to 500. We also note that a tablet at the memorial site at Son My village in Vietnam lists 504 names (Tim O'Brien, "The Vietnam in Me," *New York Times*, October 2, 1994, p. SM52), more than twenty times the number ("not less than 22 victims") that Lt. Calley was found guilty of killing. Hence, we encounter multiple sources of information—journalistic, military, legal—that differ even with regard to the basic numeric facts of the case. But which of these make their way into American memories?

Now consider culpability. Was this a matter of lone soldiers "losing their cool" with grave consequences? Was it an effect of the "broader culture of American war-making" in Vietnam (Oliver 2006, 55)? Did the top brass of the U.S. Army bear any responsibility, and did they attempt to cover up the incident? Each explanation has been put forth at some point or another, and again each seems to align with the story told by the military, by journalists, or through the trial. But which, if any, has solidified a place in American collective memory?

Finally, consider the question of impact. According to a November 1969 *New York Times* editorial, the event "may turn out to have been one of the nation's most ignoble hours." The theologian Reinhold Niebuhr wrote at the time, "This is a moment of truth when we realize that we are not a virtuous nation." And *Time* magazine asserted in its April 12, 1971, issue (p. 19) that "the crisis of confidence caused by the Calley affair is a graver phenomenon than the horror following the assassination of President Kennedy. Historically it is far more crucial."[1] Adding to that assessment, the NBC news anchorman Frank McGee declared that My Lai was a name "now seared into the American consciousness" (quoted in Oliver 2006, 231). Yet there is every indication that the memories of later generations do not live up to such expectations. Writing more than twenty-five years after the My Lai incident, Tim O'Brien, a Vietnam veteran and author of books about the war, suggested that the initial claims of a "grave" event that was "seared" into the consciousness of an otherwise "virtuous" nation did not properly anticipate the potential for amnesia that is commonplace in American society. As O'Brien lamented already almost two decades ago,

> All this is history. Dead as those dead women and kids. Even at the time, most Americans seemed to shrug it off as a cruel, nasty, inevitable consequence of war. There were numerous excuses, numerous rationalizations.

Upright citizens decried even the small bit of justice secured by the conviction of Lieutenant Calley. Now, more than 25 years later, the villainy of that Saturday morning in 1968 has been pushed off to the margins of memory. In the colleges and high schools I sometimes visit, the mention of My Lai brings on null stares, a sort of puzzlement, disbelief mixed with utter ignorance. (O'Brien 1994, SM52)

Not inconsistent with O'Brien's rather dismal appraisal, our own content analysis of more than one hundred U.S. history textbooks reveals that fewer than half make any mention of the My Lai massacre. Of those mentioning My Lai, the median word count is less than 80 words (as a point of comparison, the preceding quote by O'Brien is 102 words). Hence, it is not so clear that Americans recall My Lai as something "more crucial" than the Kennedy assassination.

Because of its alleged significance at the time and the various narratives of My Lai that emerged in the years after 1968, the constructed memory of the My Lai massacre provides an unusual opportunity to explore new ground in the realm of law and collective memory. The response to the massacre began with a cover-up by the U.S. Army. After the cover-up was exposed a year later, three narratives emerged about the incident, each in a distinct institutional setting. The first was a Pulitzer Prize–winning book by Seymour Hersh (1970) titled *My Lai 4*. The second was the U.S. Army's Peers Commission report, named after Lt. Gen. William R. Peers, who led an investigatory commission examining the events. This four-volume report remained guarded until 1974, when two volumes were released. The first of these volumes was later published, with an introduction and some supplementary materials (Goldstein, Marshall, and Schwartz 1976). The third narrative was based on the findings of a criminal court in which Lt. William Calley Jr. was found guilty and sentenced to life in prison in 1971.[2] In line with the guiding questions of this book, the following section contrasts the legal narrative with the journalistic and executive accounts before we set out to examine whether and how these alternative narratives have been reflected in news media reporting and in American high school history textbooks, both of which are important indicators of, and active players in, the formation of collective memory.[3]

Uncovering how the legacy of My Lai unfolded arguably takes on new relevance today as we find ourselves engaged in a war that gave "Abu Ghraib" and "Haditha" specific and pernicious meaning—the first referring to abuse and torture of detained prisoners, the second to the killing of many civilians—again, mostly women and children—in the recent war in Iraq. This is also a time in which the legitimacy, not to mention the legality, of torture is again part of the public discourse, as is the willingness to tolerate civilian casualties. We might then ask whether the memory of My Lai informs these issues (see chapter 4).

The case of My Lai allows us to partially evaluate whether legal trials powerfully contribute to the writing of history and the shaping of collective memory. As mentioned in the previous chapter, some jurists and prominent politicians have claimed, and in some cases promoted, the idea that trials could serve precisely this end. At the same time, research on cultural trauma and the institutional conditions of knowledge production warn us that historical narratives constructed through legal proceedings present a selective depiction of past events that differs in kind from, and competes with, not only historians' accounts but also narratives created in other institutional spheres, such as journalism. We use this case to observe how institutions such as mass media and textbook industries make selective use of trial narratives before these reach a broad audience. The cultural processing of the My Lai massacre thus provides an opportunity to examine many prominent claims from the worlds of scholarship, politics, and law and to examine the complex interactions between diverse social forces that contribute to the construction of collective memory.

The My Lai Massacre: A Trio of Tales

The *Report of the Department of the Army Review of the Preliminary Investigations into the My Lai Incident,* more commonly referred to as the Peers Inquiry or the Peers Report, was a rather thorough investigation of the My Lai incident. Lieutenant General Peers was originally directed by Gen. William C. Westmoreland, the U.S. Army chief of staff, and Stanley Resor, secretary of the army, with the following charge: "To explore the nature and the scope of the original U.S. Army investigation(s) of the alleged My Lai (4) incident which occurred 16 March 1968 in Quang Ngai Province, Republic of Vietnam. Your investigation will include a determination of the adequacy of the investigation(s) or inquiries on this subject, their subsequent reviews and reports within the chain of command, and possible suppression or withholding of information by persons involved in the incident."[4]

But as noted in the introduction of the report, "It became apparent at an early stage that the adequacy of those reports and investigations could not be evaluated intelligently without a thorough understanding of what actually took place during Task Force (TF) Barker's operations in the Son My area on 16–19 March 1968. . . . For these reasons, the scope of the Inquiry included a complete examination into the operational situation throughout."[5]

The Peers Commission summarized the events as follows, addressing various dimensions of organizational and individual behavior (marked by us in brackets; we did not include all items):

1. During the period March 16–19, 1968, U.S. Army troops of TF [Task Force] Barker, 11th Brigade, Americal Division, massacred a large number of noncombatants in two villages of Son My Village, Quang Ngai Province, Republic of Vietnam. The precise number of Vietnamese killed cannot be determined but was at least 175 and may exceed 400.

2. The massacre occurred in conjunction with a combat operation which was intended to neutralize Son My Village as a logistical support base and staging area, and to destroy elements of an enemy battalion thought to be located in the Son My area.

3. The massacre resulted primarily from the nature of the orders issued by persons in the chain of command within TF Barker ... [Organizational responsibility]

5. Prior to the incident, there had developed within certain elements of the 11th Brigade a permissive attitude toward the treatment and safeguarding of noncombatants which contributed to the mistreatment of such persons during the Son My operation. [Organizational culture]

6. The permissive attitude in the treatment of Vietnamese was, on 16–19 March 1968, exemplified by an almost total disregard for the lives and property of the civilian population of Son My Village on the part of commanders and key staff officers of TF Barker. [Organizational and individual responsibility]

7. On 16 March, soldiers at the squad and platoon level, with some elements of TF Barker, murdered noncombatants while under the supervision and control of their immediate superiors. [Individual and organizational responsibility]

8. A part of the crimes visited on the inhabitants of Son My Village included individual and group acts of murder, rape, sodomy, maiming, and assault of noncombatants and the mistreatment and killing of detainees. They further included the killing of livestock, destruction of crops, closing of wells, and the burning of dwellings in several subhamlets. . . .

19. At every command level within the Americal Division, actions were taken, both wittingly and unwittingly, which effectively suppressed information concerning the war crimes committed at Son My Village. [Organizational responsibility and individual responsibility across several levels of command][6]

The summary includes additional sections on the inadequacy of reports, investigations, reviews, policies, directives, and training and on the actions of individuals involved in the massacre. The report covers only the period between March 16, 1968, and March 29, 1969, the date on which Ronald Ridenhour, a Vietnam veteran, sent a letter to President Richard Nixon, Pentagon officials, and members of the U.S. Congress that revealed information he had gathered on the massacre and the cover-up. Owing to the secrecy of the commission's work, Ridenhour believed that the cover-up was continuing. His subsequent contact with Seymour Hersh resulted in Hersh's 1970 book *My Lai 4*, which drew considerable public attention to the case. The journalistic narrative adds graphic detail to the commission report. For instance, consider the following excerpt from Hersh's (1970, 49–54) account:

> The killings began without warning. . . . [One witness reports he saw] "some old women and some little children—fifteen or twenty of them—in a group around a temple where some incense was burning. They were kneeling and crying and praying, and various soldiers . . . walked by and executed these women and children by shooting them in the head with their rifles."
>
> There were few physical protests from the people; about eighty of them were taken quietly from their homes and herded together in a plaza area. . . . [First Platoon commander Lt.] Calley left [subordinates] Meadlo, Boyce and a few others with the responsibility of guarding the group. "You know what I want you to do with them," he told Meadlo. Ten minutes later—about 8:15 A.M.—he returned and asked, "Haven't you got rid of them yet? I want them dead." Radioman [Charles] Sledge who was trailing Calley, heard the officer tell Meadlo to "waste them." Meadlo followed orders: "We stood about ten to fifteen feet away from them and then [Calley] started shooting them. Then he told me to start shooting them. I started to shoot them. So we went ahead and killed them. . . . Women were huddled against their children, vainly trying to save them. . . ."
>
> By this time there was shooting everywhere. . . . Brooks and his men in the second platoon to the north had begun to systematically ransack the hamlet and slaughter the people, kill the livestock and destroy the crops. Men poured rifle and machine gun fire without knowing—or seemingly caring—who was inside. . . .
>
> [Herbert] Carter testified that soon after the third platoon moved in, a woman was sighted. Somebody knocked her down, and then, Carter said, "[Commander of Company C, Capt. Ernest] Medina shot her with his M16 rifle. I was fifty or sixty feet away and saw this. There was no reason to shoot the girl." The men continued on, making sure no one was escaping. "We came to where the soldiers had collected fifteen or more Vietnamese men, women and children in a group. . . . Medina said: 'Kill every one. Leave no one standing.' A machine gunner began firing into the group. Moments later one of Medina's radio operators slowly 'passed' among them and finished them off."

The events captured and narrated in the Peers Commission report and in Hersh's book were ultimately accompanied by a third narrative—the criminal trial. Initial investigations of about thirty individuals resulted in formal charges against more than half of them (Kelman and Hamilton 2002). The court proceedings addressed two types of behavior. The first covered a large number of "spontaneous" rapes and killings of individuals during the "mop-up" operation for which Lieutenant [Jeffrey] LaCross's third platoon was largely responsible. According to Hersh (1970, 72), "Le Tong, a twenty-eight-year-old rice farmer, reported seeing one woman raped after GIs killed her children. Nguyen Khoa, a thirty-seven-year-old peasant, told of the thirteen-year-old girl who was raped before being killed. GIs then attacked Khoa's wife, tearing off her clothes. Before they could rape her, however, Khoa said, their six-year-old son, riddled with bullets, fell and saturated her with blood. The GIs left her alone."

Such "unofficial" reports of spontaneous atrocities were not backed by the same hard evidence as the ordered mass killing executed by the First Platoon under the command of Lieutenant Calley, on which the charges were based. Calley stood trial for 102 of the killings he had ordered and in which he had participated. He pleaded, in his defense, that his actions were in line with superior orders. Yet as the court-martial argued, and as the judge confirmed in his instructions to the jury, "the obedience of a soldier is not the obedience of an automaton. A soldier is a reasoning agent, obliged to respond, not as a machine, but as a person. The law takes these factors into account in assessing criminal responsibility for acts done in compliance with illegal orders" (quoted in Kelman and Hamilton 2002, 209).

A jury of combat veterans eventually convicted William Calley of premeditated murder of not less than twenty-two persons. The conviction was based on witness testimony confirming that Calley had ordered and participated in the mass executions, witnessed by members of the platoon and by a helicopter crew (under Chief Warrant Officer Hugh Thompson, who eventually intervened to save the lives of some of the villagers).[7] Legal proof was too weak to link the massacre to orders from superiors, especially since Lt. Col. Frank A. Barker, Medina's immediate superior, was killed in action shortly after the Son My massacre. Captain Medina, the commander of Company C, who had given the orders for the attack on Son My on March 15, 1968, was not found guilty. Neither were other members of the company, nor those who engaged in spontaneous atrocities, nor direct subordinates of Lieutenant Calley who participated in the mass executions. Rules of evidence, in the eyes of the court, allowed only for the conviction of one participant in the massacre.[8]

We thus find a distinct difference between the accounts of the Peers Commission and the journalistic report by Seymour Hersh, on one hand, and the trial narrative, on the other.

The commission and the journalistic report find that responsibility for the massacre and the cover-up rests with the many members of Company C, including its commander, and with military personnel above the company level, which was not a conclusion reached by the court.

The commission and journalistic accounts address the organized massacre and "spontaneous" rapes and killings, whereas the verdict focuses on the organized mass execution.

The number of victims as estimated by the Peers Commission was at least 175 and possibly more than 400. Hersh's (1970, 75) account (450 to 500) exceeds the upper end of the Peers estimate. The court, constrained by evidentiary rules, charged Captain Medina with the murder of 102 civilians, but in the end only Lieutenant Calley was found guilty of at least twenty-two killings. In addition, opinion polls after the trial revealed strong public disagreement with the Calley conviction.

Which of these distinct constructions of reality do we encounter in American news reporting and in high school history textbooks, if any? How powerful is the trial relative to journalism and military reports? Has the trial become a force in the shaping of the collective memories of subsequent generations?

My Lai in the Media and the Classroom

Court trials reach a broader public primarily through the mass media, but history textbooks also communicate historical events to a younger, impressionable audience. They may be highly effective in doing so, especially when linked with strong social movements such as the civil rights movement, as shown in recent work on the changing images of President Lincoln.[9]

Textbook writers, of course, draw on a variety of sources. Historical and highly significant criminal trials are likely among them, especially as these legal proceedings constitute a kind of government-certified knowledge.

Yet textbook production is driven by its own institutional rules and its own logic in which peculiar markets play a central role. Decisions on the acquisition of textbooks are typically made by school boards based on recommendations from adoption committees, themselves formed by school boards. In some states, such as Texas and California—massive customers that textbook publishers seek to satisfy—decisions are made at the state level. Guidelines that speak to the desired content of textbooks are typically taken seriously by publishers, who make enormous investments in each textbook and are eager to see returns. Diverse lobby groups guard carefully over these guidelines and the production to make sure that no "offensive" content appears in the books. These processes are described in a highly informative and provocative book by the New York University professor Diane Ravitch, a former under-secretary of education during the George H. W. Bush administration and co-chair of the California committee that was responsible for a major overhaul of that state's content guidelines in the mid-1980s.[10] They are likely to privilege state-certified views of history and not to offend powerful constituents. The latter include actors such as Mel and Norma Gabler, major conservative players in the state of Texas, and a multitude of minority constituents in California.

Textbooks thus reflect to a considerable degree what those in power and those well organized see as valid interpretations of history. No doubt, this aspect of history writing closely resonates with Halbwachs's (1992) presentist approach. And though more critical materials were included in history textbooks after the late 1960s, opinions on the degree differ in the literature.[11] While Ravitch notes a surplus of critical content about the United States in recent decades, at least in global history texts, others argue that such views on the nation continue to be underrepresented.[12] Our analysis of My Lai depictions speaks to this debate with empirical evidence.

Hence we are looking for a few things in our newspaper and textbook data sources. How much coverage existed of the My Lai massacre? Which of the three narratives described earlier seems to dominate? And is there a tendency to play down this horrific event?

Data Collection and Analysis

We obtained information from two sources. To compile a sample of high school history textbooks, we began with database searches (EBSCO: Academic Search Complete and JSTOR). Through these searches we established a list of all scholarly journal articles that used content analysis on U.S. high school history textbooks published after 1969.[13] Copies of each book and article were located and reviewed, and these sources informed a list of all cited textbooks published after 1968 (information about My Lai was released to the general public in 1969).[14] Additional sources were then located and reviewed for any cited textbooks. We subsequently identified chapters on the Vietnam War in each textbook and highlighted information pertaining to the My Lai massacre. We catalogued several types of information that speak to the aforesaid narratives. For instance, does the chapter (or passage) highlight individual or organizational responsibility? Are upper ranks of the military implicated? How are perpetrators and victims described? Is there mention of a cover-up? In the end, we were able to assemble a dataset with 105 American history textbooks (see appendix A for a bibliography of all textbooks).

We then used a similar coding scheme to assess how My Lai was discussed in news reporting. Here we used LexisNexis to identify articles discussing My Lai and published in the *New York Times* between 1969 and 2006. The articles were located and coded in a manner consistent with the procedure applied to the examination of history textbooks. This dataset resulted in 676 news articles, nearly 90 percent of which appeared in the 1970s.

The findings from our content analysis of textbooks are revealing. For one, and despite the grand conjecture immediately after the massacre about My Lai being a watershed event on par with the Kennedy assassination, this mass killing of women and children appears in only a minority of American history textbooks. In our sample of 105 textbooks, 61 percent (64) make no mention of My Lai. All textbooks contain substantial chapters on the Vietnam War, and some mention damage caused to the Vietnamese countryside or the unintentional bombing of civilians.[15] Nevertheless, the majority of textbooks avoid any explicit reference to the My Lai massacre. Also of interest is the timing of references to My Lai. Thirty-six of the books in our sample were published in the 1970s, 33 in the 1980s, and 17 and 19, respectively, in the following two decades. Interestingly, between 20 and 30 percent of the textbooks published in the 1970s and 1980s mention My Lai, but in the following two decades the number jumps to between 58 and 71 (see figure 3.1). This appears to be consistent with Ravitch's claim that textbook content on the United States has become more critical in recent decades. Yet here the onset of reporting about a problematic event occurs almost two decades later than she leads us to expect. This suggests that an explanation different from Ravitch's might carry more weight in the case of My Lai: that textbooks turn more critical as the specific event becomes more distant, possibly because vested interests by specific actors wane with growing distance.

Further insight is gained when we examine the detail with which the My Lai incident is depicted over time. Figure 3.2 plots the word count for each textbook passage relating to My Lai included in our sample by year. Using this indicator, we see that coverage begins the year after the court-martial and remains fairly steady until about 1979. Then, both the frequency and breadth of coverage noticeably decline during much of the 1980s, only to pick up again in the early 1990s. The decline during the 1980s is consistent with the rhetoric of then President Reagan, who masterfully sought to restore Americans' pride in their nation and military. Yet the 1990s and the first decade of the twenty-first century saw a recurrence of war and war-related themes, and some of the Reagan optimism gave way to disenchantment. Moreover, there often exists a

Figure 3.1   Mention of My Lai in Sampled American History Textbooks, by Decade, 1970 to 2009

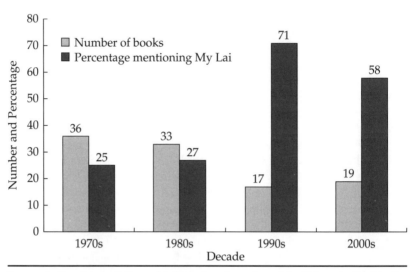

Source: Authors' compilation of information from American history textbooks. See appendix A for complete list.

period of latency between the occurrence of horrific events and their firm establishment in the telling of history.[16] As we show later, however, this modest resurgence of textbook reporting about My Lai did not generally affect Americans' attitudes toward their military.

Our data further indicate that even when My Lai is mentioned in history textbooks, such utterances are typically brief, sometimes utterly fleeting. In books that mention My Lai, the event is often given scant attention—approximately one small paragraph. The following quote is illustrative of such passages. After critically reporting on General Westmoreland's use of overwhelming firepower that drove many peasants into the arms of the Viet Cong, the authors of the 2003 edition of *America. Past and Present* inform their young readers: "Inevitably, these tactics led to the slaughter of innocent civilians, most notably in the hamlet of My Lai. In March of 1968, an American Company, led by Lieutenant William Calley, Jr., killed more than two hundred unarmed villagers" (Divine et al. 2003, 880).

Other descriptions provide even less detail, and few include the gruesome particularities noted in Hersh's book. For instance, *The American Pageant: A History of the Republic* includes only the following text: "Domestic disgust with the war was further deepened in 1970 by revela-

Figure 3.2   My Lai Word Count, by Year, 1970 to 2009

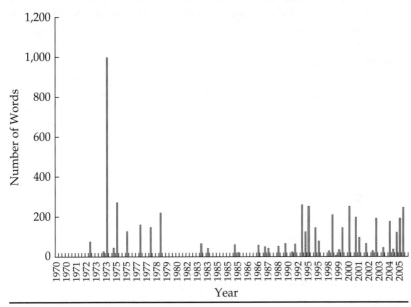

Source: Authors' compilation of information from American history textbooks. See appendix A for complete list.
Note: The highest value was top-coded at 1,000, although the actual word count exceeded this value.

tions that in 1968 American troops had massacred innocent women and children in the village of My Lai" (Bailey, Kennedy, and Cohen 1998, 967).

Some of the books include lengthier passages that report the details of the massacre, but the modal description of the My Lai massacre—when one is found at all—is both terse and generic.[17] Most of the text-books treat the massacre either as a microcosm of combat stress that overtook soldiers after North Vietnam's Tet offensive (42 percent) or as an episode that contributed to changing attitudes about Vietnam on the home front (47 percent).[18]

Moreover, and most pertinent to this chapter, the trial narrative appears to be more prevalent than the commission's and Seymour Hersh's accounts in both the textbooks and the *New York Times* articles. The history textbooks show evidence of the legal narrative in multiple places. An initial and rudimentary comparison of sampled textbooks that mention My Lai revealed no direct mention of the Peers Commission report, and we found only four explicit references to Hersh's book. References to the trial, however, are more frequent. For instance, one of the earliest books in our sample to mention My Lai includes the following: "For many in the nation the disclosure of American atrocities committed against North Vietnamese at My Lai were gruesome evidence of both the nature and futility of that war. *These revelations came out mainly in the trial of Lieutenant William Calley.* He was found guilty by a military court for allowing and encouraging troops under his immediate command to shoot at unarmed and helpless men, women, and children" (Leinwand 1975, 646; our emphasis).

Lieutenant Calley is explicitly mentioned in nearly 60 percent of the books addressing the My Lai incident. Almost all of these books also make a general reference to U.S. troops; one refers to "a U.S. Army Officer" (likely Calley), yet few others are personally implicated. The only other name explicitly mentioned is that of Capt. Ernest Medina (one mention), who was court-martialed but found not guilty in the My Lai massacre. In addition, the trial made scant reference to the cover-up or the plausible culpability of military members of superior rank to Captain Medina. This omission is particularly striking in contrast to the Peers Commission report and Hersh's book. In the textbook analysis we count only thirteen mentions (about a third of cases mentioning My Lai) of a cover-up, eight of which appear after 1990. Nine books (less than a quarter) implicate higher ranks. Although the books are hardly monolithic in their coverage of My Lai, the trial narrative appears to have stronger effects on textbook accounts than the two competing sources.

The *Times* analysis corroborates these findings. For instance, our analysis deemed articles to fit a "script" (that is, that of Peers, Hersh, or the court-martial) if the source itself is cited specifically by name in an article. A multiple-response analysis showed that when a script is mentioned, it is overwhelmingly the one provided by the military trial. Forty-three percent of articles make reference to the trial, compared with 2 percent that mention Hersh's investigation and 7 percent that refer to the Peers Inquiry.[19]

A similar multiple-response analysis was employed for alleged perpetrators in the massacre. In all, nearly seventy different names or groups appear in the 676 articles we analyzed. As with the history textbooks, the modal category is Lieutenant Calley (180 mentions). A general reference to "U.S. troops" comes in a distant second (84), followed by Col. Oran Henderson (72) and Captain Medina (65).[20] This pattern is particularly evident after the court-martial and conviction of Calley. Before 1971, the *Times* articles often make reference to U.S. troops as perpetrators at My Lai (21 percent of articles in our sample). In this early stage, ending three years after the massacre and during the year in which the trial concluded, Colonel Henderson was mentioned in fewer than 2 percent of the articles, Medina in fewer than 4 percent, and Calley in 18 percent. After the trial ended, mention of the My Lai culprits moved in the direction from the general ("U.S. troops") to the particular (Calley,

Medina). In the posttrial period, Calley was mentioned in 31 percent of cases, Henderson in 15, and Medina in 13 percent.

Hence, in much the way that law enforcement can apotheosize an individual within a larger struggle, law can also defile individuals and render them symbols of a sinister crime.[21] In the process, we encounter a collective forgetting of the larger milieu of circumstances surrounding the event. This sentiment is largely consistent with Kendrick Oliver's recent conjecture. As Oliver (2006, 55–56) writes, "That the legal process emphasized the agency of a small number of individuals no doubt reinforced the inclination of the media to adopt what was in any case a common news practice when engaging with events as complex and enigmatic as those which had occurred at My Lai (4): to gain narrative and analytical traction by reducing the frame of reportage focusing upon the fate of one or two actors. This was most evident with regard to William Calley."

Finally, we examined the discussion of victims in both the history textbooks and the *Times* articles. Compared with the other aspects of our inquiry, the issue of victims revealed a greater variety of depictions. Looking first at the textbooks, we found that those published in the early years of our study period stay rather close to the trial narrative. They refer, for instance to "more than 100 villagers, including women, infants, and old people" (Lippe 1972, 161), or they report that "over one hundred unarmed and unresisting women, children, and babies were butchered in cold blood" (Bailey 1973, 999). Before 1980, only two books mention body counts that do not align with the trial narrative. The 1974 edition of *United States History: Search for Freedom* (Current, DeConde, and Dante 1974, 642) refers to a massacre of about five hundred men, women, and children, and the 1978 edition of *Freedom and Crisis* (Weinstein and Wilson 1978, 864) makes reference to 347 civilian casualties. Again, the discussion of My Lai appears somewhat muted in history textbooks during much of the 1980s. One book in our sample (Bailey and Kennedy 1983, 882) refers to Calley's conviction of murdering "some twenty victims" in 1983, but this is one of only a few mentions of My Lai between 1979 and 1986. Then, beginning in 1986, a substantially higher proportion of textbooks mention the number of victims as exceeding two hundred, although they continue to range from very general references ("dozens of women and children"; see Carnes and Garraty 2003, 806) to "at least 450 women, children, and elderly men" (Ayers et al. 2007, 975).

The *New York Times* tells a comparable story, although these articles appear to stay closer to the trial narrative. When we restrict our analysis to general articles (omitting obituaries, op-ed essays, and letters to the editor), about 42 percent make no reference to the number of casualties, mentioning only "civilians" or "women and children." More than one-third, however, report a number of causalities that seems to reflect the trial narrative. Precisely 40 percent of general articles in our sample cite the number of civilian deaths as somewhere between 10 and 125. These numbers are close to either the number of charges (for 102 deaths) or convictions (not less than 22) achieved in the trial. Only about 10 percent of articles mention civilian deaths consistent with Hersh's investigation (350–400) or the Peers Report (175; perhaps as many as 400).

We close with a note on the context in which My Lai is discussed. We observe that textbook depictions of My Lai rarely occur in the frame of human rights or related themes. Rather, My Lai is frequently invoked where growing American doubts about the war are articulated. The following quotation from the 1981 edition of *The National Experience: A History of the United States* primarily presents the judicial narrative, but it also alerts students to challenges to that account:

> People watched with growing discomfort as the tiny screen showed Vietnamese children horribly burned by American napalm or Americans systematically setting fire to Vietnamese villages. The disclosure that American soldiers had massacred more than a hundred unarmed Vietnamese civilians at My Lai in March 1968 made war atrocities a national issue. The subsequent arrest and conviction of Lieutenant William F. Calley, Jr., produced strong if confused reactions. Some defended Calley; Nixon interceded sympathetically on his behalf. Some thought it unfair that Calley should be the only man convicted for the massacre. Some demanded the prosecution of top military and civilian leaders as war criminals. Whatever else, My Lai forced many Americans suddenly to see the war from an appalled new perspective, to wonder if the United States had not brutalized itself in Vietnam, and to conclude that the means employed and the destruction wrought had grown out of all proportion to the interests involved and the goals sought. (Blum 1977, 793–4)

The conviction of Lieutenant Calley is obviously reported. But so are the challenges, directed at the individualizing and decoupling nature of the legal narrative. Responsibility is so widely diffused that individual responsibility is no longer recognizable. However, demands are cited to attribute liability to Calley's superiors along the military and civilian hierarchy, though each of these potential challenges is limited to one sentence. The narrative then moves away from the massacre to speak critically to the war's consequences for the United States.

How Do Americans Feel About Their Military Four Decades After My Lai?

How does the mix of silencing and selective accounting in American textbooks and the references in the reporting of one of the most prominent and generally liberal newspapers, the *New York Times*, affect the lived collective memory of the American people? While a satisfactory answer to this question awaits future survey research, existing data provided by the International Social Survey Programme show that the brutalities of the war have certainly not inflicted any enduring damage on the standing of the American military in public opinion or national pride generally.[22] While Americans are a world leader in national pride (competing only with Venezuelans for that position), domain-specific data show that part of this position derives from the population's pride in its armed forces. When asked in 2004, "How proud are you of America in each of the following?" almost three-quarters (73.5 percent) of a representative sample of Americans expressed pride in "America's armed forces." This compares with around one-third who answered "the way democracy works" (32 percent) and "America's economic achievement" (38.3 percent) and somewhere between one-half and two-thirds who acknowledged "its scientific and technological achievements" (57.1 percent) and "its history" (60.6 percent). No other nation shows this level of pride in its military.

While some of this extraordinarily high esteem of America's military, measured three years after 2001, may be a result of the trauma of the September 11 attacks, the fight against terrorism, and the ongoing war in Iraq, 1996 domain-specific measures also show the military's esteem to be at a very high level, with slightly more than 47 percent holding this view, tied for second place with "America's history" and only slightly lower than "its scientific and technological achievements" (48.6 percent).[23] Longer term trends show that the military has held a leading position in public opinion for many decades, albeit at a lower level than today, and that its position has strengthened in the past two decades. During the 1970s and much of the 1980s a nationally representative sample of respondents, when expressing "a great deal of confidence" in diverse institutions, put medicine in the lead, with between 50 and 60 percent in most years, while religion and the military competed for second place (between 30 and 40 percent, respectively, in most years). Yet around 1990 the military experienced a tremendous rise in "confidence" to finally become the leading domain by the middle of the first decade of the twenty-first century. Public regard for medicine, religion, the press, and Congress declined throughout most of the study period.[24]

While the lessons from My Lai thus do not appear to have had a strong or enduring effect on the American public's esteem for the military, they also seem to have had little effect on the mindset of the American military until recently, with the war in Iraq. A report released by the U.S. Army in the fall of 2006 shows that more than one-third of soldiers believe that torture should be allowed if it helps gather important information about insurgents—despite the illegality of torture in international law. Two-thirds of marines and half of army troops respond that they would not report a team member for mistreating a civilian or for destroying civilian property unnecessarily.[25]

Changes in public attitudes toward the Vietnam War are also reflected in the renewed prominence of war memorials, including memorials of the Vietnam War. For instance, in St. Paul, the capital of Minnesota, a memorial was established in 1992 at the foot of the hill that is crowned by the magnificent State Capitol. The memorial attempts to reconcile mourning with the reaffirmation of honor for those who served in Vietnam. A quote from the memorial's website states that the Minnesota Vietnam Veterans Memorial "was designed to express honor and remembrance, while acknowledging valor and service, and affirming the need to grieve as well as to experience an earlier time of innocence before the war. It was designed also to remind us that the price of war is high: young men and women die, and others have their lives forever altered."[26] Grief is clearly a central component of this memorial. At the same time, the reaffirmation of honor, valor, and service are highlighted, while the context of a problematic war is not articulated.

Consider also previous research on the changing character and uses of the Vietnam Veterans Memorial in Washington, D.C.[27] An influential article published in 1991 in the *American Journal of Sociology* provides a detailed analysis. It describes how the somber appearance of the horizontal, black-marble memorial, dug deep into the earth in which those are buried whose names are engraved, was partially neutralized by the later erection of a massive flag post and a realist bronze statue of three soldiers. Visitors to the memorial also contribute to the change in appearance. To be sure, thousands have reinforced the original somber mood with the tears they shed when facing the dark marble wall and the engraved names of their loved ones. Simultaneously, however, visitors have displayed thousands of items, including patriotic symbols that are regularly collected by the park service and stored in archives. These changes and uses move the appearance of the memorial closer to the traditional heroic, rather than mournful, commemoration of past military engagements. They provide another expression of the shifting ways in which the Vietnam War has been remembered, away from a shameful and primarily mournful chapter of American history, in which the lives of so many young men were sacrificed on the altar of highly controversial political philosophies, toward a glorified and patriotic engagement. Not surprisingly, today we even find political candidates who pretend that they fought in Vietnam, in the belief that such lies will improve their chances of getting elected.[28]

American remembrances of American warfare contrast strangely with epochal changes diagnosed by prominent historians. Such scholars describe a shift from commemorating the experience and suffering of soldiers in the battlefield, characteristic of World War I remembrance, toward a focus on civilian victims during the post–World War II era.[29] Official American remembrance of the Vietnam War instead continues to highlight the suffering (and valorize the service) of common soldiers. American war memorials certainly neglect the civilian victims of American warfare. One possible explanation is that American wars since the Civil War have not typically involved American civilian victims.[30] Yet this chapter confirms the Yale historian Jay Winter's (2006, 282) conclusion that the civilian victims' "words appear in [such sites as] tribunals [or] in commissions of inquiry," mechanisms—albeit selective ones—to keep alive some memories of some of the civilian victims of American atrocities.

Conclusions and Implications

The My Lai massacre, the ways it was culturally processed, and the patterns of its remembrance in decades since fill one important cell in the analytic field laid out at the beginning of this volume (see table 1.1). It speaks to American memories of cases in which domestic courts respond to an atrocity. It concurrently, and not coincidentally, addresses a type of case in which only relatively low-ranked military personnel are found guilty in the court of law. How then do expectations vis-à-vis My Lai, and theoretical arguments regarding the ritual power of law—and its institutional selectivities—hold up in this case?

It seems clear that the trial against a group of military men involved in the My Lai massacre did not succeed in securing confirmation of initial predictions by prominent intellectuals and highly visible media. Profound changes in the American collective conscience did not materialize. At first glance, this appears to conflict with Durkheimian expectations regarding the ritual power of trials. We do not know, though, how much of the event would be reported in textbooks and media had there been no criminal trial; empirically assessing the counterfactual in this case is not possible.

Some might argue, of course, that the event is appropriately played down, as it should not overshadow the otherwise brave and flawless performance of American soldiers in Vietnam. Yet reports from participants such as the Marine lieutenant Philip Caputo, a Vietnam veteran, challenge that assumption.[31] They are supported by other sources that suggest, in the words of Randall Collins's (2008, 88) seminal book on violence, that "incidents of this type [My Lai] were fairly common in the Vietnam war. . . . At a minimum these were orgies of destruction, vandalism on an extreme scale."[32]

One of our specifications of the Durkheimian thesis, however, is confirmed: Wherever trials seek to attribute guilt to selected low-level frontline agents in the perpetration of atrocities, potential effects of law on the formation of collective memory are undermined. In the My Lai case, the court's conviction and sentence to life in prison with hard labor was already disputed in the public sphere when it was passed, and politicians responded to such challenges, including several governors and state legislatures, President Nixon, and Howard Callaway, secretary of the Army. A series of decisions resulted in William Calley being moved from prison to house arrest and in his sentence being reduced first to twenty years and later to ten years. In 1974 he was released after serving three and a half years of house arrest and received a limited presidential pardon. It is conceivable that the public uproar was a protest against the individualizing (or decoupling) function of criminal law.[33]

Another thesis, derived from Weberian insights into the specific logics of distinct institutional spheres, is also confirmed and simultaneously supports ideas about the cultural power of legal trials: Our analysis reveals a narrative of the My Lai events that more often than not closely reflects the historical account as established through judicial proceedings. Clearly, textbook narratives that do account for the My Lai massacre focus on Lieutenant Calley, the lone convict in the My Lai trial; the offenses committed directly under his command; and the number of victims killed directly through the mass execution he ordered. Competing narratives from the Peers Commission report and Seymour Hersh's book are not absent, but they are underrepresented for most of our analytic categories. While they indicate how law as a constitutor of history must compete with other institutions, law's dominant position is confirmed in the case of My Lai.

In short, the My Lai massacre, committed by American soldiers in the course of the Vietnam War, did not affect the telling of American history and the public esteem of the American military as profoundly as some had expected at the onset of the 1970s. To the degree to which powerful social actors have an interest in the untarnished reputation of the American military, the finding supports presentist claims regarding the cultivation of collective memory that had been so influentially made by Maurice Halbwachs. For now the question is raised as to how the processing of the My Lai massacre colors the depiction of mass killings in more recent wars. We set out to examine this question for one particular case, the killing of many unarmed civilians, including women and children, in the town of Haditha in the course of the Iraq War.

= Chapter 4 =

From Vietnam to Iraq: Bridging Metaphors, Mnemonic Struggles, and Haunting

WITH JEREMY MINYARD

I
N THE preceding chapter we showed a cleansing of American memories of atrocities committed by members of the country's military during the Vietnam War, especially the My Lai massacre. The reputation of the military, already protected by the court's attribution of guilt to a single lieutenant, the leader of a platoon within one company, continues to appear relatively untarnished. Approval ratings of the military also remain high. This constellation of memories and attitudes became most relevant, visible, and consequential as the United States engaged in a series of new wars in the late twentieth and early twenty-first centuries. The Gulf War of 1991 had been relatively short, with a clear and limited military mission and a victorious outcome. Almost a decade later, responding to the 2001 terrorist attacks targeting New York City and Washington, D.C., the United States responded with military force, first in Afghanistan, where the Taliban regime had provided the Al Qaeda terrorist organization with a safe haven. This war received broad approval, domestically and internationally, with doubts spreading only in the past few years.

Yet since March of 2003, the United States has also been involved in a war and occupation in Iraq. The justifications for this war were indeed contentious, the entire effort largely resting on a disputed claim that Iraq possessed and was ready to use weapons of mass destruction along with the second Bush administration's dubious attempts to link Saddam Hussein to Al Qaeda. At least partly owing to public doubts about these justifications for the military campaign, which were enhanced by the initially chaotic situation and massive violence accompanying the first years of occupation, the Iraq War has had tenuous and variable support from the American people. Its legitimacy has also faced considerable challenges internationally.

For many in the American media and public at large, the Iraq War conjures memories of the largely unpopular U.S. war in Vietnam, despite large differences in the number of soldiers deployed and killed and the duration of the conflicts. Descriptive terms such as "quagmire" that had lain dormant since Vietnam resurfaced in many reports from the Iraqi war zone.[1] These memories of Vietnam both inform and limit the public's understanding of the Iraq War. In a survey of a cross-section of Americans in five states in December of 2004 and July of 2005, about two-thirds of respondents likened the Iraq War to the Vietnam War rather than to World War II. The latter, as opposed to Vietnam, had a clear justification and ultimately a victorious outcome.[2] Yet in line with our arguments about the group-specific nature of collective memory, this view was not unanimous. Republicans, for example, were almost evenly split, likening the Iraq engagement as much to World War II as to Vietnam. Furthermore, the youngest cohorts were more likely to mention World War II as an appropriate comparison than were those who were alive during the Vietnam War, indicating that the consternation surrounding the Vietnam War is not firmly settled in the collective memory of younger cohorts.

Even those who likened Iraq to Vietnam were not of one mind. While the American failure to achieve its objectives in Vietnam and the eventual withdrawal of troops made it a useful analogy for those who opposed the Iraq War and preferred the withdrawal of American troops from Iraq, others used Vietnam's legacy to encourage persistence. For them, Vietnam was evidence of the potentially tragic consequences of domestic opposition to an ongoing war and failure to adequately commit to a mission.

Debate over the Iraq War and references to historic wars provide an opportunity to contribute to a number of themes addressed here and to answer further questions raised in this book. The concepts introduced in earlier chapters can be put to fruitful use as we seek to understand the processing of present-day conflicts in light of the past. Here we see mnemonic struggles unfolding in real time, those fights over the interpretation of the past in light of conflicting present-day political interests. Furthermore, bridging metaphors are again deployed, those attempts at using past events metaphorically to color our interpretation of later occurrences. The concern with bridging metaphors here resonates with work by the sociological theorist Jeffrey Alexander, who has shown that use of the Holocaust as a bridging metaphor by journalists and political leaders helped mobilize opposition to Serbian dictator Slobodan Milosevic.[3] By connecting the traumatic memory of the Holocaust and associated ideas about the necessity of intervention in mass atrocities to the issue of intervention in Serbia, actors shaped the way a current event was understood. In doing so, they effectively overcame political obstacles on the path toward military and judicial intervention. Different societal arenas lend themselves to the introduction of bridging metaphors as they respond to highly visible events. These societal arenas include the public sphere, with its commemorations and special institutions and with such actions as legislative debates and court trials, which might be thought of as "applied commemorations."

One incident during the Iraq War lends itself to an examination of the use of bridging metaphors in mnemonic struggles over war and atrocities: the killing of a large number of civilians in the small town of Haditha in the Al Anbar province of western Iraq in November of 2005. This event not only evoked massive public debates; it also resulted in the initiation of courts-martial against several members of the military involved in the incident. The public debate about both the event and the trial invoked references to My Lai as a bridging metaphor, and it clearly represented a mnemonic struggle. This chapter examines this struggle by analyzing the different ways in which mass media of distinct political leanings handled the issue. Furthermore, the trial inspired social movement activity in support of soldiers involved in the Haditha incident. We use such movement activity to illustrate ways in which trials can generate conflicting responses to interpretations of the past and link collective memories to events of the present. Such responses are likely to alter the effects that trials and other applied commemorations have on the construction of collective memories.

In addressing the Haditha incident we examine the recent and ongoing cultural and legal processing of a mass killing committed by U.S. soldiers, a case that may or may not feed into future remembrances. We thereby continue to move in the same cell of our analytical scheme (table 1.1): the study of American memories of American killings of civilians, processed in domestic courts. We go beyond the previous chapter, though, as we examine the effect of collective memories of past atrocities, specifically My Lai, on the processing of later events. We also shift the time horizon to investigate present-day constructions. In our closing comments, we suggest one additional lens through which affective components of memory may be effectively addressed: a process that anthropologists and others have captured in the concept of haunting.[4]

The Haditha Incident

The United States–led invasion of Iraq that began on March 20, 2003, resulted in the eventual removal from power of Saddam Hussein and an ongoing U.S. occupation. The fighting in Iraq became a battle against an insurgency that blended in with the rest of the Iraqi citizenry and attacked with ambushes and homemade bombs. Only in 2009 did a substantial pacification unfold. One incident in the early phase of the occupation was the violent deaths of a large number of Iraqi civilians at the hands of the U.S. military. The initial reports of the incident are the result of journalistic work, first by *Time* magazine journalist Tim McGirk in a 2006 report ("Collateral Damage or Civilian Massacre in Haditha," *Time*, March 19, 2006) and later in a detailed report on CBS's *60 Minutes*, partly confirmed by various sources, partly debated to this day.

What, then, occurred in Haditha during that fateful, but not atypical, period of August through November of 2005? Many journalists begin the sequence of events on August 8, when fourteen marines were killed by a roadside bomb near Haditha (Wuterich 2007). A little more than two months later, on November 19, a four-vehicle convoy of marines from First Squad, Third Platoon, Company K, Third Battalion, First Marine Regiment, First Marine Division was traveling through Haditha when the fourth and final truck of the small convoy was struck by an improvised explosive device (IED; McGirk, "Collateral Damage or Civilian Massacre"). The truck was destroyed; one marine, Lance Cpl. Miguel Terrazas, was killed; and two others were wounded. The marines also reported receiving small arms fire after the explosion, to which they forcefully responded. By the end of the engagement, U.S. marines had killed twenty-four Iraqi civilians. The marine unit involved in this incident was made up mostly of Iraq War veterans on their second or third tour of duty. The squad leader, however, was Staff Sergeant Frank Wuterich, a marine near the end of his service. The engagement at Haditha on November 19 would be Wuterich's first combat experience (Wuterich 2007).

Once the marines had tended to their wounded comrades, Wuterich immediately began looking for the "trigger man" who had set off the explosion (Wuterich 2007). He did not have to look far. A short distance up the road, he noticed a white car carrying five young Iraqi males. Four of the men were students on their way to school, and the fifth was the cab driver who was taking them there (David S. Cloud, "Contradictions Cloud Inquiry into 24 Iraqi Deaths," *New York Times*, June 17, 2006, A1). In broken Arabic, Wuterich ordered the men to get out of the car, and one of the other marines instructed them to get on the ground (Wuterich 2007). When the men did not obey instructions, Wuterich shot and killed all five (McGirk, "Collateral Damage or Civilian Massacre"). He reported that the men were attempting to run, but this point has been disputed by other witnesses, both American and Iraqi. A photograph taken at the scene, supposedly of the bodies of the five men lying where they fell, shows that none of the five was more than a few feet from the car when shot (Wuterich 2007).

After killing the five men in the taxi, Wuterich and his men perceived small arms fire coming from the direction of a nearby house (Wuterich 2007). When Wuterich's superior officer, Lt. William Kallop, arrived on the scene a few minutes later, he agreed that the men should assault the house in question ("What Happened at Haditha," *Wall Street Journal*, October 19, 2007, A18). Over the next few hours, the marines entered four houses near the site of the explosion. There, they killed another nineteen Iraqis, mostly women, children, and elderly men. They found no weapons in the first three houses but confiscated two assault rifles from the fourth (McGirk, "Collateral Damage or Civilian Massacre").

The marines claimed that they first cleared the houses primarily by throwing grenades through any doors behind which they heard threatening sounds, then entered the rooms and terminated any remaining threats (Wuterich 2007). However, Iraqi witnesses disputed this claim, stating that the marines entered the rooms and shot their targets with full knowledge that they were killing women and children (McGirk, "Collateral Damage or Civilian Massacre"). An Iraqi doctor on duty that night at the morgue to which the corpses were taken confirmed that the bodies had few shrapnel injuries, as one would expect from an IED or grenade blast. Instead, most of the dead appeared to have been shot in the head or chest at close range (McGirk, "Collateral Damage or Civilian Massacre"). U.S. government experts investigating the incident have reached the same conclusion (Paul von Zielbauer, "Forensic Experts Testify That 4 Iraqis Killed by Marines Were Shot from a Few Feet Away," *New York Times*, June 15, 2007, A10).

The next day, the marines issued a preliminary report claiming that on November 19 an IED killed one marine and fifteen Iraqi civilians and that U.S. and Iraqi forces killed eight insurgent combatants in a subsequent firefight. That next day, November 20, an Iraqi videotaped the scene of the killings and the morgue to which the bodies of the victims had been carried. This tape was obtained by the Hammurabi Human Rights Group and eventually found its way into the hands of the American journalist Tim McGirk. After viewing the tape, McGirk went to Haditha to interview Iraqi witnesses to the killings. He shared the tape and the testimony of witnesses with marine spokesman Col. Barry Johnson, who recommended a full investigation (McGirk, "Collateral Damage or Civilian Massacre").

The first media reports of the investigation appeared on March 16, 2006, and many political leaders and journalists began to make strong statements about the incident (McGirk, "Collateral Damage or Civilian Massacre"). These included media descriptions of the event as a "massacre" and U.S. representative and Vietnam veteran John Murtha's claim that marines had killed innocent civilians "in cold blood" at Haditha ("What Happened at Haditha," A18). The Naval Criminal Investigative

Service delivered its report on the Haditha incident to Lt. Gen. James Mattis in August of 2006, and on December 21, 2006, the Marines Corps filed charges of unpremeditated murder against four enlisted men, including S.Sgt. Wuterich, and dereliction of duty for failure to adequately investigate against four officers (Paul von Zielbauer and Carolyn Marshall, "Marines Charge Four with Murder of Iraqi Civilians," *New York Times*, December 22, 2006, A1).

Since these charges were filed, the prosecution's case has largely disintegrated. Although none of the Haditha cases has gone to trial, there has been a long series of legal proceedings. These have mostly taken the form of Article 32 investigations, the military justice equivalent of a grand jury. In these hearings, the evidence against the accused is presented to a military judge who recommends either proceeding to trial or dropping charges, depending on whether the judge believes there is enough evidence to convict. The commanding general, in this case Lt. Gen. James Mattis, decides whether or not to proceed to court-martial. Charges against three of the enlisted men and two of the officers have been dropped, and S.Sgt. Wuterich is the only marine still facing homicide charges, though the investigator in his case has stated that the prosecution would be unlikely to prove any charges greater than negligent homicide ("What Happened at Haditha").

There are numerous possible explanations for the collapse of the government's case. First of all, it is unclear whether the marines definitely knew they were killing innocent civilians as opposed to responding to a perceived threat. These men may have been acting in the only way possible in an environment in which "hesitation equals getting killed" (Wuterich 2007). Second, the marine investigators have been skeptical about the accuracy of the testimony of Iraqi witnesses. Finally, the lack of the kind of photographic evidence available in the My Lai case has caused the hearings to come down to a credibility contest between witnesses (Paul von Zielbauer, "The Erosion of a Murder Case Against Marines in the Killing of 24 Iraqi Civilians," *New York Times*, October 6, 2007, A8). The one video of victims in the morgue was discredited by military reports early on. Those sources claimed links between Taher Thabet, the Iraqi who made the video, as well as the Hammurabi Human Rights Organization, to which Thabet belonged, and Iraqi insurgent groups. No independent assessments of such allegations are known.

Conflicting Reports

How was the Haditha incident depicted in American media of different political leanings, and what role did reference to My Lai play in these depictions? Data suited to answer this question come from news reports and editorials about the Haditha incident and investigations published in three major American news sources: the *New York Times*, the *Wall Street Journal*, and *Time* magazine.[5] We conducted content analysis of all articles with a reference to Haditha published by these three sources from the date of the Haditha incident, November 19, 2005, until April of 2008. A ProQuest search of *New York Times* and *Wall Street Journal* articles identified 123 and 38 entries, respectively.[6] A search of the *Time* magazine online database identified 47 relevant items.[7] The total population of printed documents thus consists of 208 articles, columns, and letters to the editor.

Being especially concerned with identifying those articles within this population that made reference to the My Lai massacre, we undertook three steps. First, we identified and described the ways in which My Lai was discussed in Haditha coverage and the uses of such references. In particular, we were interested in whether My Lai was used as a bridging metaphor by journalists covering Haditha, as well as whether this bridging metaphor was used to analogize or distinguish the My Lai and Haditha cases. Second, we identified the institutional source of the My Lai narrative presented in each commemoration to determine the extent to which the judicial, political, or journalistic narrative of My Lai was represented in activations of collective memory of My Lai. Third, we considered shifts in the content of applied commemorations of My Lai over the course of the Haditha investigation. We were especially interested to see whether the timing of such shifts coincided with stages of the legal process, suggesting an impact of legal proceedings on the construction of collective representations and memories.

We coded any reference to My Lai or the principal individuals involved in the My Lai case within the context of a report or opinion piece on Haditha. In general, the proportions of Haditha articles containing references to My Lai are not high: of the 123 *New York Times* articles on Haditha, only 10 mention My Lai (8.1 percent), compared with 6 of the 47 *Time* articles (12.8 percent) and 3 of the 38 *Wall Street Journal* articles (7.9 percent). While references to My Lai are thus relatively infrequent, the proportions are fairly consistent across the three news sources, and no other event is referenced in Haditha reports nearly as often as My Lai.

Each article containing a reference to the atrocities of My Lai then underwent in-depth content analysis. We sought to identify cases in which the use of My Lai can be considered a bridging metaphor and the ways in which that bridging metaphor was used. We then coded the articles for the particular My Lai narrative—judicial, political, or journalistic—reflected in the content of the applied commemoration. Finally, we compared dates of publication for each article with the timeline of the Haditha investigation and legal hearings.

Linking and Unlinking Haditha and My Lai

Of the sample of 208 articles, 19 contain references to the My Lai massacre. In each of these, the reference is used as a bridging metaphor that compares or contrasts the Haditha event, which we, as readers, do not yet know about, with one we are expected to be familiar with, My Lai. The ways in which the bridging metaphor of My Lai is used are varied, and 2 of the 19 articles were coded as containing more than one of the uses identified.

> Five items use the bridging metaphor of My Lai to establish that Haditha is an example of the same phenomenon, a massacre of innocent civilians committed by out-of-control U.S. troops.
>
> Three articles link My Lai and Haditha to demonstrate a connection between the broader contexts of the Vietnam and Iraq Wars.
>
> Seven articles use the link between Haditha and My Lai to predict the consequences of Haditha for the Iraq War by describing the consequences of My Lai for the war in Vietnam.
>
> Finally, six items use the bridging metaphor of My Lai to show that Haditha is not an example of the same phenomenon and that analogies between the two events are false.

These uses of My Lai are not evenly spread across the three news sources examined, a first indication of the importance of political affiliations involved in this unfolding mnemonic battle. For instance, all of the articles that link My Lai and Haditha as examples of the same phenomenon appear in the *New York Times*, while all articles that use the link between Haditha and My Lai to connect Iraq and Vietnam appear in *Time*. The diversity of uses suggests the further specification of the tool of bridging metaphors into four subtypes: mimetic bridging, prognostic bridging, contextual bridging, and bridging challenge.

"A My Lai Acid Flashback": Mimetic Bridging

Several writers use references to My Lai as a means of establishing that Haditha and My Lai are instances of the same type of phenomenon. A June 2006 letter to the editor of the *New York Times* describes Haditha as a "21st century equivalent of My Lai" (Syed M. Majid, June 6, 2006, A20). The writer argues that Haditha is "equivalent" to My Lai, ignoring the fact that the details of the cases differ substantially, particularly in terms of the scale of the killings and the occurrence of other crimes at My Lai. Similarly, Maureen Dowd, a regular columnist for the *Times*, uses her col-umn to describe Haditha as a "My Lai acid flashback" ("Don't Become Them," *New York Times,* May 27, 2006, A13). The Haditha incident, in her mind, evokes bitter memories of the images of the My Lai massacre in the late 1960s.

Other writers provide more explicit explanations of how and why Haditha evokes memories of My Lai. A July 10, 2006, *New York Times* opinion piece by Bob Herbert ("A Vietnam Lesson, Unlearned," A17), for example, describes his reaction to the accusations against American marines, including "slaughtering 24 Iraqis, including women and children . . . a case that in its horror . . . recalls the My Lai massacre of Vietnam." An earlier *New York Times* report from May 30, 2006, discusses the impact of evidence of "execution-style killings, including gunshots to the head. As more details about the Haditha . . . incident surface, [the incident] has conjured disturbing memories of the My Lai massacre in Vietnam for many former marines and in other circles of war veterans" (Carolyn Marshall, "On a Marine Base, Disbelief over Charges," *New York Times,* May 30, 2006, A11). A Navy veteran quoted in the report saw a different connection between the Haditha investigation and the My Lai trials: "The young guys took the heat for the higher-ups there too" (Marshall, "Disbelief over Charges," A11). We refer to this type of reference to a past event as *mimetic bridging,* indicating an attempt to establish the similarity between the past and the current event.

From Infamous Places to Contentious Wars: Contextual Bridging

Other writers use the bridging metaphor of My Lai in their discussion of Haditha as a way to link the contexts of the Iraq and Vietnam Wars. These writers may draw very different conclusions though, as illustrated by two articles from *Time* magazine. In the June 12, 2006, issue of *Time* ("Rules of Engagement," 42), Reuel Marc Gerecht writes, "We have done terrible things—in World War II, the Korean War, Vietnam and now, it strongly appears, in Haditha in Iraq." However, he is quick to point out that "these dark moments—indiscriminately bombarding German civilians in World War II, mowing down Vietnamese peasants at My Lai—do not necessarily diminish the rightness of the cause for which we fight." Gerecht thus argues that though Haditha is, indeed, a dark moment, such moments have occurred throughout U.S. military history. Gerecht believes it is important to view these incidents as exceptions to the rule and not let them tarnish memories of the broader context and justifications of war.

In the same issue of *Time,* Michael Duffy ("The Shame of Kilo Company," 32) writes about the connection between the Iraq and Vietnam contexts in a very different way. He sees Haditha and My Lai as evidence of the failings of the military command structure in both the Iraq and

Vietnam conflicts. "So why did some men in Kilo Company apparently snap? Perhaps because of the stress of fighting a violent and unpopular war—or because their commanders failed them. Military psychiatrists who have studied what makes a soldier's moral compass go haywire in battle look first for a weak chain of command. That was a factor in the March 1968 My Lai massacre in Vietnam, when U.S. soldiers, including members of an Army platoon led by Lieut. William Calley, killed some 500 Vietnamese."

Duffy thus reminds the reader of the circumstances of My Lai and the Vietnam War, especially problems with the organizational context of the fighting units, conditions that were diagnosed by the Peers Commission and Seymour Hersh's journalistic accounts and have been accepted by many as explanations for that massacre. He further suggests that the Haditha incident constitutes evidence of similar conditions in the present conflict in Iraq.

We call this way of drawing parallels to the past *contextual bridging*, as the focus is on the context of the incident in question more than on the incident itself. In other words, it is about the war at large, not a specific alleged atrocity.

Common Consequences: Prognostic Bridging

The most frequent references to My Lai predict consequences the Haditha incident might have on the Iraq War, particularly in terms of public support. A *New York Times* report quotes Senator John McCain, who states that the event is reminiscent of the My Lai massacre, adding that "it certainly is harmful, but I can't assess the extent of the damage" to support for the Iraq War generally (Richard A. Oppel, "Iraqi Accuses U.S. of 'Daily' Attacks Against Civilians," *New York Times*, June 2, 2006, A1). Another *Times* article argues that "the politics surrounding the war are likely to become more volatile with disclosures about alleged killings of Iraqi civilians by marines in Haditha, a case that has prompted comparisons to the My Lai massacre in the Vietnam War" (Adam Nagourney, "Votes on Iraq War Put Senators at Disadvantage in '08," *New York Times*, June 2, 2006, A18). One *Wall Street Journal* article critically assesses the way journalists have connected My Lai and Haditha. Its author suggests that these journalists seek to use the bridging metaphor to provoke specific political consequences: "My Lai significantly altered the political status of Vietnam in the U.S. . . . So it is only natural that the My Lai template, however ill-fitting, would be pressed against Haditha to see if this one lurid story would break the back of the entire Iraq enterprise" (Daniel Henninger, "Wonder Land: U.S. Soldiers Aren't Guilty Before a Verdict," *Wall Street Journal*, July 7, 2006, A12).

Some reports explore potential political consequences specifically from the perspective of military leaders. According to a June 12, 2006, *Time* magazine report, "To some U.S. officers, the impact of the daily stream of accusations about the actions of the men of Kilo Company is conjuring up comparisons with the blow from the country's most searing example of battlefield misconduct, the My Lai massacre of 1968" (Michael Duffy, Tim McGirk, and Aparisim Ghosh, "The Ghosts of Haditha," *Time*, 29) Another *Time* article describes the reaction of one officer in greater detail:

> It's a disorienting time for the U.S. Marine Corps in the wake of the alleged massacre of civilians in the Iraqi town of Haditha. One senior Marine officer, for example, is spending his days with grim reading, as Congress, the Pentagon and the press investigate charges that the Marines were responsible for the deaths of some two dozen Iraqi civilians. He has gone through Congressional reports about the My Lai massacre. He has read *America in Vietnam* by Guenter Lewy. . . . This officer knows that the entire Marine Corps will be hard hit if the Haditha allegations are true. (Sally B. Donnelly, "After Haditha: What Makes Top Marines Worry," *Time*, June 2, 2006, online)[8]

Thus military commanders must be prepared to deal not only with enemies on the battlefield but also with the perceptions of the American public. A basic knowledge of the commonly held understandings of My Lai is essential for these actors to predict how the public will respond to Haditha.

This form of bridging may be best referred to as *prognostic bridging* as it deals with likely future consequences of events that are considered similar. Here, political consequences are the focus of attention, but different kinds of consequences may be highlighted in other cases.

Disconnecting Haditha from the Memory of My Lai: Bridging Challenges

Several articles on Haditha reference My Lai to distinguish the events and undermine the connection made by other commentators on Haditha. A *Wall Street Journal* report claims that "the casualties have drawn an extraordinary amount of political attention, becoming an emblem for everything critics say is wrong with the Iraq war—in the common telling, another My Lai" ("What Happened at Haditha," October 19, 2007, A18). The author goes on to criticize this "common" account of Haditha and those that have created it. In the June 12, 2006, issue of *Time* magazine ("Rules of Engagement," 42), Gary Solis argues that "even if proved, Haditha is no My Lai, with its victims in the hundreds, attendant sexual crimes, direct officer involvement and high-level cover-up by a dozen officers, including colonels and generals." These writers invoke the memory of My Lai and carefully distinguish it from Haditha to establish clearly that Haditha is not the same type of event as My Lai.

In "A Marine Tutorial on Media Spin," Paul von Zielbauer describes a memo produced by Lieutenant Colonel Jeffrey Chessani, Major Nathan Gonzalez, Captain Lucas M. McConnell, and First Lieutenant Adam

Mathes in response to Tim McGirk's initial inquiries into the Haditha incident. This memo was introduced as evidence at a hearing for one of the accused officers and provides some insight into the importance of the memory of My Lai and its investigation for guiding the actions of the marine officers accused of covering up the Haditha incident. Rather than answer McGirk's questions, the memo describes the "sneaky tactics" of reporters and the ways in which the questions are an attempt to characterize Haditha as the Iraq War's My Lai: "One common tactic used by reporters is to spin a story in such a way that it is easily recognized and remembered by the general population through its association with an event that the general population is familiar with or can relate to. For example, McGirk's story will sell if it can be spun as 'Iraq's My Lai massacre.' Since there was not an officer involved, this attempt will not go very far" (quoted in Paul von Zielbauer, "A Marine Tutorial on Media Spin," *New York Times,* June 24, 2007, C5). The memo also identifies the absence of an officer during the killings as a reason why Haditha must be distinguished from My Lai and why the My Lai connection ultimately fails to define Haditha.

Rather than likening Haditha to My Lai, these articles cite the bridging work done by others in order to challenge the metaphor. We call this type of argument a *bridging challenge.*

My Lai Narratives in Haditha Reporting

The references to My Lai that appear in media coverage of the Haditha incident and investigation are usually brief. Reports often do no more than mention My Lai, assuming that the reader knows enough about the event to understand its importance to the discussion of Haditha. Others provide a brief summary of the My Lai massacre or the court-martial of William Calley. These reports rarely provide enough information to identify one of the particular narratives of My Lai distinguished in chapter 3. The most common distinguishing element is the number of victims reported. Two reports describe the My Lai massacre as an attack that claimed more than five hundred victims (Michael Duffy, "The Shame of Kilo Company," *Time,* June 5, 2006; Michael Duffy, Tim McGirk, and Bobby Ghosh, "The Ghosts of Haditha," *Time,* June 12, 2006). Solis's description of My Lai in *Time* ("Rules of Engagement," June 12, 2006) claims "victims in the hundreds, attendant sexual crimes, direct officer involvement and high-level cover-up by a dozen officers, including colonels and generals."

Such depictions are based on past journalistic narratives of My Lai but also on the diagnosis presented in the Peers Commission report. While none of the articles clearly reflects the judicial narrative, one does indicate the importance to the writer of the legal evaluation of the incident, arguing that "the Marines implicated in the Haditha incident are largely anonymous now, but each is being auditioned to play this war's Lt. William Calley. But first they have to be convicted of something" (Henninger, "Wonder Land"). The focus on the journalistic narratives should not be surprising given that the data in this analysis come from journalistic accounts, and the journalistic account of My Lai is the most shocking and provocative of the different institutional narratives.

Influence of the Legal Process

The influence of the legal process partially reveals itself in the timing and content of reporting about Haditha. Media reports about Haditha that contain references to My Lai appear almost exclusively during a period stretching from May to July of 2006: sixteen of the nineteen articles (84.2 percent) that reference My Lai were published during this period. This was a time when the accusations were still fresh, as the details of the civilian deaths began to come to light in March of that year, especially through journalistic reports. The Marine Corps had not released the results of their investigation at that time, and the charges against the accused marines were still months away. The construction of the Haditha incident during the summer of 2006 showed clear parallels to the acknowledged facts of the My Lai massacre, but that image would change after months of hearings and testimony of the accused. The *New York Times* reports most clearly demonstrate the influence of the legal process on the content of My Lai commemorations. Only the three most recent *New York Times* items contain bridging challenges. This group includes the only two reports published after the pretrial hearings for the accused marines had begun on May 8, 2007. The most recent *New York Times* article to refer to My Lai illustrates the effect of the hearings on the Haditha–My Lai connection:

> Last year, when accounts of the killing of 24 Iraqis in Haditha by a group of marines came to light, it seemed that the Iraq war had produced its defining atrocity, just as the conflict in Vietnam had spawned the My Lai massacre a generation ago. But on Thursday, a senior military investigator recommended dropping murder charges against the ranking enlisted marine accused in the 2005 killings, just as he had done earlier in the cases of two other marines charged in the case. The recommendation may well have ended prosecutors' chances of winning any murder convictions in the killings of the apparently unarmed men, women and children. (von Zielbauer, "Erosion of a Murder Case," October 6, 2007, A8)

Obviously, as the facts of the Haditha incident are adjudicated and distinctions between Haditha and My Lai are publicly drawn, references to My Lai do not cease. Yet My Lai no longer serves as a mimetic, contextual, or prognostic bridge; rather, the purpose of the comparison shifts from analogizing the two cases to distinguishing them—that is, toward bridge challenging.

It is not the task of social scientists to adjudicate adjudication. It is, however, our task to seek to explain the outcome of legal processes. Legal literalists would likely point to the nature of evidence that challenged parallels between Haditha and My Lai. They would argue that the case of Haditha did not allow for the production of sufficient evidence. Yet a sociological perspective on law will ask what evidence was produced by whom and was awarded what weight.[9] It will ask for the social structure of the case and, based on that structure, predict the outcome of the legal process. In the case of Haditha, social movements, partly inspired by the legal process itself, played a central role. Their involvement apparently strengthened the perspective of the defense.

Social Movements and Mnemonic Struggles: Contesting Legal Narratives

Since the Haditha investigations began, much support for the accused soldiers has been expressed by those opposed to the portrayal of the events in mainstream media. Media have also communicated the voices of the accused themselves to a broad public. Yet statements from pro-soldier actors appear most often on websites devoted to supporting the accused marines or as comments posted in response to online news stories. Many of these statements directly attack accusatory media reports or statements of politicians and other public figures who oppose the war in Iraq. The late U.S. representative and former marine John Murtha is but the most vocal example. Murtha was the first major American political figure to address the incident, condemning the killings as criminal acts committed "in cold blood" by Marines who snapped under the unbearable pressure of war (quoted in "What Happened at Haditha").

Support for the accused marines is not limited to the public sphere but percolates into the court process through fund-raising efforts to support their legal defense. Defense attorneys offered to the accused soldiers by the military tend to be overworked and generally less experienced and lower in rank than military prosecutors, much like public defenders in the civilian criminal justice system. Yet thanks to the fund-raising efforts, most of the accused marines have obtained more experienced, and much more expensive, civilian counsel. On pro-soldier websites, links to fund-raising groups for the Haditha marines have become common (Ken Maguire, "Vietnam Vets Come to Defense of Accused Troops," *Boston Globe*, October 7, 2006, AP).

Commentary on these websites is emotionally charged and sharply critical of the investigation and the ongoing prosecutions. Pro-soldier activists decidedly oppose the military's attempt to place responsibility on individual soldiers. In other words, they challenge the decoupling function of criminal trials. Pro-soldier movement participants often are pro-military only to the extent that the interests of the military are in line with those of soldiers themselves.

The development of social movement organizations devoted to promoting the welfare of American soldiers and veterans is not a new phenomenon, nor is the opposition of such groups to the interests of the military. Organizations like the Vietnam Veterans Against the War were founded to voice the concerns of veterans who believed the military was putting its soldiers in unacceptable and unnecessary danger and failing to adequately care for them when they returned home with serious physical and psychological injuries. The perceived need for assistance to veterans of the Vietnam era gave rise to other groups, as well, such as the Vietnam Veterans of America. These organizations have remained devoted to a wide range of activities, including securing the provision of counseling services, raising and distributing money and supplies, lobbying government actors for better treatment of veterans, and holding protests and demonstrations to raise awareness for their cause. While pro-soldier organizations take differing positions regarding support for or opposition to war, their goals for improving the treatment of soldiers and veterans, as well as many of the tactics they employ to reach those goals, are similar. This is also true of pro-soldier organizations that have developed in the context of the Iraq War.

Many of the statements made in support of the Haditha marines exhibit a strong emotional response to the incident, investigation, and prosecutions. The speakers are often former marines or other veterans of the Vietnam War, the Gulf War, or the current conflicts in Iraq and Afghanistan. Others are family of soldiers currently serving or recently returned from the war.

More specific to our case, legal defense fund-raising is not a new tactic for pro-soldier movements. During the Vietnam War, organizations raised money to support the defense of American soldiers accused of a wide range of crimes (see Maguire, "Vietnam Vets Come to Defense of Accused Troops"). The fund-raising groups included pro-soldier organizations as well as antiwar groups who saw the prosecution of soldiers as a tactic by which the U.S. military and government could cleanse themselves of guilt for atrocities that, in this view, naturally resulted from the conduct of the Vietnam War itself. Both constitute examples of legal mobilization, only recently addressed by sociolegal and social movement scholars, as the translation of a desire into a legal "demand as an assertion of one's rights" (Zemans 1983, 700), typically combined with other movement strategies.[10] Furthermore, while stressing rationalist explanations for the adoption and success of legal tactics, researchers have invested much less into the role of emotions in legal mobilization. While the law formally channels the use of emotions, it simultaneously allows for emotional pleas at several points in the legal process. For instance, judges and sometimes juries hear demands for justice from victims' families, as well as calls for compassion from witnesses for the defense during the sentencing phase of criminal trials. Some plaintiffs in civil cases are even allowed to recover for emotional damages.

Most important in our context, emotions are a potential motivator of legal claims, challenges, and mobilization. Several scholars have addressed the importance of collective rituals in generating the emotional charge needed to motivate and sustain movement activities.[11] Most significant here, scholars view rituals as a means of generating solidarity and an opportunity to build emotional energy. Others focus on the role of leadership in organizing and managing the emotional reactions of movement members to turn moral outrage into effective and sustainable collective action. Central to this theme is the use of "injustice frames" (Gamson 1992) in the process of identifying the problematic social conditions to be addressed and the groups or individuals responsible for those conditions. However, anger must be paired with positive feeling such as compassion, sympathy, or hope if mobilization is to succeed.[12]

What role, then, do social movements play in the Haditha case? Specifically, how does emotion-driven legal mobilization challenge a legal process that seeks to attribute liability to low-level soldiers while decoupling the larger organization and larger society from their role in the killings of innocent civilians? More specifically yet, how do such challenges torpedo the bridging strategies of other actors who seek to link the Haditha killings to the My Lai massacre of Vietnam?

Movement Messages

To better understand these questions, we conducted content analysis of Internet sites dedicated to fundraising for the Haditha marines' legal defense and linked sites devoted to covering the investigations and prosecutions. We focus on the websites DefendOurMarines.com, which provides information and commentary on the Haditha investigation, and FrankWuterich.com, the site devoted to raising funds for Staff Sergeant Wuterich's defense. FrankWuterich.com contains a variety of appeals for donations to the legal defense fund as well as updates on the course of the investigation. DefendOurMarines.com is the most significant resource on the web for information about the Haditha investigations and prosecutions. The site contains links to most stories about the incident and the legal proceedings from major American newspapers. It also links to numerous conservative blogs and news sources for reporting and commentary. In addition, it provides transcripts of testimony from the hearings that have been conducted to date, includes photographic and video evidence related to the case, and directs readers to web pages devoted to raising funds for the remaining Haditha defendants.

Among the most interesting links on DefendOurMarines.com is a set of sixty-six reader responses to the question, "The Haditha Marines: Why do you care?" posted on a conservative commentator site named FreeRepublic.com.[13] The original question was posted by David Allender, one of the major contributors to DefendOurMarines.com. This post asks readers to explain why they support the Haditha marines, and it asks those who have donated to the defense fund for one or more of the soldiers to explain why they took that extra step. Of these sixty-six responses, fifty-two are answers to this question.

We conducted content analysis of the DefendOurMarines.com and FrankWuterich.com websites as well as the commentary responses. The content of each of these sources was examined qualitatively for evidence of emotional content, particularly emotional pleas for support. We identify emotional content as that which expresses the evaluative or interpretative feelings and reactions of the writer, especially in relation to the Haditha incident, investigation, or legal process. We then categorized the type of emotion displayed, such as anger, compassion, love, gratitude, pride, or injustice. Feelings of injustice are among the most significant and common type of emotional response to the legal process, and we expect them to be particularly prominent among those seeking or giving support to the defense in criminal proceedings.

In addition, we conducted quantitative coding of the responses by supporters of the Haditha marines. We coded each response for several characteristics of the writer, including military or veteran status, relationship to current military personnel, and whether a respondent had donated to one or more defense funds for the Haditha marines. We then coded for the presence of emotional content, the type of emotion displayed, and the objects of the emotional response (enemies for feelings of anger or injustice; allies for feelings of sympathy, pride, or compassion). The characteristics of the respondents, where available, were coded based only on any identifying information provided by the writers themselves. Emotions were coded based on our evaluation of whether the content met the definition provided (fifty of the fifty-two responses did so).

Results: Depicting Haditha and the Legal Process on Movement Websites

Our analysis of the content of the DefendOurMarines.com and FrankWuterich.com websites identified a range of emotions expressed by the different respondents. All types appear regularly on these web pages.

They are provoked by and directed toward a range of targets, including enemies like the media and the political Left; allies like the legal defense team, the Haditha marines themselves, and the friends and family of the accused; and more ambiguous groups that can be characterized as neither friend nor foe, like the Marine Corps or the military broadly.[14]

Our analysis reveals that commentary is often charged with anger and feelings of injustice over the investigation and prosecution. In an article from October 11, 2007, titled "Our Massacre, We Loved It So: *New York Times* Deeply Saddened That Justice Is Being Done," Nathaniel Helms, contributing editor of the DefendOurMarines.com website, blasts Paul von Zielbauer's report on the reduction of charges against Staff Sergeant Wuterich. He describes the American media as "self-anointed purveyors of truth, justice, and the American way." Helms suggests that it might be difficult for reporters like von Zielbauer (who actually reports from Baghdad) to "occupy the same high morale [*sic*] ground in an atmosphere filled with lethal objects rather than hot air." Similarly, David Allender wrote a piece for DefendOurMarines.com on August 9, 2007, titled "Dear Mainstream Media: You and Congressman Murtha Must Set the Record Straight." Other commentary expresses and evokes different emotions, including pride and compassion. Don Dinsmore's report on "Ride & Rally," his motorcycle ride down the West Coast to raise awareness for the Haditha marines, describes the need to raise money to support the "honest, hard-working" families of the marines.

FrankWuterich.com is expressly devoted to raising funds for Staff Sergeant Wuterich's legal defense. Compared with DefendOurMarines.com, this site focuses much more on the needs of Wuterich's family and the difficulties of his position in order to elicit sympathetic and compassionate emotional responses. However, it does not completely ignore those it sees as enemies of the pro-soldier movement. One page on this site is dedicated to providing information on Frank Wuterich's defamation suit against Representative Murtha, although the page only contains links to the court documents from the suit, without any of the angry and maligning language found in the commentary on DefendOurMarines.com. The opening statement on the FrankWuterich.com front page is illustrative of the site's balance between feelings of anger toward enemies and sympathy for the accused: "YOU Can Help Support Our Troops . . . Against the Media Bias and Others Who Ignore Our Constitutional Right to a Fair Trial. In America, where one is 'Innocent Until Proven Guilty in a Court of Law' Marine Staff Sgt. Frank D. Wuterich, a family man and squad leader at Haditha incident needs our help NOW with Legal Defense Funding. He has always maintained his innocence and is financially responsible for his own legal counsel" (quoted from www.frankwuterich.com).

FrankWuterich.com, like DefendOurMarines.com, contains numerous links to favorable news reports from various outlets. However, it has a much greater proportion of content that relates to the accused's family and the need for support or expresses pride in the soldiers or the Marine Corps generally. A prominently featured story quotes Frank Wuterich's father, David Wuterich, as saying that Frank is "a good Marine. He's a good dad." There is a link to a story titled "Staff Sgt. Frank Wuterich, Our Son, Our Hero," written by Wuterich's parents, and the following statement appears at the bottom of the page: "This could happen to you or your loved one, who proudly serves this country. It did for Dave and Rosemarie Wuterich's son, Frank."

Our analysis of the FreeRepublic.com responses has found expressions of anger, injustice, pride, compassion, sympathy, and gratitude. By far the most commonly expressed emotions are feelings of injustice over the prosecutions. Thirty-one of the fifty-two responses coded express feelings of injustice about the investigation or legal process and those conducting it. Twelve of the fifty-two responses express anger toward a variety of enemies, including the media, the political Left, and the military command structure. Anger toward the media is occasionally directed specifically at the news outlets *Time* magazine and the *New York Times* or at reporter Tim McGirk. Anger toward the Left, when an individual target is specified, is most commonly directed toward John Murtha, but John Kerry and Bill and Hillary Clinton are also mentioned. Eleven responses display feelings of compassion or sympathy for the defendants and their families; seven express pride in the accused soldiers or the Marine Corps generally; one post expresses gratitude toward these men for their service, and one expresses frustration with those who are "trying to lose this war."

The types of emotions displayed are not evenly distributed across the various categories of respondents. Five of the fifty-two respondents identify themselves as donors, nine as current or former military personnel, and eighteen as current U.S. military personnel. Of the five donors, two express feelings of injustice, one anger, and three compassion or sympathy. Only two of the thirty-one respondents who are motivated by feelings of injustice and one of the twelve who are motivated by anger have been mobilized as donors, while three of the eleven who are motivated by compassion or sympathy have donated. It appears that those motivated by compassion or sympathy show a greater propensity to become donors.[15]

Our analyses support expectations that while emotions generally play an important part in mobilization, feelings of compassion or sympathy for defendants and their families are particularly associated with mobilization to donate to legal defense funds. Analyses also show that the web page explicitly dedicated to fund-raising for an accused marine contains more feelings of compassion and sympathy than does one devoted to a less tangible concept of support for the same soldiers. Obviously, those behind the fund-raising campaign recognize the importance of generating sympathy and compassion as a mobilizing tool.

A Note on Haunting: Affective Dimensions of Unsettled Collective Memories

We might also think of the mnemonic struggles depicted here as instances of haunting and, most certainly, defensive responses to haunting. *Haunting* in everyday parlance and in a sense familiar to most readers refers to the presence of the ghosts of the dead among the living, regularly portrayed in popular films and television programs in contemporary (especially American) society. This idea of haunting, turned metaphorical, has recently been incorporated into the social sciences as a means of expressing the influence of the dead in present-day society. Scholars see the dead as active participants in our lives, in that memories of them (and some people's belief in their actual mingling in the lives of the living) affect interactions, institutions, and even individual identities. Avery Gordon (1997, 8), for example, approaches the concept of haunting as a description of "how that which appears to be not there is often a seething presence, acting on and often meddling with taken-for-granted realities."[16] Others have addressed the ambiguity of history as a cause of haunting.[17] Finally, Walter Benjamin has written about the activation of the dead in contemporary political struggles, an argument that is closely related to the concept of haunting.[18] Benjamin's statement, in particular, makes clear that haunting is actively produced by those who construct collective memories in ways that bring the dead, more precisely the memory of the dead, into present-day conflicts among the living.

In terms of our definition of collective memory, haunting implies that the dead become acknowledged and memories of them become mutually reinforced by collectivities. But this is an instance of remembering in which the living either are not at peace with the passing of their kin, compatriots, or fellow humans or are not comfortable with the ways in which they commemorate the dead. Heonik Kwon, in his anthropological study of the massacre in My Lai and a similar incident in the village of Ha My, demonstrates this disturbing unease for the Vietnamese villagers who lost so many members of their communities in the course of the massacres and whose culture regards such death as a "bad death." The haunting they experience is thus intensified because they are deprived of the means of appropriately honoring, in traditionally prescribed rituals, those dead who are buried in mass graves or whose resting place is unknown.[19] Kwon describes with uncanny cultural sensitivity the ritual ways in which locals attempt to find alternative means of commemorating the dead to diminish such haunting.

But what about Americans and the presence of the Vietnamese (or Iraqi) dead in their experience? Like the Vietnamese, Americans too make use of rituals to lay their dead to rest and to prevent the terror of haunting. In cases of violent death, court proceedings are often part of ritual practice. As such, legal proceedings become sites for the contestation of the past. This applies especially in the context of trials of soldiers accused of murdering civilians. The trials of My Lai and Haditha also involve complex interactions with the dead, and the concept of haunting is relevant to our understanding of such trials in three ways. First, trials against killers are mechanisms through which haunting occurs. They constitute officially sanctioned, and generally well publicized, attempts to settle disputes over the nature of the event and the perpetrator. They thereby simultaneously involve the identification and definition of the dead as either legitimate military targets or innocent victims of murder. As such, during the trial the status of the dead is unsettled, providing an opportunity for the haunting of both the military and the American public.

Second, trials are attempts to resolve the ambiguity in the status of the dead and in this way to serve as a mechanism for ending haunting. Where trials find the defendants not guilty, they relieve all Americans from responsibility. Where guilty verdicts are reached, the court's decision achieves "decoupling." Attributing guilt to one or a few individuals, "bad apples," liberates all "good" Americans, including the "good" military, from a sense of guilt. Thus trials can be compared with an exorcism ritual in which the military institution and society in general are cleansed of the presence of the ghosts of the victims of military atrocities.

Finally, the idea that a defendant is being "sacrificed" at trial, under conditions of vehement contestation, implies that a trial may, in fact, produce a new ghost and a new haunting. However, this does not appear to be the outcome of the Haditha trial, even if one case is not yet fully closed (at the final editing of this text in July of 2011). Here the legal process—never isolated from affectively loaded societal contestation—may have served its exorcism function. American society and its military, decreasingly haunted by the ghosts of My Lai, can put the ghosts of Haditha to rest as well. Bridging challenges have prevailed. This mnemonic struggle is decided—at least for now.

Conclusions: Mnemonic Struggles, Bridging Challenges, and Haunting

Consistent with arguments regarding the path dependency of collective memory, our analysis shows that memory of the past affects the way contemporary institutions and actors respond to current events. Actors use commemorations of a past atrocity to contextualize recent killings. At least some media reports of the Haditha incident and investigation link this mass killing of civilians to the My Lai massacre by using the historical case as a bridging metaphor. They stress the likeness of the events (mimetic bridging) and similarities of context (contextual bridging), and they conclude from consequences of the old event to anticipated ones of the current (prognostic bridging); but some also create a link in order to stress differences between the old and the new (bridging challenges). The legal process here does not feed but rather constrains negative media coverage. While challengers to the prosecution's case are mobilized by political antipathy toward critics of the war, many also express resistance to at least one element of the logic of the legal process: the attribution of guilt to a few individuals and its associated decoupling function.

Challenges to the prosecution are further supported by social movements that, with high emotional investment, engage in mnemonic battles against the mobilization of collective memory. They especially target such mobilization by war critics and possibly by the prosecution when it draws on legal precedent, here understood as an institutionalized form of collective memory. Our analysis of websites supports the conclusion that emotions play an important role in social movement mobilization, even for movements employing legal tactics. It also supports earlier claims that feelings of anger and injustice, on their own, are not likely to motivate collective action.[20] In our case, they are supplemented by feelings of sympathy or compassion that provide additional, positive charges leading to action.

In some respects the rest of this story about the mnemonic struggles surrounding Haditha is still to be told, and we hope future research will examine applied commemorations of My Lai for the handling of Haditha in other institutional contexts. Political hearings on the Haditha incident have been promised, and they may still occur, but not until the criminal justice system has run its course. From a presentist perspective, the activation of collective memory of My Lai within these hearings will likely depend on who is in power more than what actually happened. Close scrutiny of such hearings, should they ultimately occur, would provide important comparative material for this analysis of media reports.

Our analysis of the Haditha case has added new insights to what we learned in examining the cultural processing and remembrance of My Lai in the previous chapter. Our understanding of that cell of table 1.1 that focuses on American memories of American atrocities as processed in domestic courts has been further enriched. Indeed, findings from these combined extended case studies of My Lai and Haditha speak to our basic theses presented in chapter 1. They support central parts of the argument and suggest further specifications: First, legal trials are indeed an arena in (and around) which struggles over the construction of collective memory occur. Second, memories constructed in past trials are mobilized by actors involved in current legal disputes through different types of bridging strategies. Third, the affective and unsettled aspects of memories can be conceived of as haunting the living and trial outcomes as potential and partial remedies. Fourth, selectivities inherent in the institutional logic of law have the potential to torpedo the legitimacy of trials in cases of the military, especially where only selected low-level actors are charged. Fifth, attaching criminal responsibility to only a few low-level individuals undermines the potential of trials to serve as arenas for the construction of collective memories of past atrocities in ways that may serve as platforms for learning and for the avoidance of future atrocities. This latter conclusion was already suggested by the My Lai case, but it is demonstrated all the more convincingly for the Haditha killings.

It would be premature, however, to conclude that Justice Jackson and President Roosevelt were altogether wrong when they invested their history-writing hopes into criminal tribunals. Instead, we now set out to ask what shape American memories may take when high-level actors of foreign regimes are tried in international tribunals. Consider the case of the late president Slobodan Milosevic of Yugoslavia to see what it teaches us about that cell of table 1.1 that speaks to American memories of foreign atrocities tried in international courts of law.

═ Chapter 5 ═

Slobodan Milosevic Through Lenses of Law, Diplomacy, and Media Reporting

WITH COURTNEY FAUE AND YU-JU CHIEN

IN THIS chapter we again examine the institutional contexts that are likely to shape collective memories. And again we are concerned with American memories of atrocities. Yet these atrocities are committed not by Americans, as in the My Lai incident, but by foreign powers, and they are adjudicated not in American courts but by an international tribunal. We selected the case of the Balkan conflict because it is well suited for studying the formation of American memories. The United States played a most active role throughout the unfolding conflict; it was a central player in the establishment of the International Criminal Tribunal for the former Yugoslavia (ICTY) in The Hague, and American lawyers contributed much to the court's operation.[1] The United States also took center stage in diplomatic efforts to resolve the crisis and—eventually—in military intervention. Not surprisingly, then, American media reporting on the violent conflict in the Balkans was intense. Here, discourses from the diplomatic and the judicial realms as mediated by news reporting are juxtaposed.

Two words of caution should be added at the outset. First, the case of Yugoslavia is not necessarily typical of ways in which the United States deals with foreign atrocities, and this is likely to have consequences for memory formation. We expect different patterns in cases in which the United States abstained from involvement, for example in the mass killings in Cambodia during the Pol Pot regime of the 1970s. There, the communist Vietnamese Army put an end to the atrocities. We should anticipate even more different memories in cases in which the United States was complicit in the events that led to grave human rights violations, for example in the 1973 overthrow of President Salvador Allende's government in Chile by soon-to-be dictator General Augusto Pinochet. Second, the memories of the Balkans are still quite fresh, and we do not know yet what shape they will take in future decades. But here we examine close up the images produced by competing institutional spheres that entered America's cultural "toolkit,"[2] a reservoir from which future mnemonic entrepreneurs will be able to draw. The recent death of an American prosecutor involved in the ICTY gives us a first sense of how such mnemonic practices are beginning to unfold.

Thus the case of the Balkan conflict, albeit a particular and relatively recent event, contributes important insights to that cell of table 1.1 that addresses American memories of foreign atrocities tried before an international tribunal.[3]

Milosevic and the Balkan Conflict

On February 11, 2002, a good seven months after former Serbian and Yugoslav president Slobodan Milosevic had been handed over to the ICTY, charged with grave violations of human rights and humanitarian law, the *New York Times* (A10) published a timeline under the heading "Milosevic on Trial: The Accusations." Table 5.1 shows the events marked in this timeline, organized by Yugoslav war events and atrocities, international diplomatic and military interventions, and the judicial procedures of the ICTY. We supplement the *Times* information (in quotation marks) with a history of the atrocities and of ICTY proceedings as recounted by the Northwestern University sociologist John Hagan and his collaborators in one of the most comprehensive examinations on the unfolding of the war and the simultaneous building of the tribunal.[4]

We divide this last terrifying chapter of the twentieth century into four periods, beginning in May of 1989, when Milosevic became president of Serbia, a republic within the Yugoslav Federation and home of Belgrade, Yugoslavia's capital. Second is the war period, beginning with the wars between Serb-dominated Yugoslavia and the break-away republics of Slovenia and Croatia in 1991 and 1992. The war against Slovenia lasted just weeks, but the war against Croatia was intense and was fought for half a year. Massive human rights violations were committed in its course. Both wars ended with the internationally and widely recognized independence of the break-away republics. Immediately after these wars, civil strife broke out in the Republic of Bosnia and Herzegovina, where the Muslim and Croat minorities sought independence from Serbia, a goal opposed by Bosnia's ethnic Serbs.

The resulting civil war, tacitly supported by Serbia, lasted from 1992 through 1995. It involved massive war crimes, including systematic rape

Table 5.1   Yugoslav Wars, International Intervention, and Legal Proceedings, 1989 to 2001

Year	Yugoslav History and Wars	International Intervention	ICTY
Stage 1: Before Wars			
1989	"May 8 . . . : Mr. Milosevic became President of Serbia."		
Stage 2: During Wars (as of June 1991)			
1991	"June: Slovenia and Croatia seceded from Yugoslavia. Slovenia won independence in 10 days. In Croatia, clashes between Serbian troops and Croatian defense forces erupted into full-scale war."		
	August to November: destruction of Vukovar, Croatia, and execution and expulsion of Croatian population.		
1992	Spring 1992 into 1993: Ethnic cleansing and rape houses in Foca, Bosnia (Hagan 2003, 46–51). Ethnic cleansing in Prijedor, Bosnia, and death camps of Omarska and Keraterm (Hagan 2003, 46–51).	"January . . . : Truce brokered in Croatian-Serbian war." "April 1992: Bosnia and Herzegovina's independence was recognized by the United States and European countries."	October: Commission of experts established by UN Security Council Resolution 780.
1993	1993–1995: Siege of Sarajevo.		February: ICTY established by UN Security Council. July: Richard Goldstone named first chief prosecutor.

1995	July: Massacre at Srebrenica (Hagan 2003, chap. 5).	"November . . . : Mr. Milosevic and leaders from Croatia and Bosnia reached an agreement near Dayton, Ohio, to end the war. Bosnia was divided into a Muslim-Croat federation and a Bosnian Serb republic."	First trial, against Duško Tadic.
1996			In absentia hearings against Radovan Karadzic and Ratko Mladic; Louise Arbour replaces Goldstone.
1997	"July 15 . . . : Mr. Milosevic was elected President of Yugoslavia."		
1998	"January 1998: Albanian rebels in Kosovo assassinated a Serbian official; clashes between Serbian police and Albanians grew."		
Stage 3: After Indictment (as of May 1999)			
1999	First half of 1999: Massacres of Kosovo Albanians and expulsion on a massive scale. "June . . . : Serbian forces withdrew from Kosovo."	"March 1999: NATO began bombing Yugoslavia to end the repression of Albanians in Kosovo."	May: Milosevic indicted. Carla Del Ponte becomes chief prosecutor.
2000	"October . . . : Serbs drove Mr. Milosevic from power after he tried to steal the Yugoslav presidential election from Vojislav Kostunica."		March: Beginning of Srebrenica trial. Beginning of Foca rape trial.

(Table continues on p. 80.)

Table 5.1   *Continued*

Year	Yugoslav History and Wars	International Intervention	ICTY
Stage 4: After Extradition (as of June 2001)			
2001			"June 28 . . .: Mr. Milosevic was sent [extradited] to the United Nations war crimes tribunal at The Hague." "Slobodan Milosevic's trial is scheduled to begin tomorrow at The Hague. The charges stem from the wars in Croatia, Bosnia, and Kosovo." The indictments against Mr. Milosevic are listed in a separate line: *CROATIA 32 counts:* For crimes against Croats and other non-Serbs from August 1991 to June 1992. BOSNIA 29 *counts:* For crimes, including genocide, against Bosnian Muslims, Bosnian Croats, and other non-Serbs. An estimated 200,000 people died and millions were driven from their homes from March 1992 to December 1995. KOSOVO 5 *counts:* For crimes against Kosovo Albanian citizens. Hundreds were killed and more than 800,000 were driven out from January to June in 1999."
2006			March 11: Milosevic dies in the custody of the ICTY.

Source: Authors' compilation of information from Hagan (2003) and *New York Times* articles on Slobodan Milosevic.
Note: ICTY = International Criminal Tribunal for the former Yugoslavia; UN = United Nations; NATO = North Atlantic Treaty Organization; ICC =

campaigns, and the deadly and destructive siege of Sarajevo, Bosnia's capital city. This war cost some two hundred thousand human lives and drove millions from their homes. The most horrific episode just experienced its fifteenth anniversary in July 2010: the Srebrenica massacre, named for the Bosnian town in which it was committed. Bosnian-Serb army units separated men and grown boys from women. They proceeded to kill more than eight thousand men in a gruesome execution campaign, hiding the bodies in mass graves. This was the first large-scale massacre committed in Europe since the end of World War II.

Barely one year into the Bosnian War, the United Nations Security Council established a commission of experts to examine war-related atrocities, a step that would result in the establishment of the ICTY only half a year later. The Bosnian War ended in November 1995 with Bosnia's independence through the famous Dayton peace agreement brokered under the tutelage of U.S. president Bill Clinton and with the active participation of Serbian president Slobodan Milosevic. Two years later Milosevic was elected president of Yugoslavia.

The last of the Yugoslav wars broke out in early 1999, when Serbian-lead Yugoslavia sought to repress independence moves by ethnic Albanians in the province of Kosovo. Hundreds of people were killed, and hundreds of thousands became refugees. In March 1999 the international community intervened militarily with a bombing campaign against Serbia. President Milosevic was indicted in May of the same year, marking the beginning of the immediate postwar period. The fourth and final period began when a new Belgrade administration extradited Milosevic to the ICTY on June 28, 2001. He was charged with war crimes in the Croatian, Bosnian, and Kosovo conflicts and with genocide in the Bosnian War.

Law, Diplomacy, and American Media Representations

Before we step into our analysis, a brief reminder of our central themes and a note on our methods and data are in order. We have established that each societal field, such as law, scholarship, and politics, works with its own institutional logic, types of opportunities and constraints, criteria of evidence, prescriptions and proscriptions, taboos, and rules of procedure. Various institutions produce distinct types of narratives with consequences for the ways in which atrocities will be remembered and, subsequently, for future action. We are again particularly interested in the role of legal proceedings, their inherent potency for the construction of collective memories, and their particular selectivities that are manifested, for example, in specific rules of evidence and criminal law's binary logic of guilty or not guilty.[5] We have also established in previous chapters that narratives created by legal proceedings are always contested and that legal narratives merge and interact with those generated by other institutions, such as diplomatic, scholarly, or political accounts.

In the Yugoslav case the field of diplomacy constitutes a particularly important institutional sphere. And it should play a much more powerful role than criminal justice proceedings, at least according to the influential "realist" school in international relations and its argument that the threat of trials diminishes chances of successful transitions.[6] Be that as it may, diplomacy did in fact play a central role in the unfolding of the Yugoslav story. The logic of the diplomatic field differs markedly, of course, from that of law. It is not constrained by evidentiary rules of law, nor does it focus on binary logic and the exclusion of presumed evildoers. Instead, actors in the diplomatic game seek to use established social (specifically diplomatic) capital by keeping players engaged in negotiations toward the achievement of policy outcomes. This substantive outcome orientation replaces adherence to formal rules.

Whatever their legal or diplomatic source, statements about a conflict are filtered by mass media. This institutional arena comes with its own selectivities, a limited repertoire of narrative genres, and a focus on individual actors and neglect of larger structural and cultural forces. These statements often involve simplifications and mischaracterizations of liberal principles of legal proceedings before they reach a broader audience, to finally settle in the sediments of collective memory.[7] Mass media are crucial in our context for three reasons. First, while millions of those residing within the borders of the former Yugoslavia directly observed and experienced the events, many suffering their painful and deadly consequences, those of us outside of the war zones largely learned of this violent conflict through the intense diplomatic, military, and legal involvement of the international community as reported by news media. Second, media play a particularly significant role in the foreign policy formation of U.S. administrations, as in this policy realm the vast majority of Americans are not well informed and lack strong positions.[8] Third, media matter greatly for budding international courts. We have already cited Hagan's statements about the central role journalism played in helping Justice Jackson develop his charisma at the Nuremberg tribunal and Hagan's contention that media may play an even more crucial role today in the age of twenty-four-hour news stations, with their seemingly instantaneous global coverage.

In short, legal narratives compete with others, such as diplomatic ones, and they are filtered through mass media before they reach a broader public. As we set out to examine such competition and mediation for the atrocities committed during the Balkan conflict, specifically the role played by the late Slobodan Milosevic, we analyze articles published in the *New York Times* between 1989 and 2006. This newspaper is well suited for an examination of foreign policy themes as it is considered one of two leading American newspapers in this policy realm. Its articles and opinion pieces are often reprinted in local papers across the country. Also, previous work has demonstrated that the *Times* took strong positions on the Bosnian War.[9] Here we are interested in the representation of Milosevic's role in atrocities perpetrated during different periods of the prelegal and legal stages, before and after his indictment and before and after his arrest and extradition to the ICTY. We further examine how the representation of his role varies with the types of sources on which journalistic accounts are based, especially diplomatic versus legal ones. We explore the construction of sector-specific narratives from series of disjointed statements as mediated by newspaper reporting, a method that to our knowledge has not previously been used. Finally, we supplement this approach with quantitative analyses that illustrate and largely support our theoretical expectations.

Empirical Examination: Law, Diplomacy, and Media Reporting Through Time

The non-sociologist will notice again that our methods differ considerably from those practiced by scholars in other disciplines. This applies especially to historians, who have produced remarkable studies on trials against perpetrators of crimes against humanity. Historians examine multiple archives in great depth and over many years to study one particular trial and provide us with detailed narratives; in contrast, we focus on the reception of legal proceedings. We also do not provide the same thick description of particular trials, the actors involved, their arguments, and public debates in multiple sectors of society. Instead, we engage in systematic sampling procedures and quantitative coding that allow for statistical depictions and even modest multivariate analyses. Finally, our approach allows us to incorporate several cases into one volume, thus capitalizing on the comparative potential of social science analysis. Obviously, the distinct disciplinary modes should be perceived not as competing but rather as supplementing each other. Interestingly, though, independent of method, there is a substantial degree of overlap in some of the conclusions.[10]

Seeking to identify the representation of atrocities in the Yugoslav wars, especially the role of Slobodan Milosevic, we identified all *Times* articles that mentioned the word *Milosevic* and were published between 1989, the year in which Milosevic was elected as Serb president (and two years before the outbreak of war), and the time surrounding his death in 2006 (seven years after the Kosovo War). The sample we selected consists of all articles published in January of each of these years, supplemented by articles published around particularly salient events, often referred to in the literature as critical discourse moments.[11] The selection of January articles was a convenient way of establishing a random sample and appropriate, as the events in Yugoslavia were not structured by annual cycles. Given our specific interest in the ways in which legal processing affects media reporting and the formation of collective memory, however, we decided to supplement this sample with a purposive sample. The latter focused on sets of articles published around the dates of legal events, specifically Milosevic's indictment, his extradition to the ICTY, and his death in custody in the spring of 2006. The total sample includes 152 articles.[12]

We subjected these articles to content analysis. We coded information regarding the date of publication, the articles' dominant themes (for example, elections, war, economy, diplomacy), the types of suffering mentioned in the article (killing, injury, rape, displacement), the number of victims where applicable, the place in which the articles were published (section and page number), and their length. Within these articles we identified descriptions of 504 actions taken by Milosevic (for example, he negotiated; he supported Bosnian-Serb troops with weapons) and 210 actions by others directed at the former Serb and Yugoslav president (for example, demanding his arrest; praising his cooperativeness). For each of these actions we identified the source of information cited by journalists (for example, "according to prosecutors from the ICTY" or "according to diplomats involved in the negotiations"). We thus constructed a dataset with 714 action cases nested within the 152 articles.

We analyzed the data qualitatively and quantitatively. In our qualitative analysis we used a new method of constructing quasi ideal-typical narratives. We strung together statements from diverse articles about actions taken by Milosevic, as provided by actors from a specific sector (for example, the court) that the journalist cites as the source of information. We thus arrived at sector-specific depictions of Milosevic and his role in the conflict. In addition, we conducted a standardized content analysis and, based on the resulting dataset, a statistical analysis of the set of articles and statements. Figure 5.1 illustrates the distribution of articles over the four time periods noted early in this chapter.[13] Figure 5.2 similarly depicts the number of statements about actions by or directed at Slobodan Milosevic over time.[14]

The average annual number of *New York Times* articles in which the name Slobodan Milosevic appears increases during the war years and further during the postindictment period before it declines to the wartime level during the postextradition period. This increase, however, is not a

Figure 5.1   Number of Sampled Articles and Mentions of Suffering, by Stage

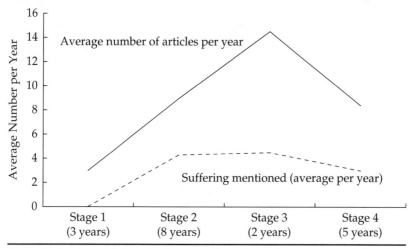

Average number of articles per year

Suffering mentioned (average per year)

| Stage 1 (3 years) | Stage 2 (8 years) | Stage 3 (2 years) | Stage 4 (5 years) |

Source: Authors' compilation of information from *New York Times* articles discussed in text.
Note: Stage 1 = Before Yugoslav wars. Stage 2 = During Yugoslav wars. Stage 3 = After indictment. Stage 4 = After extradition.

reflection of the newspaper's interest in the judicial proceedings per se. It partly reflects the fact that event-specific sets of cases within our sample focus on the legal events of indictment and extradition and on Milosevic's death in custody. The postindictment era was also particularly intense as it involved not just judicial proceedings but also the end of the Kosovo War.

More interesting to us is the distribution of articles that mention diverse types of suffering across the four periods (see table B.1 in appendix B for additional detail). Surprisingly, the horrific consequences of war and war crimes are not frequently invoked in our sample of 152 *Times* reports. In fact, torture and rape are almost never mentioned, despite the systematic use of both, in line with the traditional silencing of rape campaigns during times of war. Killings and injuries are more frequently reported, especially during the war years, while the displacement of populations is mentioned most often during the periods that involve judicial proceedings.

Finally, just as the number of articles in which Milosevic's name appears increases up until the indictment phase and then slightly declines, the number of actions by Milosevic described in the articles

Figure 5.2   Actions by and at Milosevic, by Stage

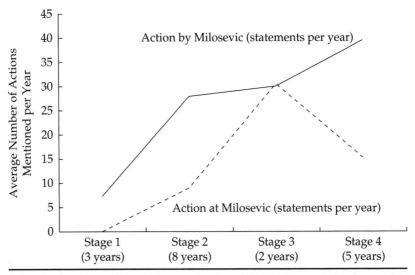

Source: Authors' compilation of information from *New York Times* articles discussed in text.
Note: Stage 1 = Before Yugoslav wars. Stage 2 = During Yugoslav wars. Stage 3 = After indictment. Stage 4 = After extradition.

grows throughout the study period, indicating an intensifying focus on the former Serb and Yugoslav president throughout the legal proceedings (figure 5.2). According to a more detailed examination (not shown), the amount of reporting about Milosevic's actions varies considerably by year: from zero (January 1998) and two (January 1989) actions at the low end to more than fifty at the high end (January 1997; January 1999). The number of actions reported at times reflects the fact that some Januaries were high-intensity months. For example, January 1997, when Milosevic annulled local elections throughout Serbia against intense and growing protests; and January 1999, the month immediately preceding the North Atlantic Treaty Organization (NATO) military campaign against Serbia, filled with negotiations and ultimatums.

However, other Januaries were also crowded with intense events but are not reflected as such in the number of reports. Examples include the Januaries of 1994 and 1995, when the Bosnian War was raging but only seven and four, respectively, actions by Milosevic were reported in the *Times*. Actions reported around special events, such as Milosevic's indictment in 1999, his extradition to the ICTY in 2001, the beginning of his trial in 2002, and his death in March 2006, are again much more numerous.

Yet the number of actions reported during the course of the trial was very low, with none at all during the Januaries of 2003 and 2004 and two and five, respectively, in the Januaries of 2005 and 2006. This pattern confirms findings from earlier research that news media are more interested in the catastrophic events that may be the basis for later trials and in the outcome of trials than in ongoing judicial proceedings.[15]

While the intensity of reporting thus varies considerably over time, one finding is constant. Slobodan Milosevic does not typically appear in a positive light. The light in which he is cast varies, however, with the institutional sector by which information is provided, and it changes across the four stages distinguished earlier. The main competitors are the worlds of diplomacy and law, with the latter increasingly replacing the former in the later stages of the unfolding drama.

Law Versus Diplomacy: Distinct Narratives on Milosevic and the Yugoslav Wars

Institution-specific narratives are best suited to examining the different ways in which law and diplomacy depict Milosevic's actions. We first merge statements citing judicial sources. The narratives address both Milosevic's actions and measures taken against him. Dates of the articles from which statements are selected are provided in parentheses. The following paragraphs summarize all narratives within our sample but a couple of irrelevant statements by court officials. Specifically, they are concerned with Milosevic's crimes, his command responsibility, his criminal intent, and, to a lesser extent, procedural issues.

The first paragraph concerns the aggressive acts and crimes that are at issue. We read about Milosevic's campaign, his declaration of war, his campaign of terror and violence, his killing and committing crimes. We also read about the specific types of crimes for which he was eventually charged (forced expulsion, killing, specifically killing witnesses). Here the actus reus, the criminal act, is established, a necessary requirement on the way toward a criminal conviction:[16]

Chief Prosecutor Carla Del Ponte announces an extended indictment against Milosevic for crimes during the conflicts in Bosnia and Croatia, which may include charges of genocide (June 30, 2001). An ICTY investigator states that Del Ponte has a list of Milosevic's war crimes for actions in Kosovo, and Nancy Paterson from the prosecutor's office speaks to the evidence on which the indictment against Milosevic is based. In the same article Del Ponte is cited with a reference to an extended indictment in which five additional killing sites are addressed (July 2, 2001). Later she argues that "the common denominator of all this criminal activity was—one must never forget—forced expulsion" (January 31, 2002). Referring to his behavior in court, and again citing Del Ponte, an article reports that while "the great Milosevic" had killed and committed crimes, he stared at the floor and refused to talk to her (February 9, 2002). Although the latest statements mostly deal with Milosevic's presumably inappropriate use of medications and his death, a prosecutor is cited one final time, reminding readers that Milosevic instigated crimes in Bosnia and Croatia by supplying and financing armies (March 13, 2006).

The second set of statements is in line with the demands of criminal proceedings, especially in cases like this, in which high-ranking actors have managed to keep their hands clean: command responsibility has to be established. Thus in some of the following statements Milosevic is depicted as the top of a chain of command, as in the "Milosevic-led Serbian government" (Chief Prosecutor Richard Goldstone). This theme is also reflected in a statement on his "use of his Deputy Prime Minister" and in another on his controlling Serb forces. Such statements are meant to show Milosevic's use of the state and its organization as tools in the execution of crimes:

An ICTY investigator is cited as arguing that the court will focus on Zeljko Raznatovic ("Arkan") and Vojislav Seselj (paramilitary leaders) to climb the chain of command to Milosevic but that an indictment of all three could be very difficult (January 28, 1996). This situation changes after the Kosovo War, in which Milosevic was clearly the commander in chief, as indicated by the following statements made five years later: According to Chief Prosecutor Carla Del Ponte, considerations are under way to try Milosevic for the Croatian and Bosnian Wars as well as for Kosovo (January 10, 2002). Investigators for the ICTY refer to Milosevic's campaign against ethnic Albanians in Kosovo (July 2, 2001). Citing a prosecutor, a later article informs readers that Milosevic-controlled Serb forces killed witnesses (February 16, 2002). Nancy Paterson, a member of the prosecution team, speaks to Milosevic's use of Deputy Prime Minister Nikola Sainovic "as his trusted man on the ground" doing dirty police work (July 2, 2001).

Furthermore, criminal proceedings need to establish criminal intent. This judicial requirement is reflected in a third set of statements made by court actors about Slobodan Milosevic and cited in the *Times*. Here, terms such as "premeditated," "grand plan," and "criminal plan" speak to the murderous intent with which Milosevic ordered his underlings to engage in crimes:

The court's indictment states that Milosevic's declaration of war gave him control over republican and federal police units and over all key institutions and that Milosevic "planned, instigated, ordered, committed, or otherwise aided and abetted in a campaign of terror and violence directed at Kosovo Albanian civilians" (July 3, 2001). Later, Milosevic is presented as the instigator of Serb attacks on civilians. Del Ponte is also cited explicating the premeditated nature of his actions by referring to his intent "to forge a Serbian nation that was ethnically pure . . . , 'a common criminal plan'" (January 10, 2002). Some three weeks later Del Ponte is again quoted with a similar argument: "The grand project, the accused Milosevic's overall plan, which is already evident from 1989, was an essentially Serbian state, dominated by Belgrade" (January 31, 2002). Simultaneously, according to prosecutors, the prosecution seeks to prove that Milosevic is responsible for atrocities because he knew or should have known that they were occurring (February 19, 2002).[17]

The preceding paragraphs, made up of individual utterances about Milosevic's actions over a period of more than ten years, summarize all *New York Times* text that is explicitly based on ICTY information in the entire set of 152 articles. It concerns Milosevic's role in the Balkan conflict and the massive humanitarian and human rights crimes committed in their course. In line with our expectations, this narrative is thoroughly informed by the institutional logic of law, its individualizing focus, its stress on legal categories, its procedural demands, and its binary and exclusionary logic. Most statements depict Milosevic as an individual evildoer.

One additional observation about this court narrative concerns the time frame used by the criminal court. In the case of the Nuremberg tribunal against leading Nazis, the time frame under consideration by the tribunal was limited to the period of the war, from 1939 to 1945. The same applies to the Yugoslav case. Yet while the reduced time frame in the Nuremberg case excluded from consideration the systematic preparation of inhumanities against Jews and others in times of peace, in the Yugoslav case it excluded the complicated history of ethnic tension, including historic wars, that had served as a central tool in mnemonic battles preceding the Balkan conflict. Atrocities committed against Serbs during World War II, as well as the imposed "harmony" during the authoritarian regime under the post–World War II leader Marshall Tito, are especially relevant here. In both cases the temporal framing serves the interest of achieving criminal convictions. In Nuremberg, an inclusion of prewar crimes would have resulted in defense arguments that the trial offended against principles of national sovereignty, then sacred in international law. In the Milosevic case, however, the limitation of the time frame in the court-informed narrative excluded potentially mitigating circumstances and supported the binary logic of law in which Milosevic must be found guilty if he is not to be found innocent. Clearly, this logic also aimed at Milosevic's exclusion from political life and civil society.

In short then, the court-based narrative of the *New York Times*, constituted from many different articles over a ten-year period, specifies

Milosevic's behaviors under recognized legal categories. It attributes criminal liability to him in cases in which atrocities were committed by others, and it seeks to demonstrate that his state of mind fulfills the preconditions for a criminal conviction. Other statements explicate legal strategies to achieve a conviction. We find a depiction of a historical figure, read through the lens of a criminal tribunal. How does this compare with the image of Milosevic drawn up from *Times* statements that cite diplomatic sources? Here a different logic is at work. We expect to see this logic reflected in a different portrayal of Milosevic—and we do.

Just as the *Times*'s criminal court–based narrative reflects the logic of criminal law, so the narrative based on diplomatic sources reflects the distinct logic of the world of diplomacy. Diplomacy applies neither an exclusionary nor a binary "guilty–not guilty" logic. It is also not primarily oriented toward procedure. Instead, diplomats seek to use current political actors and diplomatic capital to settle disputes and to achieve desired outcomes. Accordingly, the Milosevic presented in statements informed by diplomatic sources appears in a radically different light. As the following paragraphs show, however, there is also some degree of heterogeneity. We see substantial variation by phases of the process. Also the specific diplomatic sources of information matter. European and United Nations diplomats are more generous with friendly assessments than are their American colleagues.

In the late stages of the Croatian War, Cyrus R. Vance, the United Nations' special envoy and secretary of state under President Jimmy Carter, informs the reporter that Milosevic formally agreed to support Vance's peace plan "should the circumstances on the ground permit it." The Belgrade government also reversed initial opposition to peacekeeping forces (January 1, 1992). An article of the same month, informed by statements of Lord Peter Carrington (chairman of the European Community peace conference), reports that Milosevic expressed condolences for the deaths of four Italian and one French peace monitor, attributing responsibility to Serbian extremists in the Yugoslav Air Force. Furthermore, Milosevic agrees for the first time to Carrington's plan of accepting Serbian enclaves in other republics' territories, as long as their minority rights are protected (January 10, 1992).

Diplomats, in this early stage of the Balkan conflict, primarily during the Croatian War, thus portray a picture of Milosevic that differs radically from the image we encounter in the judicial statements. Milosevic appears as an actor who is conciliatory and interested in negotiations and peace. Astonishing in hindsight, this portrait continues into the yet crueler Bosnian War. Once again, Cyrus Vance plays a central role in this period in collaboration with former British foreign secretary Lord David Owen. Vance and Owen were crucial in developing the Vance-Owen Peace Plan in January 1993. This plan was eventually agreed upon in Athens in May of 1993. Later, however, it was rejected by a Bosnian-Serb Assembly meeting during which Radovan Karadzic, president of the self-declared Serbian Republic of Bosnia-Herzegovina and currently a defendant before the ICTY, played a particularly destructive role. Consider the following statements from the early stages of the Bosnian War:

In January of 1993, Cyrus Vance is cited regarding a meeting with Milosevic in which the latter agreed to help with ending the war in Bosnia and Herzegovina; Vance reportedly adds that Milosevic made and kept the same kind of promise more than a year earlier in the war between Serbs and Croats. In the same article participants in the Belgrade peace talks are cited as saying that Milosevic put pressure on Bosnian Serb leader Radovan Karadzic to agree to a peace plan and that Milosevic was in a position to deny weapons, ammunition, food, and electricity to Bosnian forces. Milosevic himself is quoted as saying to Vance, "Peace is in our vital interest. I will do everything in my power" (January 7, 1993). Vance reports about another line of conflict, albeit not yet war, that Milosevic "was prepared to reopen primary schools for Albanians, permit improvements in their health care and allow an independent census." According to statements by Vance and Owen, Milosevic's attitude had made the two chairmen optimistic. They will seek to include Milosevic on talks about ending the Bosnian War (January 8, 1993). Milosevic is quoted accordingly: "We are here to support peace. I hope all sides will use this opportunity to end that cruel war" (January 12, 1993).

Milosevic is not portrayed simply as a conciliatory contributor to peace efforts. As the following statements make clear, he is depicted even as an antagonist to those aggressive actors who seek to drive Bosnia further into its destructive civil war, most noteworthy president Karadzic:

Just one day later officials close to the talks report that pressure from Milosevic caused Karadzic to change his mind about the UN agreement. Cyrus Vance is cited as presenting the information that Milosevic and President Dobrika Cosic of the Yugoslav Federation agreed to the UN peace plan. According to "a person who took part in the process," Milosevic and Cosic "squeezed" Karadzic for about two hours before he gave in. Fred Eckhard, a spokesperson for Vance and Owen, refers to Milosevic and Cosic as "a persuasive team and persuasive force" (January 13, 1993), and Vance is quoted as saying that the Serbian leader acted as "a broker in the process that led to the Serb-Croat armistice" (January 19, 1993). Later that month a UN spokesperson reports that Milosevic "agreed to try to use his influence to end the battles" (January 24, 1993).

The image of Milosevic drawn from diplomatic sources differs dramatically from that provided by the ICTY. It is certainly not dictated by an exclusionary logic. Instead, Milosevic appears mostly as a politician who is cooperative and concerned with the establishment of peace. The depiction is also concerned not with evidentiary criteria or procedural matters but with the achievement of policy goals in the context of peace negotiations.

We have to be careful not to contrast this narrative too quickly with the very distinct portrayal that is based on ICTY-issued statements, as this diplomatic depiction of Milosevic is drawn from a much earlier period. To be sure, these earlier years were already an era of horrendous cruelty. Yet potential mutations of the diplomatic narrative warrant closer inspection, controlling for the era from which the court narrative is constructed. In other words, are diplomatic and court statements as distinct as they appear when we examine only those made in a specific period? In addition to controlling for time period, we also have to distinguish between the different regimes under which diplomats work, as these governments or international organizations ultimately determine the policy goals toward which diplomatic action is oriented.

Diplomats cited in the preceding narrative represent European governments, the European Union, and the United Nations. Distinctly more ambivalent, even outright negative, depictions of Milosevic originate from American diplomatic sources as early as January 1993. During this period the Clinton administration was unwilling to give up on Milosevic as a potential partner in peace negotiations, but it was concerned that the proposed peace settlement would legitimize, or at least implicitly acquiesce to, Serbian aggression and atrocities.

Warren M. Christopher, Clinton's secretary of state, is quoted for the first time with a call "for war crimes trials for atrocities in both Iraq and the Balkans" (January 24, 1993). Simultaneously, Lawrence Eagleburger, a former secretary of state, suggests that Milosevic be listed as a war criminal, along with Karadzic and others, despite his involvement in the European Community peace negotiations. A Clinton administration report sent to the UN for possible use in future war crimes trials "details dozens of incidents of murder, torture, the abuse of civilians in detention centers, the wanton destruction of property and forcible deportations of civilians by Serbian authorities and soldiers in Bosnia and Herzegovina" (January 27, 1993). Unspecified diplomatic sources are also cited with the observation that Milosevic exploits a recent Croatian attack on Serbian rebels to maintain the appearance of Serb victimization by Croatia (January 29, 2003).

In addition to distinct policies staked out by different national governments, historical time also affects the message from diplomatic sources as constructed by the *Times*. Space does not allow for a presentation of all statements about Milosevic that reference diplomats as informants. However, selections illustrate how the narrative on Milosevic becomes markedly more negative despite a simultaneous desire to maintain him as a negotiation partner up to the point of his indictment. A January 30, 1995, article, anticipating the Dayton peace negotiations, cites Western officials expressing the hope that Milosevic will play a crucial role by recognizing the international borders proposed for Croatia. Later in the same year, Milosevic indeed traveled to attend the Clinton-brokered peace negotiations at the Wright-Patterson Air Force Base near Dayton, Ohio. There, in November 1995, a peace agreement was reached. The agreement was formally signed in Paris on December 14, 1995. This accord was significant as it put an end to the three-and-a-half-year war in Bosnia. Yet shortly after Dayton, we again read mixed evaluations of Milosevic's role. While a January 23, 1996, article cites John Shattuck, U.S. assistant secretary for human rights, with positive comments on Milosevic's cooperation regarding human rights investigations and a pending tour of mass graves, the same edition of the *Times* points out that Milosevic had not settled a crucial dispute with Croat president Franjo Tudjman about a peninsula of strategic importance (Prevlaka Peninsula).

One year later, we still find a mixed assessment, but the rhetoric becomes more negative overall. Western diplomats remind journalists of Milosevic's support for the Dayton peace accord and inform them of his attempts to have Yugoslavia rejoin European organizations and enter into bodies such as the UN and the International Monetary Fund. But a letter by Warren Christopher from the same month warns of further isolation of Serbia should opposition election victories not be recognized by the Milosevic administration (January 4, 1997). At this point, Milosevic's standing in the international community has clearly weakened, as the following quotation from a European diplomat indicates: "Milosevic has lost a lot of his power, his image of invulnerability and his prestige. He can only come out of all of this a loser, the question is how big a loser" (January 13, 1997). Part of the loss of prestige is attributed to his reputation for unreliability. Nicholas Burns, a U.S. State Department spokesman, for example, states in the dispute over election results that the Milosevic government periodically offers the opposition an olive branch, only to take it away (January 15, 1997).

Clearly, the positive portraits from earlier years, which read like nomination letters suggesting Milosevic for the Nobel Peace Prize, have given way to considerable skepticism among diplomats. This impression intensifies two years later, during the build-up to the military confrontation in Kosovo.

James Rubin, a State Department spokesman, is cited as saying that Milosevic will be held responsible (along with Kosovo Albanians) for the security of peace monitors (January 16, 1999). In response to a massacre of Kosovo Albanian civilians, the State Department demands that the Milosevic administration remove extra soldiers sent to Kosovo in recent months, and Rubin says, "Mr. Milosevic was being asked to iden-tify and 'take action' against those who . . . ordered the massacre and to allow the International War Crimes Tribunal for the former Yugoslavia . . . into Kosovo to investigate" (January 17, 1999).

The last quotation is significant as it illustrates that the fields of law and diplomacy are not just competitors. Once diplomats begin to execute policies aimed at the exclusion of political actors, they may use the exclu-sionary and binary logic of criminal courts to support their new position. Yet with Milosevic still in power, ambivalence remained, not just among European and UN diplomats but also among their American counter-parts. We do not wish to burden the reader with too detailed a depiction of that part of media reporting that is fed by diplomatic sources. The essential points we seek to make are expressed in the preceding reports. The remaining reports continue the recent, increasingly critical tone toward Milosevic. In 1999, while Milosevic himself is still cited in a January 20th article making comments on the provocative nature of actions by the Kosovo Liberation Army, articles on the following two days depict him openly as an enemy of the West and criticize his expul-sion of an American human rights diplomat from Serbia.

Yet although diplomacy begins to threaten with war, it continues to hold the door open for a diplomatic resolution. Milosevic, still in power, is simultaneously portrayed as aggressive but worthy as a participant in negotiations. Both Robin Cook, the new British foreign secretary, and, four months later (now with NATO attacks against Serbia under way), U.S. State Department officials comment on the need to involve Milosevic in meetings with international arbiters (articles of January 31 and May 15 of 1999).

With the end of NATO warfare and the defeat of Yugoslavia approaching, and after the indictment of Milosevic by the ICTY, all in the spring of 1999, diplomatic activity involving Milosevic almost comes to a halt. News media cite few diplomatic sources in this phase. Most excep-tions are from two of Serbia's fellow Christian Orthodox countries. One is neighboring Greece, interested in maintaining Serb strength vis-à-vis Albania and Macedonia, neighbors to both Serbia and to Greece that Greece views with skepticism. The other is Russia, a longtime Serbian ally. Shortly before the ICTY issued its indictment against Milosevic, even the Clinton administration still indicated that the pending "indict-ment . . . would not preclude direct negotiations" with Milosevic (May 27, 1999). Yet eight months later the *Times* reports that "Secretary of State Madeline K. Albright has told senior aides that one of her goals, before leaving the office a year from now, is to see Mr. Milosevic out of office" (January 24, 2000).

Our analysis shows that the distinct institutional logics of the diplomatic and legal fields, despite some similarities, produce very different narratives, as reflected in journalistic accounts. Both narratives focus on specific individual actors, and Milosevic clearly is the prime character in these stories. Yet the diplomatic field's depiction of Milosevic is more ambivalent and varied than that produced under the logic of the criminal court. This variation reflects the nation- and time-specific policy goals under which diplomatic action unfolds. Over time, the growing weight of the criminal proceedings, progressing from investigation through indictment to trial, in combination with the shifting policy goals that direct diplomacy result in an increasingly close association between Milosevic and the atrocities committed during the Yugoslav wars.

Narratives in Numbers: Counting Arguments and the Weight of Sector Versus Time

How do these conclusions, derived from an interpretive analysis of narratives, hold up under statistical examination? What do numbers say about the relative impact of judicial versus diplomatic sectors and distinct stages on the depiction of Milosevic? A cursory look at statements about actions taken by Slobodan Milosevic reveals that relatively few are informed by court sources (22). More are based on information provided by diplomats (32), by diverse governments in Yugoslavia and the Western world (38), and by Milosevic himself and by his representatives (113). Almost half of the statements about Milosevic do not name a source of information (308 combined). The relative scarcity of statements for which the court is cited as a source likely reflects the lack of a permanent *Times* correspondent at the ICTY, attesting to resources, budgets, and media priorities as potential contributors to stories and narratives that may partly shape collective memory.

Nevertheless, journalists explicitly refer to court actors as sources of information in twenty-two statements about Milosevic's actions. Most of these statements are concentrated in the postindictment and postextradition or trial phases. Not surprisingly, their character differs considerably from that of statements informed by diplomats and those for which no source is provided.

As figure 5.3 illustrates, more than 30 percent of ICTY-informed statements address hostile actions by Milosevic, such as the inflammation of nationalism and hatred, military action to advance the Serbian cause, advancing authoritarianism, and uncooperativeness with the West. Almost 20 percent address issues such as human rights or humanitarian law offenses and their preparation, and nearly 10 percent comment on

Figure 5.3   Depictions of Milosevic's Actions, Based on Sources

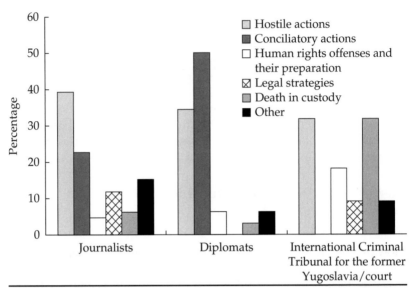

Source: Authors' compilation of information from *New York Times* articles discussed in text.

Note: Other categories of sources, including Milosevic or his representatives, Western governments, and others, are omitted from the figure. Hostile actions include enhanced nationalism and conflicts, military action to advance the Serbian cause, uncooperativeness with the West or the United Nations, and advancement of authoritarian causes. Human rights offenses and their preparation include (advancing) human rights offenses and commanding of these actions.

legal strategies. More than 30 percent speak to Milosevic's death in custody of the ICTY. These last are mostly defensive in nature, attributing the death to Milosevic's deliberately improper use of medications to impede legal proceedings and to force release to medical care in Russia.

Even the basic information provided in figure 5.3 indicates that the image of Milosevic is quite different when accounts rely on diplomatic sources for information. Half of these statements describe a man who engages in conciliatory action. Yet diplomats do not consistently paint a rosy picture of Milosevic. About one-third of statements refer to hostile actions generally, and 6 percent to human rights offenses specifically. The many statements about Milosevic for which journalists do not cite sources mention his hostile actions most frequently, but a good 20 percent also depict a conciliatory Milosevic. Here we see reflected traces of both the accusatory nature of the criminal law discourse and the conciliatory tone of diplomacy.

Figure 5.4   Individualizing Nature of Articles Mentioning Suffering and
Milosevic's Actions, by Stage

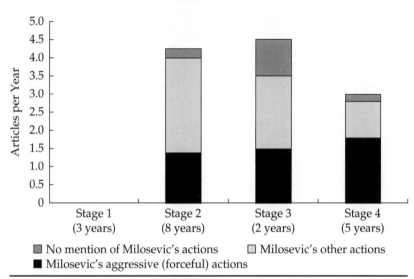

Source: Authors' compilation of *New York Times* articles discussed in text.
Note: Aggressive (forceful) actions include general forceful aggressive actions (military
action to advance the Serbian cause, forceful action to advance an authoritarian cause)
and human rights offenses and their preparation (advancing and commanding human
rights offenses). Stage 1 = Before Yugoslav wars. Stage 2 = During Yugoslav wars. Stage 3
= After indictment. Stage 4 = After extradition.

The association between negative depictions of Milosevic and the
timing of events is reflected in figure 5.4, which illustrates patterns from
articles in which atrocities are reported and shows simultaneously the
proportion of articles in which different types of actions by Milosevic are
depicted. While Milosevic's actions are referred to in almost all of these
articles, the proportion of aggressive and forceful actions as well as
human rights offenses and their preparation is highest in the final, postextradition, or trial, stage.

In an attempt to separate time and sector effects we conducted a multivariate analysis in which we regressed the type of action undertaken
by Milosevic on the sources of information and on time periods (see
table 5.2). Looking first at the likelihood of references to conciliatory
actions, we find that model 1 shows that information provided by diplomats is significantly more likely to view Milosevic as a conciliatory actor
than are journalistic and judicial sources. We also see that Milosevic is significantly less likely to be portrayed as a conciliatory actor after extradition

Table 5.2   Logistic Regression Coefficients

	Model 1 Conciliatory Actions	Model 2 Aggressive (Forceful) Actions
Sources[a]		
Milosevic and representatives	.127	−.934[#]
	(.326)	(.499)
Diplomats	.848*	.560
	(.401)	(.769)
Judicial		1.098*
		(.453)
Western governments	−.061	−.040
	(.403)	(.435)
Other source	−.147	−.069
	(.313)	(.365)
Stages[b]		
After indictment	.126	.126
	(.314)	(.385)
After extradition	−2.021***	.158
	(.409)	(.403)
Constant	−.805	−2.342***
	(.188)	(.263)
−2 Log-likelihood	478.60	430.27

Source: Authors' compilation of data from *New York Times* articles about Slobodan Milosevic.
Note: Standard errors are in parentheses. Conciliatory actions include cooperating with the West or the United Nations, stressing peaceful means, advancing Yugoslavian unity, and making concessions. Aggressive (forceful) actions include military action to advance the Serbian cause, (advancing) human rights offenses, commanding human rights offenses, and forceful action to advance an authoritarian cause.
[a]"Journalistic" is the omitted reference category in model 2. Journalistic and judicial sources are the reference category in model 1. In the latter case there were extremely small cell frequencies for the "journalistic" dummy variable, and thus it is used as part of the reference category. Additional analyses that eliminated cases coded as "1" on judicial source and analyses using alternative reference categories yielded the same substantive results.
[b]"Before war" and "during war" are omitted as the reference categories.
[#]$p<.10$; *$p<.05$; ***$p<.001$

than during the prewar and war years (the latter two periods omitted as reference categories in table 5.2). Even when we controlled for the source of information, it appears that the collaborative Milosevic is more likely to be depicted in the earlier phases. The trial phase puts an end to that image, and his portrayal in the media reverses course after extradition.

In a second analysis we examined the sector and time effects on the likelihood that Milosevic is associated with aggressive and forceful actions. Here we find that judicial sources are more likely than other sources to link Milosevic with such actions. Neither model indicates that any stage is significantly associated with statements about aggressive and forceful actions. While the low number of cases warrants a cautious interpretation of our findings, we may conclude, in line with our expectations, that Milosevic is more often associated with conciliatory action when diplomats are sources of information and when he is reported about in the prejudicial stages. He is most likely associated with aggressive and forceful actions when speakers of the court inform *Times* reporting.

Reflections of Milosevic Discourses in American Memories

It may be too early to diagnose American memories of Slobodan Milosevic and his role in the atrocities committed during the Yugoslav wars. Yet a review of recent U.S. press reports in which the former Serb and Yugoslav president and defendant before the ICTY is mentioned provides a first indication. We scanned all contributions published in American papers in the year 2010 through the time of this writing (July 2010) as documented in the search engine ProQuest. This procedure allows for at least a brief illustration of the way Milosevic is remembered four years after his death; eleven years after the cruel repression he unleashed over Kosovo; fifteen years after the worst single event of the Bosnian War, the genocidal mass killings in Srebrenica; and almost two decades after the beginning of the disastrous wars over which he presided. Substantive articles or editorials are relatively rare in 2010, especially in U.S. media as compared with European outlets, and in the following pages we present statements selected from those few reports that most explicitly refer to Milosevic.

The most recent occasion that brought Milosevic to media attention was the issuing of an opinion by the International Court of Justice that strengthened Kosovo's newly declared independence from Serbia. On July 26, 2010, the *Wall Street Journal* issued an editorial commenting on the court's opinion and remembering Milosevic's role in this context: "There certainly can be no doubt that Kosovo had suffered 'a long train of abuses and usurpations' at the hands of Slobodan Milosevic's brutish government before it was saved by NATO intervention."

Here the editorial combines a renewed condemnation of Milosevic with praise for the military action undertaken by NATO forces. The *International Herald Tribune* of July 23, 2010, commenting on the same event, discusses Milosevic's role as follows:

Kosovo's declaration of independence on Feb. 17, 2008, marked the culmination of a showdown between Serbia and the West in which the United States and a majority of European nations argued that Serbia's violent repression of Kosovo's majority ethnic Albanians under former President Slobodan Milosevic had forfeited Serbia's moral and legal right to rule the territory. . . . Mr. Milosevic, the former Serbian leader, revoked Kosovo's autonomy in 1989 and fiercely repressed ethnic Albanians, who make up most of its population. Some of them eventually turned to armed rebellion. NATO intervened in 1999 to halt Mr. Milosevic's violent response to the rebels.

Just before the International Court of Justice's opinion was issued, July 10 of 2010, provided another occasion for commemorative events and commentaries: the fifteenth anniversary of the Srebrenica massacre, in which some eight thousand men were killed in a massive genocidal act. Remarkably, Milosevic's name barely appears in reports and editorials that commemorate this date. Almost all contributions emphasize the role of Ratko Mladic, the Bosnian-Serb general only in May 2011 extradited to the ICTY. Here the memory appears to focus on the actor who bore the most direct command responsibility. One exception is the *Wall Street Journal*'s July 12, 2010, comment on Belgrade's recent first formal condemnation of the Srebrenica killings. Both Milosevic and Bosnian-Serb president Karadzic are referred to here: "Serbia has arrested and handed over numerous alleged war criminals, including former Serbian President Slobodan Milosevic, who died while on trial, and former Bosnian Serb leader Radovan Karadzic, currently on trial in The Hague."

A very different occasion for Americans to remember the crimes committed in the Balkan conflict was the death of the former American ICTY prosecutor Nancy Paterson. An obituary, written by Dennis Helvesi and first published in the *New York Times* on April 8, 2010, was reprinted in other papers such as the *Boston Globe* on April 10 and the *Pittsburgh Post-Gazette* on April 11. We quote at some length as, in this obituary, the memory of Paterson is closely intertwined with that of Milosevic, spelling out his crimes in greater detail than any other article or opinion piece published in 2010:[18]

Nancy Paterson, an international war crimes prosecutor who played a leading role in building the case linking the former Yugoslav president Slobodan Milosevic to massacres, mass rape and ethnic cleansing in the Balkans in the 1990s, died March 27. . . .

From 1994 to 2001, Ms. Paterson was one of the prosecutors commissioned by the United Nations to investigate war crimes, crimes against humanity and sexual crimes during nearly a decade of bloodshed that killed more than 200,000 people in the former Yugoslavia.

With Clint Williamson, who later became the United States ambassador at large for war crimes issues, Ms. Paterson led a team of more than 50 lawyers and investigators who gathered evidence leading to the indictment of Mr. Milosevic, whose role in the bloodshed earned him the sobriquet Butcher of the Balkans.

The 54-page initial indictment by the International Criminal Tribunal for the former Yugoslavia, which focused on war crimes in the Kosovo region, was written by Ms. Paterson and Mr. Williamson. It was the first time that a sitting head of state had been charged by an international tribunal. The indictment was later expanded to include crimes in Croatia and Bosnia.

Mr. Milosevic, the Communist leader whose embrace of Serbian nationalism ignited the ethnic strife, was president of Serbia from 1989 to 1997 and president of Yugoslavia from 1997 to 2000. As he rose to power by inciting dreams of a Greater Serbia, he became the prime engineer of conflicts that pitted his fellow Serbs against the Slovenes, the Croats, the Bosnians, the Albanians of Kosovo and ultimately the combined forces of the NATO alliance.

By the fall of 2000, Mr. Milosevic's appeals to nationalism were no longer sufficient to keep him in power.

After comments on Milosevic's ouster, trial, and death, the obituary continues:

Louise Arbour, chief prosecutor for the tribunal at the time of the initial indictment of Mr. Milosevic, said the Paterson-Williamson team "showed that Milosevic was commander of the army and the police; that everything came under his command both in the political and the military sense."

"That," she said, "established his responsibility for the crimes that were being committed."

. . . While investigating mass murder in the Balkans, it was not always possible for Ms. Paterson to maintain a veil of detachment.

There were, she told the British newspaper *The Guardian* in July 2001, "dead animals lying in the fields, houses still burning; then we would examine the crime scenes and the bodies."

Ms. Paterson said: "On one level, you think, I am doing this from a professional standpoint. Then, these are men, women and children. I remember going down the steps to a cellar in which 19 women and children had been burned; there was a child's slipper burned on the step. These things you remember."

The crimes for which responsibility is attributed to Milosevic are clearly spelled out in this obituary, and his command responsibility is restated. Another obituary, written by Emma Brown and published in the *Washington Post* on April 8, 2010, similarly links the memory of Nancy Paterson with that of Milosevic, whom she prosecuted. Brown specifies the numbers of victims as charged at the ICTY with "340 counts of murder and 740,000 forced deportations of ethnic Albanians from their homes in Kosovo." She also reinforces the notion, discussed at the beginning of this book, that the indictment did not further extend the war, quoting

Paterson's statements from 2001 toward the British newspaper *The Observer:* "We decided that this was not going to prolong or shorten the war; we had the case, we had the evidence, the satellite photos and the witnesses." The obituary confirms this assessment, noting that "Milosevic surrendered just days after he was indicted." It also tells of Paterson's travels to Kosovo where, continuing to collect evidence against Milosevic for the trial, she "found about 500 mass graves and a country ripped apart by the horrors of war." The reader is reminded of the "about 200,000 civilians dead and millions more displaced."

Elsewhere Milosevic and his crimes are used as a historical contrast to new and hopeful developments in Serbia. On January 16, 2010, the *New York Times* published a biographical essay, titled "Recasting Serbia's Image, Starting with a Fresh Face" and written by Nicholas Kulish, on Vuk Jeremic, the new Serbian foreign minister (A7). Here, the foreign minister argues his position against the autonomy of Kosovo and seeks to legitimize it through the memory of his opposition to Milosevic and by distancing himself from the former Serbian leader. Jeremic highlights his opposition to the "regime of Mr. Milosevic," his contribution to the 1997 foundation of the Organization of Serbian Students Abroad, his support for the Otpor (Serbian for *resistance*) student movement, and the steps he took—after the ouster of Milosevic—with the new president Tadic, even while taking a break from his education at Harvard's John F. Kennedy School of Government. This interview-based report may speak more to Serb memories than to American ones. While the statements of the young Serbian foreign minister are much more guarded than Western commemorations of Milosevic, they clearly challenge the notion that Milosevic is unavoidably remembered in Serbia as a national hero.[19]

In short, media articles published in 2010 that tell us about the American memory of Milosevic nowhere reflect the image of Milosevic that we have constructed based on diplomatic narratives. Clearly, the narrative created by the ICTY has the greater staying power in this case of a foreign leader and enemy to America. It would be surprising to find different depictions of other foreign leaders in similar positions. Saddam Hussein of Iraq is but one example.

Conclusions: Contrasting American Memories of Milosevic with My Lai and Haditha

We have presented a composite picture of all statements made in a sample of *New York Times* articles reporting 714 actions involving the former president of Serbia and Yugoslavia and later defendant at the ICTY, the late Slobodan Milosevic. In times of easily retrievable media archives such written documentation may already be interpreted as an element of collective memory. We expect, and our brief exploration of 2010 media representations suggests, that these depictions provide a repository out of which those entrepreneurs will avail themselves who seek to forge American memories of the Balkan conflict, of the evildoers involved, and of the role America played in resolving the conflict. Memories will eventually be sedimented in the minds of social actors, as measured through survey research.[20]

In line with our expectations regarding the impact of judicial proceedings on collective memory, we have found that the trial changed the categories under which media reports presented Milosevic's motivations and actions. The criminal court was the decisive institution in the depiction of Milosevic as a force of evil in the unfolding history of the Yugoslav wars. The judicial field sought to disqualify its target by attributing criminal liability for the collective crimes committed to the individual who was at the helm of the Yugoslav government. The image of Milosevic that emerges in this discourse is one of a power-hungry nationalist preacher of ethnic hatred who supported, mentally and materially, those engaged in mass atrocities and who permitted or ordered troops under his direct command to engage in such atrocities. His actions, cast in a negative light from the beginning, are finally subsumed under the crime categories of The Hague and Geneva Conventions and of the Genocide Convention.

This portrayal, originating in the court, was communicated to a broader audience by the *Times*, and it eventually colored the image of Milosevic independently of the utterances of specific informants. This finding confirms Fine's argument that reputational entrepreneurs are involved where difficult reputations emerge.[21] To this notion, our analysis adds the insight that reputational entrepreneurs act in the context of institutions with their specific logic and institutional rules.[22] Our findings also confirm the ritual potency of criminal trials, especially when media reporting disseminates their message, in line with hopes of historical actors such as President Roosevelt and theoretical expectations developed by the classical French sociologist Emile Durkheim and today's neo-Durkheimian scholars.[23] This finding is all the more impressive as the trial's ritual effect was only partially realized because of Slobodan Milosevic's untimely death in March 2006, presumably shortly before a verdict would have been reached.

We found other aspects of the institutional logic of criminal law also reflected in the depiction of Milosevic, especially as the court strengthened its position among the competing fields. The binary logic of criminal law prevailed, as positive aspects of Milosevic's role in the Yugoslav conflict diminished in the unfolding narrative. Furthermore, under the judicial perspective, a focus on Milosevic as an individual, rather than on a structural analysis of the conflicts and atrocities, gained ground. Finally, the role of evidentiary rules became important as the events reached a crucial turning point in the Kosovo conflict. This was a moment at which the actions of troops could be directly attributed to Slobodan Milosevic as their commander in chief. The prosecution accordingly worked initially only with an indictment for crimes against humanity committed in the Kosovo conflict. Other effects of specifically legal evidentiary criteria may also come to bear as they contribute to the systematic production of evidence through the excavation of mass graves and through interviews with hundreds of witnesses and victims.[24] The production of such evidence most likely contributed to the growing public recognition of atrocities and to a deterioration of Milosevic's image over time. The substantial media skills of Chief Prosecutor Louise Arbour can only have advanced acknowledgment of the atrocities at this time.

Knowledge claims from the judicial field compete throughout with claims from diplomacy, which is driven by a different institutional logic, one that is oriented toward the achievement of policy outcomes rather than adherence to a strict set of formal rules. Diplomatic logic aims toward the maintenance of players in the diplomatic game, or the cultivation of diplomatic capital, as long as peace settlements are the policy goal. In our case, the image of Milosevic that emerged initially was that of a willing negotiator whose actions contributed to the avoidance, or at least ending, of bloodshed. Once decisions have been made, however, to replace diplomacy by military force (or once valuable players have been thoroughly delegitimized, for example, through court proceedings), actors in the diplomatic field may discard their former collaborators and contribute to their negative depiction. In these instances courts and diplomats no longer appear as competitors. Instead, diplomatic actors may use court deliberations or outcomes to legitimize their new strategies or their yielding to the pursuit of military force.[25]

The case study on Milosevic's role in the atrocities committed during the Balkan conflict thus contrasts with the more disappointing history-writing outcomes of the My Lai and even more the Haditha stories. It is a case of a high-level defendant who fell from grace and power in a situation of at least partial regime change and military defeat. Studies conducted by historians confirm the history-writing potential of trials in such historic situations. Consider conclusions from the historian Devin Pendas's impressive study of the Auschwitz trial held in Frankfurt from 1963 to 1965 and its public representation and perception: "[The trial] proved to be much more than simply a trial. It was a cultural watershed. It was both a focal point and a wellspring for the politics of memory of the Federal Republic" (2006, 251).[26]

In addition, and in a note of caution, Pendas draws three further conclusions for the Auschwitz trial that support central arguments developed in this volume. First, the particular institutional logic of a criminal
trial colored the way history was told. Being primarily concerned with
"concrete guilt of the individual defendants" (291), the trial played
down the organization of a criminal state. Furthermore, the court deval-
ued "the experiential truth of Auschwitz recounted by the survivor witnesses" for the benefit of "the judicial truth of individual agency" (291).
Finally, the types of crime brought to the eyes of the public were also colored by the evidentiary rules of trial proceedings: "Torture and other
individual atrocities represented in many respects an 'easy case,' compared with the ambiguous domains of responsibility and obedience that
characterized bureaucratically organized genocide. . . . Consequently,
atrocity [here understood more narrowly than in our study] tended to
occupy a privileged terrain compared to genocide" (291).

Second, it was not the Auschwitz trial in itself that affected the public
mind (other trials had not succeeded in doing so) but the fact that it
attracted massive public attention and was extensively reported in the
media. Third, and related, the fact that much of the attention was dependent on media reporting caused a certain coloring of the accounts before
they reached the public's view. In Pendas's terms, the use of "realist" tech-
niques, like selected strings of exchanges between trial participants to
increase the sense of drama, and of "novelist" methods such as atmos-
pheric descriptions that extended to the defendants, in the service of narrative fealty contributed to "what might be termed the characterological
style of objective newspaper reporting," a style that "entailed both a concern with personality and a tendency to reduce it to monadic types. And
in this, a strong homology existed with the juridical emphasis on the subjective disposition of defendants and the assumption of a causal nexus
between motivation and action" (Pendas 2006, 262).

In short, we have built here on our My Lai and Haditha studies of
American memories of American atrocities adjudicated in domestic
courts by addressing the related but distinct story of the build-up of
American memories of foreign atrocities adjudicated by a U.S.-supported
international tribunal. More than before, we find support for both arguments presented at the outset of this volume. Clearly, supporting our
findings from the My Lai case and previous insights by historians, the
institution-specific selectivity of criminal court narratives has to be
accounted for.

At the same time, we have also found considerable confirmation
regarding our thesis about the narrative power of trials. In fact, in this
respect the ICTY has been more effective in laying the seeds of future

collective memories of evil than those courts that tried the defendants of My Lai and Haditha. While the Milosevic case did alert us to the courts' competitors, specifically diplomacy, American challengers to the criminal justice narrative are largely absent in the Milosevic process, especially in its late stages. In obvious difference from the American responses to My Lai and Haditha, no American reputational entrepreneurs were at work on behalf of the defendants at the ICTY. Also, Yugoslavia, unlike the United States, did not experience regime continuity after its encounters with crimes against humanity and war crimes. America had fought the perpetrator victoriously, and his portrayal as a criminal in the court of law could only justify her government's decisions and people's sacrifices. Finally, this is a case in which a former head of state, not a few selected frontline agents, was charged and would almost certainly have been found guilty in the court of law were it not for his premature death. Slobodan Milosevic clearly did go down as guilty in the perceptions of most Americans who followed the Yugoslav story. President Roosevelt and Justice Jackson would almost certainly have approved of the history writing of the ICTY.

By contrasting three extended case studies, we have gained insights into two cells of the analytic field outlined at the beginning of the book (table 1.1). Clearly, exploring these proved fruitful. Future research will add more evidence and insights into the cells we have examined and into others we did not empirically address. Here we move on, however, to ask what structure of memory emerges when cases like the ones described so far accumulate to shape a nation's collective memory. Many actors are involved in the cases described, including perpetrators, judicial personnel, politicians, movement organizers, journalists, and textbook writers. Their pursuits contribute to the shape our memories of specific events take. But how do all these memories of specific events interact and add up to affect the structure of memory that guides a nation, its foreign policy, and its lawmaking and law enforcement?

= Chapter 6 =

The Shape of
American Memories—and a
German Comparison

P ARTICULAR processes such as legal interventions against atrocities accumulate to shape larger cultural patterns, including collective memories. Having examined in detail how American or United States–supported institutions process domestic and foreign mass killings such as My Lai, Haditha, and the Balkan massacres, we now take a brief look at the composite picture. This picture is simultaneously affected by omissions in processing, through courts or alternative mechanisms, other atrocities in the course of American history, such as those committed during the Indian Wars and in the context of the slavery and Jim Crow systems. Note that instances in which no legal or quasi-legal processing occurred constitute an overwhelming part of all cases of atrocities noted in table 1.1.

We depict here hegemonic memory structures, those reflected in national holidays and memorials in the nation's capital. No doubt, dominant patterns meet challenges, resistance, and mnemonic struggles, all claims for different narrations of the past. New generations of history textbooks, parts of the heritage movement, and slavery museums in cities with predominantly African American populations provide examples.[1] Yet what is highlighted by the federal government and displayed in the nation's capital carries particular weight. Through it the nation projects itself and likely influences the collective memory that is sedimented in the minds of a majority of Americans. These depictions of history are the most visible remembrances, capable of spreading their message more effectively than their localized competitors. They paint a glorious portrait of American history, filled with American heroes and fights against foreign villains.

As we present this composite picture of America's collective memory, we contrast it with that of Germany, a country that is similar in many respects. Germany, like the United States, is a western democracy, specifically a federal republic, with an advanced capitalist economy. Yet, different from the United States, and this is a key point for our purposes, well-publicized trials have played a more central role in addressing past German atrocities, at least in the post-Nazism era. Legal proceedings have involved high-ranking perpetrators, most notably at Nuremberg. As discussed in chapter 2, legal responses after World War II were likely to inform the collective memory of the Holocaust (or Shoah) in the United States and Germany, albeit in different ways. In this chapter we highlight differences in collective memory in the two nations. At least partially informed by law, these differences are consequential, as we argue later in the book, for legal institutions and law enforcement.

To be sure, the conduct and the nature of trials involving perpetrators of atrocities is but one of many differences between the two countries. We could surely point to the nature of atrocities. Germany under Nazi rule was the perpetrator of perhaps the deadliest and most meticulously planned genocide in human history. Germany was defeated in war, and some of the trials were conducted by the victorious powers. Moreover, the country has been exposed to considerable scrutiny by an international community on which it has been highly dependent, economically, politically, and strategically.[2] These and other factors no doubt contributed to a distinct macrostructure of memory.

Histories of Hate and Cruelty

Reasons to remember are plentiful in both countries. Each has a history of hate and inhumanity that is well known and needs only brief mention here. In America, the early destruction of much of the Native American population during the colonial era was continued after independence by further atrocities, wars, broken treaties, forced migration and death marches, and the general devastation of American Indian livelihood. The slave trade and the system of slavery caused immense suffering and massive loss of life to Africans and their descendants. While the figures are likely to go into the millions, the exact death toll is unknown. Inhumanity did not end with the abolition of slavery. Long-standing racial hatred reached new heights during the Reconstruction period. Jim Crow laws, the rise of the Ku Klux Klan, and the history of lynching are well known, as are the anti-immigrant Know Nothing movement of the late nineteenth century, anti-Catholicism, anti-Semitism, and hateful resistance to desegregation projects in the wake of the civil rights movement.[3]

Today, large portions of Native Americans and African Americans live in miserable conditions, partly owing to a legacy of discriminatory practices. Additionally, the federal and state governments have used massive force against members of these groups.[4] The so-called war on drugs, for example, has been a major contributor to the vast over-representation of blacks in America's prisons, and federal authorities anticipated this consequence from the outset.[5] Felon disenfranchisement laws have been motivated by aggressive attitudes against African Americans and have contributed to a weakening of their political representation.[6] The practice of capital punishment has also been driven by resentments against minorities, and it continues to disproportionately affect blacks.[7] Finally, excessive cruelty in foreign wars and occupations committed by U.S. military has been made public despite manifold attempts to conceal such occurrences.[8] Recent offenses against human rights in places such as Guantánamo Bay, the Bagram Air Force Base in Afghanistan, and the Abu Ghraib prison certainly made the news. But are they visible where America remembers its history most prominently?

Certainly, perpetrators of these acts of inhumanity have almost never been found guilty in a court of law. In some cases, including selected war crimes, low-ranking actors have been sentenced, thus absolving the majority and the political and military leadership of responsibility. In other cases, those responsible for discriminatory policies and the use of violence that is all but certain to adversely affect many civilian lives are often supported by the majority of Americans, as expressed in elections and opinion polls.[9] Almost all the atrocities and human rights violations mentioned here thus fit into those cells of table 1.1 that represent cases in which no judicial responses occurred. A few must be placed in the other cell where the law stepped in to target only low-level offenders.

Germany's history of hate and inhumanity is even better known than America's. The legacy of anti-Semitism dates back to the Middle Ages, with pogroms and expulsions of Jewish populations from many towns as early as the twelfth century.[10] Early twentieth-century colonial rule was marred by genocidal acts against the Herero and Namaqua in today's Namibia. These atrocities are supplemented by discriminatory practices and aggression against Polish immigrant labor in the late nineteenth and early twentieth centuries and against mostly Southern European and Turkish labor immigrants in the second half of the twentieth century.[11] But all of this history is overshadowed by the hatred cultivated against Jews and other groups in the decades preceding and especially during the Nazi regime. Nazi policies culminated in the Holocaust, with its industrialized murder machine and uncounted acts of individual cruelty that resulted in the death of some 6 million Jews and additional millions of victims, other minorities such as Sinti and Roma (Gypsies), homosexuals, nationalities such as Poles, and political opponents.

While the histories of both countries thus include chapters of deadly hatred against minorities, they also differ in important respects. With regard to timing, the greatest excesses of German cruelty occurred in the twentieth century. Furthermore, the Holocaust is unique in its purposely planned, industrialized destruction of millions of human lives. We argue though that such variation does not sufficiently explain distinct collective memories and the way such memories inspire legal interventions. Country-specific memory patterns reflect differences between the two countries with regard to carrier groups, national institutions, and exposure to global scripts. But we begin with a simple depiction of the structure of national memories in the United States and contrast this structure with Germany's.

Collective Memory

A comparative examination of memorial days and holidays, monuments and memorial sites, and national history exhibits indicates the official representation of collective memory in both the United States and Germany. We are especially interested to learn whether and how collective memory attributes evil and hate, and liberation from them, to the home country or to foreign powers. Furthermore, which groups are recognized as victims of collective cruelty? Finally, are evil and liberation discussed in historical context or in abstraction from the historical reality of the country in question?

Before we shed some empirical light on these questions, a few words about our data are in order. Our sources of information are diverse. For the identification of publicly certified collective memory at the national level, we searched government websites and scholarly publications on national holidays, monuments, and memorials in the nations' capitals, and we reviewed catalogues and websites of prominent historical exhibits supported by the national governments. We were interested in the structure of memories some sixty years after the end of World War II, thirty years after the Vietnam War came to a close, and after the violence in the Balkans and the hot phase of the Iraq War had just run their bloody course. We thus examined the picture that presented itself around the middle of the first decade of the twenty-first century. Needless to say, hegemonic memory changes slowly in the absence of revolutionary change. The patterns we identify thus apply to more extensive periods of time.

Days of Commemoration

National days of commemoration and celebration are relatively few in number. In the United States, national holidays are formally state matters. Yet several holidays have been designated by the U.S. Congress and are observed in the majority of states (see table 6.1). The Federal Republic of Germany, by comparison, has constituted ten days of celebration (Feiertage) and commemoration (Gedenktage) on which public congregations and sessions of the legislature remember crucial historic events. These American and German holidays and memorial days fall into five meaningful categories. Most common in the United States is the celebration of domestic achievements, foundational events, personalities, or symbols (Presidents', Flag, Independence, and Thanksgiving Days).[12] This type of holiday is also prominent in Germany (Constitution Day, the Day of German Unity, and Memory of the Fall of the Berlin Wall Day).

Just as common in Germany are days that commemorate domestic resistance against or liberation from evil (Labor Day; Memorial Day for the Assassination Attempt against Hitler and the German Resistance; and the Memorial Day of the German People, celebrating the 1953 East German uprising). The United States knows two such days, honoring labor (albeit depoliticized) and Martin Luther King Jr., the civil rights leader. While these days imply histories of national evil and hate such as labor exploitation, racism, and political repression, they focus on celebratory domestic events and personalities who fought these evils. Distinct from the United States, however, Germany commemorates national evil directly with the Day of Commemoration of the Victims of National Socialism Day (Auschwitz liberation date) and the Memory of the Reichspogromnacht Day. One further German particularity is the Day of the End of the War and the Liberation from National Socialism, which commemorates liberation from domestic evil by foreign powers. Finally, common to both countries is the commemoration of soldiers killed in war (in Germany, the People's Day of Mourning; in the United States, Memorial Day), to which the United States adds a day on which veterans of the military are celebrated.

The German commemoration of national evil and hate and of liberation through foreign powers has no equivalent in the United States. Those events that are commemorated in Germany are a selection from the universe of grave human rights violations. They all refer to World War II and to the Holocaust and its preparation, events that stand out because of their enormity but also because they are the ones that were addressed in the court of law.

Memorials and Monuments

Given the considerable number and diverse types of memorials and monuments and the unclear boundaries between those with historical

Table 6.1   Official Days of Commemoration in Germany and the United States

Type of memory	Germany	United States
Domestic achievements	May 23, Constitution Day (passing of the Basic Law in 1949)	February 16, Presidents' Day (originally Washington's and Lincoln's birthdays)
	October 3, Day of German Unity (new states [former German Democratic Republic] joining the Federal Republic of Germany)	June 14, Flag Day (celebrating national symbol)
		July 4, Independence Day (commemorating the country's founding)
	November 9, Memory of the Fall of the Berlin Wall (events of 1989)	November 25, Thanksgiving (commemorating friendly encounters between Europeans and Native Americans in early colonial history)
Domestic resistance	May 1, Labor Day (past working-class struggles and present-day labor issues)	January 19, Martin Luther King Jr. Birthday (commemorating the civil rights leader)
	June 17, Memorial Day of the German People (1954 East German revolt against Communist regime, crushed by East German and Soviet military [before 1990 Day of National Unity])	September 1, Labor Day (removed from symbolically significant day of May 1, Chicago Haymarket riot)
	July 20, Memorial Day for the Assassination Attempt against Hitler and the German Resistance	

National evil	January 27, Day of Commemoration of the Victims of National Socialism (anniversary of the liberation of Auschwitz concentration and extermination camp)	None
	November 9, Memory of the Reichspogromnacht 1938 (night of murder and destruction against Jews, synagogues, and Jewish property)	
Liberation by foreign powers	May 8, Day of the End of the War and the Liberation from National Socialism (see Olick 1999b)	None
Commemoration of military	November, People's Day of Mourning (day of mourning for soldiers killed in wars, typically last weekend in November)	May 23, Memorial Day (honoring America's war dead) November 11, Veteran's Day (honoring military veterans, originally Armistice Day, scheduled on date of end of World War I to honor veterans of foreign wars)

Source: Savelsberg and King (2005, 592–93). Reprinted with permission of University of Chicago Press.

significance and others, we sought guidance in listings by national political institutions. By doing so, we highlight those memorials and monuments that were advertised on high-level government websites at the time we conducted this research (2003 to 2004). Again, this strategy necessarily omits many types of memorials, such as slave plantations that have been reconstructed by private groups or individual historical conservationists and memorials that receive no federal funding (for example, the Crazy Horse Memorial).[13] The advantage of our approach is that we can effectively examine those historical memorials and museums that the government wishes to highlight.

We screened, for each country, the websites of both chambers of the legislature and, to capture the international representation of each country, the two countries' state department websites.[14] In Germany, the Bundestag website contains an entry on the history of German parliaments over the past two hundred years.[15] It also provides a link to an exhibit and a catalogue on Germany's history. Only the two chambers of Congress and the German state department (Auswärtiges Amt), however, provide guides to memorials and monuments in their respective nation's capitals. In the United States, a Senate website lists ten monuments and memorials (as of May 28, 2004), to which the House website adds two.[16] The German state department's website lists ten sites.[17] The focus of these memorials differs dramatically (see table 6.2).

The categories for memorials and monuments are similar to those for national holidays. On the U.S. government websites, memorials for domestic achievements and personalities, mostly focusing on great men of American history, constitute one of two important categories. This type of memorial is missing completely on the German government website. However, the German website lists one memorial for acts of resistance (against Nazism) and devotes most of its sites to events that reflect national evil and hate (committed by Germans during the Nazi era). The latter types of memorial, which highlight dark chapters of the country's own history, are completely missing from the U.S. government websites. Neither site offers commemoration of liberation by foreign powers, but the American sites reference foreign evil by directing the visitor to the United States Holocaust Memorial Museum. Finally, the largest category of memorials in Washington, D.C., listed on the U.S. Senate and House websites is dedicated to the memory of the American military and wars, as places of mourning and as reminders of national sacrifice for democracy and for the liberation of the world from evil. These memorials, mostly created in recent decades, are differentiated by specific wars, gender, and branches of the military. This latter category of memorials is absent from the German government website.

Table 6.2   Memorial Sites in or Near Nations' Capitals, Germany and the United States

	Germany	United States
Type of memorial		
Domestic achievements	None	Washington Memorial (honoring first president)
		Lincoln Memorial (honoring defeat of slavery and preservation of national unity [references to Gettysburg and second inaugural addresses])
		Ford's Theatre (site of assassination of Abraham Lincoln)
		Jefferson Memorial (honoring writer of the Declaration of Independence)
		Roosevelt Memorial (honoring "world leader who brought America through the depression and World War II")
Domestic resistance	German Resistance Memorial	None

(Table continues on p. 116.)

Table 6.2 *Continued*

	Germany	United States
National evil	Anne Frank Center (exhibit on her life, hiding, and death in Bergen-Belsen concentration camp) Plötzensee Memorial Center (honoring victims of Nazi regime and its "justice" system) Sachsenhausen Memorial Center and Museum (commemorating victims of concentration camp closest to Berlin) Köpenick Week of Bloodshed June 1933 Memorial (recognizing brutal mistreatment of political opponents by Sturmabteilung in Berlin neighborhood of Köpenick) House of the Wannsee Conference (site where leading Schutzstaffel and high civil servants outlined the Holocaust on January 20, 1942) Memorial to the Murdered Jews of Europe (massive memorial to the Jewish victims of the Holocaust in Berlin's center)	None

Foreign evil	None	United States Holocaust Memorial Museum
Military and war	None	Korean War Memorial ("determined to support the world's imperiled democracies, the United States immediately sent troops")
		Vietnam Veterans Memorial (honoring "the men and women of the armed forces that served in Vietnam")
		Women's Vietnam Veterans Memorial ("honoring . . . women . . . who served in the Republic of Vietnam during the Vietnam era")
		Iwo Jima Memorial ("dedicated to all marines who have given their lives in defense of the United States")
		United States Navy Memorial
		Arlington National Cemetery ("the final resting place of thousands of American soldiers, sailors, and airmen" [also listing the tomb of the Unknown Soldier, John F. Kennedy and Robert Kennedy graves, Arlington House, and the Women in Military Service for America Memorial])

Source: Savelsberg and King (2005, 594–95). Reprinted with permission of the University of Chicago Press.
Note: Memorial sites as listed on legislatures' and state department websites.

In short, notwithstanding the international showcase function of the German state department website, the central, highly visible, or widely known sites listed there focus on the history of domestic evil and hate, especially as committed by Germans against Jews during the Holocaust. Such sites abound in the capital city of Berlin. American memorials instead focus on great presidents and on the military and its fights against foreign evil. Domestic injustices, such as the decimation of the Native American population and the system of slavery, do not appear. Differences between American and German commemorations are thus even more pronounced when we consider monuments and memorials in the nations' capitals in addition to national days of commemoration.

Museums and Exhibits

While memorial days and monuments deliver powerful symbolic messages, history museums and exhibits provide more detailed accounts of a nation's reading of its history. A 1971 government-sponsored exhibit on the political, economic, and social history of modern Germany, prominently set up in the building of the former Reichstag in Berlin (now the new seat of the German Bundestag), provided insights into the German government's remembrance of history, including the history of hate.[18] The exhibit's catalogue, more than four hundred pages long, displays only a few instances of hate and discrimination beyond resentment, conflict, and riots or assassinations in the context of political conflict (Deutscher Bundestag 1983). Examples are discussion of "insensitive" and "bureaucratic approaches" toward the integration of national minorities into the German Empire after its establishment in 1871 and the "Germanization" of Polish farms (that is, the expropriation of Polish farmers) in 1908.

The only major section that deals with issues of hate is the Holocaust. The text includes accounts and photos of the persecution (Judenverfolgung) and annihilation (Judenvernichtung) of Jews. Other victim groups are not mentioned, with the exception of political opponents (Deutscher Bundestag 1983, 202–3, 223, 309). The Holocaust exhibit is embedded in the chapter on the Nazi regime and the demise of the Weimar Republic (Deutscher Bundestag 1983, 313–17). Further references to the terror of Nazism and the Holocaust appear throughout the remaining sections of the exhibition and its catalogue. They begin with a discussion on the deliberations of the Parliamentary Council (Parlamentarischer Rat) against the background of the Weimar experience: "Based on experiences with the Weimar Constitution, in clear rejection of any kind of dictatorship and in line with liberal democratic traditions of the 19th century, a broad majority supporting the Basic Law subscribes to the order of law, parliamentary democracy, the welfare state, and the federalist principle" (Deutscher Bundestag 1983, 345–6).[19]

Subsequent chapters include sections on "shadows of the past," with accounts of the trials of former Schutzstaffel (SS) guards of the Auschwitz concentration and extermination camp; the parliamentary debate on the temporal extension of criminal liability of Nazi crimes; and the temporary successes of the newly founded National Democratic Party, a neo-Nazi party, in the late 1960s: "Especially abroad, the rise of Neo-Nazi forces evokes memories of the late phase of the Weimar Republic" (Deutscher Bundestag 1983, 392).

Additional memorials and museums have since been established in Berlin. They include the Holocaust Memorial in the city's center, right next to the Brandenburg Gate and the Reichstag building, the seat of the legislature. Close by, near Potsdamer Platz, the Topography of Terror memorializes the horrors committed by the SS, the Gestapo, and the Reichs Security Main Office, those agencies that had inhabited this city block and that executed the genocide and multiple other crimes. Other memorials to the terror of Nazism abound across the city.[20]

On the American side, the United States Holocaust Memorial Museum in Washington, D.C., listed on the U.S. House website, is one of two exclusively historical museums in the nation's capital that is supported by the U.S. government. The other historical museum, the Smithsonian National Museum of American History, lists, among twenty-three collections and almost fifty exhibits, one on *Brown v. Board of Education*, one on the internment of Japanese Americans during World War II, and one on the sweatshop system.[21] Yet neither its exhibits nor any of the more than 180 publications associated with them deal with the annihilation and mistreatment of Native Americans, the slave trade or the slavery system, or the repression of African Americans.

The Holocaust Memorial Museum, in contrast, is entirely dedicated to the issue of hate and genocide. The museum was opened in 1993, adjacent to the National Mall, to "broaden public understanding of the history of the Holocaust through multifaceted programs," as the purpose statement on the museum's website declares. "The United States Holocaust Memorial Museum is America's national institution for the documentation, study, and interpretation of Holocaust history, and serves as this country's memorial to the millions of people murdered during the Holocaust. The Holocaust was the state-sponsored, systematic persecution and annihilation of European Jewry by Nazi Germany and its collaborators between 1933 and 1945" (www.ushmm.org, "United States Holocaust Memorial Museum: Mission Statement"; see also Jeshajahu Weinberg, the museum's director, in Berenbaum 1993, 30).

The website also invokes the role of the United States as liberator and place of refuge for survivors of the Holocaust: "As Allied forces moved across Europe in a series of offensives on Germany, they began to encounter and liberate concentration camp prisoners, as well as prisoners en route by forced march from one camp to another. In the aftermath of the Holocaust, many of the survivors found shelter in displaced persons (DP) camps administered by the Allied powers. Between 1948 and 1951, almost 700,000 Jews emigrated to Israel, including 136,000 Jewish displaced persons in Europe. Others emigrated to the United States and other nations" (www.ushmm.org, "United States Holocaust Memorial Museum: Introduction to the Holocaust").

In addition to Jews, a variety of other victim groups are prominently displayed. The mission statement summarizes what the later text elaborates on: "Jews were the primary victims—six million were murdered; Gypsies, the handicapped, and Poles were also targeted for destruction or decimation for racial, ethnic, or national reasons. Millions more, including homosexuals, Jehovah's Witnesses, Soviet prisoners of war, and political dissidents, also suffered grievous oppression and death under Nazi tyranny" (www.ushmm.org, "United States Holocaust Memorial Museum: Mission Statement"; see also Berenbaum 1993, 6).

In short, while the German government's exhibit on its country's history elaborates the historical conditions leading to the breakdown of the Weimar Republic, the rise of Nazism, and the conditions and execution of the Holocaust committed by Germans, the American museums focus more on specific groups of victims of a brutal foreign regime and the role of America as a liberator and provider of refuge. The plea for engagement against hate remains decontextualized from American life and elevated to general principles of humanity and citizenship.[22]

Conclusions: Contrasting Legal Responses, Contrasting Memories

American memories, as depicted in the most visible places and highlighted on national days of remembrance, focus on glorious national events and actors and on foreign evil. Such a pattern is not necessarily characteristic of a nation's way of cultivating its memories, as the German experience illustrates. Again, official national memories are always contested. We have discussed the notion of mnemonic struggles. The construction of memories is the result of conflicts between different social groups that carry and may seek to spread their specific views of the past. At times the official recognition of historic events by the political establishment, in school curriculums, and in the public consciousness itself provokes the construction of contrasting memories at the local level. For Germany, this is illustrated by the work of a group of social psychologists led by Harald Welzer on German family memory of the Holocaust.[23] Welzer, Sabine Moller, and Karoline Tschuggnall find that families tend to redefine, minimize, and rationalize the involvement of their grandfathers, especially in light of the growing public acceptance of the horrors of the Nazi past. Fittingly, the title of this book is "Grandpa Was No Nazi." Also at the macro level, interested groups regularly challenge established historic memory, of which the German debate in 1985 and 1986 on the conditions of the Holocaust, the so-called Historikerstreit, is but one example (Olick and Levy 1997, 931–33).

Yet such differentiations do not change the fact that some groups are more successful in these struggles than others, and their relative success is reflected in commemorative events such as major national holidays, memorials, historical museums, and highly visible exhibits in capital cities (Schwartz 1982). At this level American memories are exceptionally glorious, certainly when compared with German memories. This is not surprising, initially, in light of the enormity of German crimes.

But the difference between American and German memories is also not surprising if Justice Jackson's and President Roosevelt's hopes and expectations have any validity. They wanted the history of German atrocities to be documented in the court of law, with witnesses under oath and with all the written files as supportive evidence. They believed that such documentation would prevent the incredible horrors from ever being disputed. Germany's Nazi terror should become part of the broadly accepted historical record, and the trials that followed it were meant to settle in the collective memories of Americans and Germans alike. The trials initiated by the victorious powers were followed by others, conducted by German courts under the watchful eye of the international community. Perpetrators at the command level and frontline agents were found guilty. To be sure, much punishment was far too lenient in light of the enormity of the crimes, and far too many escaped justice. But the point here is this: The legal response against German perpetrators in all likelihood helped cement the atrocities committed by Germans in the historic record and in the collective memory of both nations.

It can certainly not be argued that acknowledgment comes easily in the context of German culture and society, a fact to which the collective amnesia regarding the earlier genocide against the Herero speaks volumes. By the same token, the lack of legal response in the United States to its own incidents of atrocity, except against a few low-level perpetrators, contributed to a collective memory that enjoys a glorious image of the nation's history. The processes of memory construction examined in the preceding chapters, with a multitude of contending actors involved, constitute the structure of American memory displayed here.

Why should we care? Because memories have consequences. The perpetrator people's memories of atrocities they committed can end cycles of violence. This is likely to apply to international violence. It certainly applies to efforts at intervention against domestic hate-inspired violence, as the following chapters show. Theoretical arguments (chapter 7) are followed by two empirical examinations, the first again an American-German comparison (chapter 8), the second a cross-jurisdictional comparative analysis within the United States (chapter 9).

= Chapter 7 =

From Collective Memory to Law: Theoretical Interlude

ESPITE the general cultivation of a glorified image of American history, on June 18, 2009, the U.S. Senate unanimously passed a resolution apologizing for more than two centuries of slavery in
America. This resolution was passed, not coincidentally, around the June
14 holiday once celebrated by former slaves to commemorate emancipa-
tion. It stands alongside several related resolutions enacted during the
period of just a few years. For instance, in 2008 the House passed a similar resolution apologizing for slavery and Jim Crow laws, and the Senate
apologized for atrocities perpetrated against Native Americans. In 2005 a
Senate resolution formally apologized for the federal government's con-
spicuous idleness during the lynching campaigns of the late nineteenth
and early twentieth centuries against former slaves and their descendants.

This new spate of congressional apologies for injustices and atrocities
perpetrated by the U.S. government is remarkable. Still, such apologies
are not a purely American phenomenon, nor are they unprecedented in
recent U.S. history; Congress's actions are part of an international wave
of apologies for past evils.[1] The Civil Liberties Act passed by Congress
in 1988 not only acknowledged and apologized for the injustice of relo-
cating and interning Japanese Americans during World War II; in this
case, Congress took the additional step of providing restitution to those
who were interned. The latter provision is particularly notable in light
of the Senate's resolution concerning slavery, which explicitly prohibits
the resolution from being used to support any claims for reparations to
descendants of former slaves.

The Civil Liberties Act of 1988 and the recent actions taken by Congress
with respect to slavery and Jim Crow speak to a central theme of this and
the subsequent chapters. Collective memories of past injustice and atrocity matter. We have already established that memory of past atrocities may
delegitimize and prevent future grave human rights violations. Yet
memories matter in other ways also. They may occasionally inspire social
movement activity, even nourish revolutions. Here we are especially

concerned with the possibility that memories may motivate social control responses, that they may even become institutionalized in law. It is simultaneously clear that memories of injustice do not automatically make their way into legal institutions.[2] When they do, there are notable differences in the timing and content of laws or resolutions that in some way attempt to right old wrongs. For instance, we might ask why the apology to Japanese Americans came fewer than fifty years after internment, while the congressional apology for slavery was voiced nearly a century and a half after abolition. And why did one congressional action allow for reparations while the other explicitly denied them? These questions might be subsumed under more general queries. Namely, what conditions enable collective memories to become institutionalized in law? And to what extent are collective memories successfully mobilized in efforts to influence lawmaking and law enforcement?

Although vast but largely distinct literatures exist on the topics of atrocities and law, the questions posed here receive limited attention in existing empirical research. Scholars have indeed suggested that law is sometimes used to commemorate past injustices and that collective memories are likely to influence our expectations of what constitutes justice.[3] Others have advanced the related idea that laws enshrine memories of peoples or events and thus we can think of legislation itself as a carrier of the past into the present—a kind of enduring memorial written into legal codes.[4] However, case studies and philosophical expositions of the connection between atrocities, memory, and law rarely give systematic attention to the conditions that make this nexus possible. The issue, we think, has not been sufficiently articulated. For instance, it remains unclear why justice is sometimes dispensed rather quickly following atrocity (for example, the Nuremberg tribunals) while in other cases a collective amnesia seems to preclude the possibility of legal redress for a past injustice.[5]

We do not suggest that scholarship on this topic is entirely absent. In fact, we seek to demonstrate quite the contrary. But existing work on the institutionalization of collective memory in law is scattered across multiple disciplines, focuses on disparate themes, and draws on a variety of theoretical perspectives. Our objective in this chapter is to synthesize some of this rather disconnected body of work and to tease out commonalities that help us understand how collective memory contributes to the shaping of law. Can we identify unifying concepts across disciplines? Can we move closer to a coherent theoretical model? To what extent does this set of ideas help us explain the recent growth in, and enforcement of, laws seeking to quell hate-inspired speech and violence?

We see prior work as generally coalescing around three concepts that help us think about collective memory as influencing law: analogical narratives, historical consciousness, and carrier groups. The first of these refers to a strategy through which collective memories are deployed to bolster calls for legislation or law enforcement efforts. The second and third refer to conditions that work in tandem with collective memory to influence law. These concepts are neither exhaustive nor mutually exclusive, but they assist in organizing the literature, and they provide some guidance in our effort to understand how and when collective memories are institutionalized in law. In what follows we introduce these concepts and then note selected studies that illustrate their utility.

Collective Memory as Bridging Metaphor and Analogical Device

One of the ways that collective memory and cultural trauma can influence law is through analogies between contemporary situations and past traumatic events. Research on analogical references to past atrocity and law represents a nascent and still developing line of scholarship; to date, research in this vein has largely focused on the legacy of the Holocaust. A working thesis derived from multiple theoretical lineages is that symbolic depictions of certain atrocities provide a cognitive and moral framework for impelling legal action. In other words, drawing a connection between a current social problem or a particular criminal case and a recognized atrocity imbued with lessons about good and evil can be persuasive when making an argument for legal action. This notion is grounded in the sentiment that symbols stand for larger ideas and "evoke an attitude, a set of impressions, or a pattern of events associated . . . with the symbol" (M. Edelman 1985, 6).[6] Consider the Holocaust, or Shoah, which has arguably been constructed as the universal symbol of evil in the Western world.[7] It has a distinct "metaphorical power" that can influence national and international legal institutions (Levy and Sznaider 2005, 5).

Jeffrey Alexander's work on cultural trauma provides keen insights into the notion that collective memory can be effectively employed as an analogical device in the realm of law.[8] Alexander expounds in detail the construction of the Shoah narrative in the post–World War II era, in which the Holocaust ultimately became a universal symbol of evil in the Western world. It came to define inhumanity in the modern world and "served a fundamental moral function . . . : it became a bridging metaphor that social groups of uneven power and legitimacy applied to parse ongoing events as good and evil in real historical time" (Alexander 2002, 44). This moral universal, along with its linguistic and visual symbols (for example, "mass extermination"; entrance gates to concentration and extermination camps), is capable of profoundly affecting legal and other (for example, military) action through analogical reference.[9]

The memory of the Holocaust clearly propelled American and European intervention in the conflict involving Serbian atrocities in Bosnia and Herzegovina in the early 1990s.[10] The Balkan conflict coincided with a reinvigorated Holocaust discourse, exemplified by the construction of the Holocaust Memorial Museum in Washington and the production of Steven Spielberg's *Schindler's List*.[11] The choice to intervene in Bosnia was contested, and politicians were hardly uniform in their proposed resolutions. Some politicians made symbolic analogies between the Shoah and the Balkan conflict both to motivate and to justify intervention, which ultimately took form in a peace settlement that included obligations for all parties under international law.[12] As Alexander (2002, 47) notes, "Senator Joseph Lieberman told reporters that 'we hear echoes of conflicts in Europe little more than 50 years ago,' and presidential nominee Bill Clinton added that 'history has shown us that you can't allow the mass extermination of people and just sit by and watch it happen.'"

European politicians made similar pleas. As Margaret Thatcher stated, "How many more echoes of horror do Western societies need to hear? Sealed train cars . . . ethnic cleansing . . . concentration camps. Genocidal aggression and callous indifference did not end with the Nazis. The plague has risen with Serbia's devastation of defenseless Bosnia" ("Margaret Thatcher as Churchill," *New York Times*, August 11, 1992, A18). Such political claims were accompanied and buttressed by pictures and descriptions of prisoners that ultimately served a similar analogical purpose. One infamous reference depicted an emaciated prisoner named Fikret Alic apparently reaching through barbed wire to shake hands with reporters. "With his rib-cage behind the barbed wire of Trnopolje, Fikret Alic had become the symbolic figure of the war, on every magazine cover and television screen in the world" (Alterman 1997, 17). The picture, the veracity of which was the subject of much ensuing debate, conjured up images of Nazi concentration camps, and analogies between the Balkan conflict and the years preceding the Holocaust helped mobilize international law.

The Holocaust narrative not only impelled legal intervention in the Balkans; it also spurred a new vocabulary for human rights law. While the memory of the atrocities perpetrated during World War II immediately brought about the Universal Declaration of Human Rights (1948), more recent human rights mandates are also products of Holocaust memory. As Daniel Levy and Natan Sznaider (2004, 143) concisely put it, "It is just at this moment, when people are asked to sacrifice blood and treasure for human rights ideas . . . that the memory of the Holocaust emerges from its tacit presence to become something consciously put into the foreground and invoked as a frame of reference justifying action. . . . Nothing legitimizes human rights work more than the slogan, 'Never Again!'"

Once the end of the Cold War removed an obstacle to the lessons of the Shoah, Holocaust memory moved from a particular act against those who were victimized to a universal symbol that referenced inhumanity more broadly.[13] This revised discourse paralleled renewed calls for international law to address human rights violations. As Alexander (2002, 49) remarks, "Representatives of various organizations, both governmental and nongovernmental, have made sporadic but persistent efforts to formulate specific, morally binding codes, and eventually international laws, to institutionalize the moral judgments triggered by metonymic and analogic association with the engorged symbol of evil."

Recent discussions of the relevance of Holocaust memory for reparations movements are much in line with Alexander's exposition of the Shoah in his work on cultural trauma. In demonstrating the benchmark status of the Holocaust, for example, John Torpey refers to a host of reparations movements that analogically refer to the Shoah in support of their plea.[14] These movements share the commonality of employing Holocaust memory to garner attention and propel legal action in the international arena. "Such references to the exemplary character of the response to the *Shoah* for those who have suffered violence and degradation elsewhere demonstrate that . . . the emblematic status for our time of the Jewish Holocaust has helped others who have been subjected to state-sponsored mass atrocities to gain attention for those calamities" (Torpey 2001, 341).

The Holocaust as analogical device informs other efforts to reform law as well. The 1970s and 1980s witnessed a new discourse on Japanese internment during World War II, where "internment camps" became "concentration camps."[15] Drawing parallels between the Holocaust and the treatment of Japanese in the United States helped secure formal apologies along with legal recourse in the form of monetary reparations.[16] With respect to reparations, Torpey suggests that late-twentieth-century calls for monetary reparations for past injustices "share the common characteristic that the Holocaust is regarded as a standard for judging the seriousness of past injustices and [serves] as a template for claiming compensation for them"; it constitutes the "central metaphor" for the politics of reparations and redress for past injustice (Torpey 2001, 337–8).

While the bulk of work in this domain concerns international law, we also see evidence of Holocaust memory deployed as an analogical device in domestic law, particularly law relating to intergroup conflict and hatred. We build on this idea in the following two chapters, but as just one example consider the testimony of Kevin Berrill of the National Gay and Lesbian Task Force, who drew an analogy with the Shoah to underscore his support for the pending hate crime law: "I would like to point out that many of the witnesses at this hearing will be wearing a pink triangle, which was the badge that identified homosexual inmates of Nazi concentration camps. Although it is an often overlooked fact, tens of thousands of gay persons were herded into the camps, and, along with the Jews, gypsies, and others, were gassed and incinerated. We wear the triangle to remember them and to remind people of the terrible cost."[17] As with movements in the realm of international law, references to the Nazi atrocities are again deployed to advance the cause of legislation.

In sum, an evolving body of scholarship suggests that symbols of past evil can serve as analogical references to effectively bolster calls for legal (and other) intervention in conflict or to marshal support for a law enforcement effort. Holocaust memory, in particular, holds a singular place in this body of work. But what can be said of collective memories of other injustices, such as slavery or civil rights abuses in the United States? And what other factors must we consider in the nexus between collective memory and law?

Historical Consciousness

Memory of past atrocity can also penetrate into the legal realm through the mediating role of historical consciousness, an admittedly nebulous concept that has various connotations across multiple disciplines. Indeed, some writers note that the concept is sometimes used synonymously with collective memory.[18] For our purposes, *historical consciousness* is the outcome of the collective exploration and evaluation of the past that entails conscious reflection on the relationship between historical events and their significance for the present. This consciousness can be present or absent in a society, and where it is present, it can be relatively unified and agreed on or disparate and contested. It is, in essence, socially constructed and variable. Moreover, we concur with historians that "different forms of historical consciousness are supported by and, in turn, promote different social and political arrangements" (Seixas 2004, 11). The latter two points, taken together, are consequential for understanding the association between atrocities, collective memory, and law. To the extent that historical consciousness is absent, suppressed, or contested, it is increasingly difficult to mobilize the memory of atrocities to justify a policy or legal action. In the following paragraphs we seek to illustrate this point by guiding the reader through the arguments of two related studies.

The first such study that comes to mind is Lawrie Balfour's (2003) elaboration of historical consciousness and the legacy of slavery. Balfour draws heavily on the writings of the great African American intellectual W. E. B. Du Bois to suggest that a "willful national amnesia prevented black citizens from enjoying in fact the freedom and equality they were guaranteed by law" (Balfour 2003, 33). Du Bois indeed argued that the suppression of an overt and critical reflection on slavery, or in other words the absence of a historical consciousness about the experiences of slaves, particularly among whites, seems to preclude the possibility of reparations. Balfour illustrates accordingly how consciousness of the past parallels legal and policy debates concerning equality and civil rights. Following Du Bois, she suggests that "any understanding of American history must take seriously the view of that history from the perspective of the former slaves and that, for white Americans, this requires an openness to reevaluating everything they believe" (Balfour 2003, 38).[19] In the absence of this acknowledgement, let alone a sustained debate, support for a substantial reparations program remains highly unlikely (Balfour 2003, 43).

Following Balfour's argument along with the notion of historical consciousness, we might suggest that the collective memory of slavery lacks reflection on the relationship between the era and its significance for blacks today, thus limiting the likelihood of policies that directly address the legacies of slavery.[20] As a point of comparison, we might contrast the diffuse historical consciousness about slavery in the United States to the memory of the Holocaust in Germany. Themes such as responsibility, moral lessons, and implications for contemporary Germany are common in the German discourse, including those in the parliament.[21] At the same time, the German government continues to allow for reparations payments under certain conditions.

The second example for literature on the role of historical consciousness and the context in which collective memories can be effectively mobilized in legal institutions is the sociologist Francesca Polletta's (1998) work on commemoration of Martin Luther King Jr. in the halls of the U.S. Congress. Polletta examines how, when, and why African American legislators invoke King's memory. The dominant collective memory of King, at least in Congress, involves a narrative of unity and progress while playing down themes of social change, extra-institutional activism, and the continuing consequences of discrimination. In the words of the historian Jacquelyn Hall (2005, 1234), "Erased altogether is the King who opposed the Vietnam War and linked racism at home to militarism and imperialism abroad." Although Polletta does not directly make the claim, we again see a muted discussion of the relationship between King, a symbol of the civil rights era, and the continuing significance of race today. Legislators' speeches consequently invoke King's memory to "encourage speakers to call for more commemoration rather than for new legislation, more appropriations, better enforcement of existing laws, or an otherwise interventionist federal stance" (Polletta 1998, 504).

While King's name may sometimes be used to bolster calls for legislative action, such as federal legislation to assist in the fight against church arsons, the number of times King's name is invoked in the context of legislative debates pales in comparison with the frequency with which it is invoked on more commemorative occasions, such as tributes to individuals (for example, Thurgood Marshall), honoring of historical events (for example, black history month), or other nonlegislative topics.[22] The manner in which King's legacy can be employed is thus constrained, in part, because the dominant narrative of progress and unity trumps the subordinate narrative of the enduring problems in the area of race relations.[23] For instance, African American politicians who invoke the memory of Martin Luther King to call for redistributive policies meet resistance, often from white speakers who emphasize progress that has already been made.[24]

These stories suggest that actors are constrained by weakly developed historical consciousness in their attempts to mobilize collective memories of the past for purposes of legal change. Not all collective memories of injustice involve a historical consciousness as we define it. Under this condition the mobilization of collective memory for legal change is less efficacious. A point worth emphasizing, and one that we return to in the following chapters, is that collective memory of the Holocaust is markedly different from collective memories of U.S. slavery or civil rights abuses, particularly as invoked for purposes of legal action.

Carriers of Collective Memory

A line of neo-Weberian scholarship emphasizes the role of carrier groups as essential to the study of collective memory and law. *Carrier groups* are bearers of social action who maintain a discourse on ideas and promote social values.[25] Weber had cultural carriers in mind, typically dominant groups in society. We use the concept more liberally to include interest groups and marginalized groups. The link to our theme is obvious in discussions on cultural trauma, where—as in Alexander's foundational essay—carrier groups are thought of as collective agents of the trauma process.[26] Individual actors or entrepreneurs matter, but they first have to convince the carrier group before the trauma process can spread into other societal groups that were not directly (or not at all) affected by the event to which cultural trauma is attached.

The importance of carrier groups becomes visible in discussions of righting old wrongs, the phenomenon of seeking legal redress for past injustices.[27] The sociolegal scholar Marc Galanter (2002, 108) claims that a "proliferation of efforts to reform the past" has characterized recent decades, particularly with respect to prejudicial and often violent injustices in the United States and abroad. Advocates of reform pursue various remedies, including reparations, formal government apologies, and pardons. The apparent spike in government action in response to injustices that occurred decades or centuries ago raises numerous questions that at this time can be explained only if we take mobilized carrier groups into consideration. Government action on behalf of civil rights during the 1960s and beyond would have been unlikely had it not been for the contributing role of African Americans who carried memories of black repression more than any other group in society, the civil rights movement that grew out of the black American population, and specific moral entrepreneurs who articulated the messages that resonated in the minds of African Americans. These groups are necessary to publicly articulate a grievance, remind public officials of a past injustice, mobilize wider support, and ultimately offer a vision of the past to compete with "the hegemonic stories of the majority" (Galanter 2002, 122).[28] Such carrier group mobilization is particularly likely for injustices against ascriptive groups (that is, ones based on caste, tribe, ethnicity, religion) compared with groups defined by class, residence, or political affiliation.[29]

This notion that ethnic groups mobilize collective memories of injustice for purposes of legal redress is similarly evident in the story of the repeal of Title II of the Internal Security Act of 1950. This law authorized the protective detention of citizens in order to safeguard internal security and essentially legalized the types of internment camps in which Japanese Americans were imprisoned during much of World War II. The movement to repeal Title II, which floundered in the early stages, initially lacked involvement from Japanese Americans. African American and Jewish organizations took the early lead. Only later did groups representing Japanese Americans join the cause, "reconstruct[ing] the memory of internment among the public as an injustice based on racial prejudice rather than wartime necessity" (Izumi 2005, 177). Masumi Izumi suggests that collective memory of Japanese internment profoundly influenced public support to repeal the act.

This case indicates that the mere collective memory of internment was insufficient to achieve legal change. Mobilization and protest by previously interned Japanese protesters, however, effectively added credence to the movement. Groups representing Japanese Americans were able to redefine the memory of internment. For instance, *relocation centers* were redefined as *concentration camps*, a discursive shift that enabled members of Congress to make analogies to the "ugly symbol of totalitarianism" (Izumi 2005, 192), a thinly veiled reference to the Nazi atrocities. In short, carrier groups of collective memory may give birth to social movements. In the case of Japanese Americans, such a movement successfully engaged in the use of bridging metaphors to achieve legal change. We thus see how forces of collective memory addressed in this chapter interact to achieve legal change.

Yet even in the absence of an organized effort, members of aggrieved groups can serve as carriers of collective memory and inspire movements for legal change. One mechanism through which this can be achieved is *micromobilization*—interactions among actors in which meanings of past events and identities are formed, which in turn motivates activism.[30] Fredrick Harris examines the way collective memories are used as catalysts for an individual's involvement in collective action. Stories of triumph and tragedy by elders who witnessed civil rights abuses can inspire younger cohorts to become politically active.[31] As Michael C. Dawson (1994, 51) observes, "The collective memory of the African-American community continued to transmit from generation to generation a sense that race was the defining interest in individuals' lives and that the well-being of blacks individually and as a group could be secured only by continued political and social agitation." Collective memories can then have an effect on political and legal action when grievances are articulated, or carried, across generations. The memory of the well-known murder of Emmett Till offers an example. Till, a young African American from Chicago, was kidnapped and murdered in Money, Mississippi, in 1955 for allegedly flirting with a white woman. This was a galvanizing case that attracted much media attention, including the iconic image of Till's mutilated body on the cover of *Jet* magazine, which mobilized black advocacy organizations and inspired civil rights leaders. Former representative Charles Diggs dubbed the *Jet* magazine photo the "greatest media product of the last forty or fifty years," and the civil rights activist Amzie Moore cited Till's death as "contributing to the beginning of the civil rights movement in Mississippi" (quoted in Harris 2006, 38). Harris suggests that even years after the murder the narrative of Till's slaying reinvigorated a commitment to racial justice and ultimately motivated some African Americans to engage in collective action. Collective memories of traumatic events can thus serve as catalysts that carrier groups articulate and mobilize for purposes of political action and legal change.[32]

Summary and Future Directions

In this chapter we have tried to identify some common and recurring themes and to synthesize existing work that either explicitly or implicitly speaks to the institutionalization of collective memory in law. Three concepts provide insight into how and why, or under what conditions, collective memories are effectively mobilized for purposes of lawmaking, law enforcement, or commemoration in a legislative body. First, collective memory can be used strategically as an analogical device to bolster a claim for legal action. Second, the absence of a sustained historical consciousness limits the extent to which collective memories can be drawn on for purposes of legal change. Finally, carrier groups and their activists appear necessary, although not sufficient, for constructing and articulating collective memories. These concepts and the processes to which they speak are obviously interrelated. Representatives of carrier groups may, for example, use collective memory as an analogical device to push for legal action. They may further use the same strategy to advance historical consciousness and thereby strengthen the force of collective memory in calls for legal change.

Arising from such conceptual and theoretical groundwork regarding the institutionalization of collective memory in law is a series of questions we ask in the subsequent empirical chapters. First, how does it matter that domestic as opposed to foreign injustice is part of a nation's collective memory? It is at least conceivable that collective memories that entail critical reflection on domestic injustice appear more apt to be institutionalized in law, as seems to be the case in Germany (more on this in chapter 8).

Second, and related, we might inquire about the framing of collective memory in a nation. The work of Polletta and Balfour suggests that American collective memories of slavery and the civil rights era tend to emphasize progress already made and unity achieved. The themes are dehistoricized and treated abstractly. As Balfour argues, sustained attention to the continuing ramifications of past injustice remains muted. For example, reconstructed plantations in the United States lack the solemnity and fail to depict the cruelty of the slavery system, at least in comparison with the concentration camps now reconfigured as memorials across Europe. Under such conditions collective memories are unlikely to be institutionalized in law. We speak to this issue in more detail in the following two chapters.

Third, who are the carriers of collective memory? Following Galanter and to some extent Izumi, we can speculate that victims of injustice or atrocity with ascribed characteristics (for example, race or religion) are better positioned to articulate collective memories than groups based on class or political affiliation. Moreover, attention should be paid to whether collective memory is defined by groups in civil society or by groups representing the state, in collaboration with interest groups. Finally, the current status of the Holocaust as a universal symbol of evil suggests that it should have particular significance in the legal realm. We expect that collective memories of the Shoah, deployed as an analogical device or through the symbolism of Holocaust memorials, are especially likely to exert an influence on lawmaking and law enforcement.

In short, analogical bridging, historical consciousness, and carrier groups have been suggested as crucial mechanisms through which collective memory affects law and its enforcement. They unfold in the public sphere and under specific political institutional conditions. In the following two chapters we empirically explore these mechanisms and the questions we raised throughout this chapter. As we do so, we focus on the substantive case of memories of hate and legal responses to hatred and hate-motivated crime. Our comparative analysis of hate crime laws in the United States and their functional equivalent in Germany illustrates how nation-specific collective memories and political arrangements converge to inform the content and enforcement of hate crime laws. We then look more closely at the American case in chapter 9 to examine how commemoration of the Holocaust and the civil rights movement are associated with the implementation of hate crime law across jurisdictions. Each case demonstrates that collective memory matters for legal change or law enforcement. Still more specifically, these chapters explore how the shape of collective memory affects the nature of laws that respond to hate-motivated violence.

═ Chapter 8 ═

How American Memory Shapes Hate Crime Law—and a German Comparison

A s the previous chapters have established, collective memories of atrocities differ across societies, and past legal intervention contributes to those differences. Moreover, collective memories of past atrocities have consequences for the likelihood that cycles of violence will be brought to an end. They may at least enhance chances that governments will act to prevent such recurrence. Memories also contribute to the shape legal interventions ultimately take. This expectation applies both to large-scale atrocities and to those small occurrences of hate-inspired threats and violent acts, often referred to as hate crimes, that instill fear in the minds of many ethnic, racial, and religious minorities in countries around the globe. Hate crimes and the steps governments take to prevent them are the focus of this and the following chapters.[1]

Concerns about hatred, and hate-inspired violence, are not limited to a few countries. Rather, they have grown globally in recent decades. At present, nearly every country in the Western world has enacted some type of law to combat hate crime or to restrict hate-inspired speech. For instance, hate crime laws are found in nine of every ten states in the United States, and many American universities prohibit "hate speech" on their campuses. Most countries on the other side of the Atlantic go even further. In addition to punishing criminal acts that are motivated by bigotry, many European countries criminalize offensive speech and the denial of historical atrocities. For example, Austria prohibits certain types of speech that play down or otherwise attempt to excuse Nazi atrocities. The Czechs criminalized not only Holocaust denial but also denial of atrocities perpetrated by communists. In Romania, one can be imprisoned for five to fifteen years for establishing a xenophobic organization, and the Council of Europe recommends prohibitions against various forms of intolerance. Moreover, the creation of such laws is accompanied by a surfeit of international human rights mandates that seek to outlaw hatred (for example, Article 20 of the International Covenant on Civil and Political Rights). "Anti-hate" laws are now commonplace; they are the rule rather than the exception.

While laws of this kind are nearly ubiquitous, their nature and enforcement take distinct forms in different countries. A closer look at American hate crime law and how it differs from its German equivalent adds detail to these variations:

American law focuses on the potential vulnerability of groups to hate crime, while German law links protection of the vulnerable with concerns for the democratic state.

American law protects individuals along a set of clearly specified dimensions (for example, ethnicity, gender, sexual orientation), while the German law seeks to protect minority groups generally. One exception is the relatively broad group "victims of the Holocaust," for whom German law establishes a group-specific right, a right incidentally not found in the United States (for example, Federal Republic of Germany Criminal Code, paragraph 194; see also Nier 1995, 260).

Also in contrast with American law and law enforcement, the protection against hate in German law involves limitations on civil rights such as the right to free speech and free association, for the sake of protecting minorities and the state against extremist activities (Nier 1995).

Unlike U.S. law, German law explicitly accepts its subordination under international law, including international human rights law (Basic Law for the Federal Republic of Germany, Article 25).

Differences in codes are reflected in enforcement. While special hate or bias crime units in American prosecutors' offices are rare, German prosecutors' offices typically have specialized units for hate-motivated offenses. These offices are often embedded within broader departments dedicated to crimes of political extremism (Extremismusdezernate). In addition, German police departments handle hate crimes in the context of specialized units "for the protection of the state" (Staatsschutz).

Finally, while American enforcement discourses are relatively free from references to both international scripts and major chapters of grave human rights violations in American history, German agencies and their discourses are rich with international references and saturated with the memory of German history, especially the Holocaust.

Why do we encounter such distinct national patterns despite the globalization of hate concerns and hate crime issues? More specifically, why are measures for the protection of minorities not linked with precautions regarding social stability and democracy in the United States, even though this link is common elsewhere, such as in Germany? Why does U.S. law not place special emphasis on the protection of victims of national inhumanity such as the near extinction of the Native American population or the slave trade and slavery system, despite regular references to foreign atrocities? Why does German law, seemingly paradoxically, limit some civil liberties in order to protect them (for example, limiting free speech so it cannot be used as a means by those seeking to abolish it), while the United States shows that democracy can work as citizens make generous use of such liberties?

The puzzle would become even more intriguing if we looked beyond American-German differences at a yet more colorful range of policies and laws across the globe. Sociologists with an eye on the global diffusion of law would face multiple questions: Why are certain political organizations outlawed in some countries but not others? Why is hate speech restricted in some countries, while it is punishable elsewhere only if accompanied by a more traditional criminal offense? Why do some nations justify such laws with reference to their own past atrocities, while others are loathe to acknowledge the darker chapters of their national history? Two straightforward answers to these questions immediately jump to mind, but neither convinces.

First, some countries have more horrid and atrocious pasts than others, which might translate into stricter and more encompassing legislation. While we think the severity and timing of past atrocity matters, such an explanation could not explain, for example, differences between Canada and the United States. The latter has a deeper history of slavery, lynching, and destruction of Native American lands, but it is also more protective of hate speech. Second, a simple legalistic answer to these questions might point to nation-specific differences in constitutional protections. The First Amendment to the U.S. Constitution, for instance, protects the right to free speech, even offensive or hateful speech. It thus makes sense that expressions of hatred cannot be restricted under U.S. law. Nonetheless, many countries, including Canada and Germany, also protect freedom of expression in their respective constitutions.[2]

Yet in practice these rights to free speech and expression have very different meanings in the three countries. For example, Germany has deemed it necessary in some cases to restrict civil rights and limit certain types of speech in order to protect the constitutional state. Canada does not go quite this far but nonetheless allows for some restrictions on expression, such as denial of the Holocaust.[3] The United States, by contrast, has been reluctant to outlaw expression that is xenophobic in nature.[4] In short, more than mere constitutional differences and past atrocities are evidently at play.

In this chapter, we offer an explanation of nation-specific laws and enforcement mechanisms that brings collective memory and cultural trauma to the fore. To unpack our argument we build on our comparison of American and German memories developed in chapter 6 and on the theoretical arguments laid out in chapter 7. We specify those arguments and illustrate them as we closely compare hate crime laws and their enforcement in the two countries. Our explanation of cross-national variation in such laws adds to previous contributions about differences of lawmaking and implementation within the United States.[5] Simultaneously, we explore basic sociological ideas about the institutionalization of culture and the interplay between globalization and the organization of local institutions. Finally, and of particular importance in this context, we hope to gain insights into the consequences of collective memory for efforts toward curbing cycles of violence. The law, we think, would certainly play a key role in such efforts.

Collective Memory, Institutions, and Control Across Nations

Three guiding arguments are crucial as we examine the impact of collective memories of hate on ways in which governments seek to control violence against minorities by means of hate crime laws. The first two were introduced at the outset, and a brief reminder will have to suffice here: First, an actor's effort to shape collective memory is restricted by the path dependency of collective memory. Political discourse about a past event, such as World War II or the Holocaust, reflects not only present-day interests and powerful constituencies, as Halbwachs (1992) might have suggested, but also past remembrances. We add to this argument the more specific point that collective memory and commemorations also affect events in which decisions are debated and made on laws and enforcement organizations. These very situations constitute, in fact, specific forms of commemoration. Imagine a parliamentary session in which German legislators meet to decide on enhancing penalties for the distribution of neo-Nazi propaganda through the Internet. Speeches will deal with legal principles such as due process, weighing free speech protections against protections of groups and the constitutional state, and the deterrent effects of enhanced penalties. These speeches, however, will also be infused with discussions of the Nazi past, the Holocaust, and the conditions of the Weimar Republic as providing fertile ground for the rise of the Nazi Party. While they may have less public visibility than purely commemorative speeches, such as those held on official days of remembrance, the decisions to which they contribute will crystallize collective memory as they mold it into institutional structures of new laws or the establishment of control agencies.

Second, concerns within countries are also influenced by global issues and a country's position relative to others in international relations. Global scripts are thus important, and their weight has increased in recent decades. For instance, after hate-inspired war crimes and genocide of the Nazi regime had been addressed by the Nuremberg tribunals, the theme subsided for almost five decades, despite massive hate campaigns and human rights abuses in many countries. The sociologist Austin Turk (1982) argues in his path-breaking work that the power balance between the United States and the Soviet Union created a barrier against intervention in human rights abuses: Neither side was interested in allowing international law in its sphere. Yet the post–Cold War era witnessed a rebirth of international concerns and intervention such as the creation of the International Criminal Tribunal for the former Yugoslavia and the establishment of a permanent International Criminal Court, ratified so far by more than one hundred countries. Indeed, the establishment of the International Criminal Court "marks a major advance in the movement to establish international authority to intervene in what traditionally has been considered 'off-limits' as 'internal affairs' of the state" (Hagan and Greer 2002, 232). Such internationalization of moral concerns and legal intervention is likely to affect nation-states, as a rich body of literature on the emergence of global norms has documented.[6]

Third, the same literature also shows that countries are differentially exposed to global pressures depending on their degree of dependency within the global community. To understand how international sensitivities affect laws at the nation level, we must thus consider such exposures. We must simultaneously take into account nation-specific political and judicial institutions and, crucial here, the specific ways in which each nation handles its collective memories of the dark chapters of its history. The link to earlier arguments is clear as those carrier groups of collective memory that use bridging metaphors and contribute to historical consciousness (chapter 7) take shape and act in specific national contexts, each with its particular set of institutions. Consider again the American and German comparison.

The public spheres of these countries are characterized by an active civil society in the United States, in contrast with neocorporate arrangements in Germany.[7] The state, in collaboration with major aggregations of social interests, should thus play a central role in the articulation of collective memory in Germany, while civil society groups should play a bigger role in the United States.

The distinct nature of public spheres in each country gains currency as a result of different citizenship laws. While currently an estimated one in every thirty U.S. residents is undocumented, most members of vulnerable groups in this country are citizens.[8] This is largely a result of the jus soli of a long-term immigration country, in which citizenship is granted by virtue of birth in the country (following the Fourteenth Amendment). Naturalization has traditionally been much more difficult under Germany's jus sanguinis, where citizenship, despite recent reforms, depends primarily on German ethnicity.[9] This has consequences for the contribution of immigrant minorities to public discourses. Minorities in Germany show relatively little involvement in domestic German issues even if they are immediately affected. When they make public claims, they address homeland politics (41.5 percent) much more frequently than xenophobia (32.1 percent) or minority integration politics (6.3 percent) of their host country, as survey analyses of a Dutch-British team of sociologists has shown.[10] Minority groups should thus play a bigger role in the transformation of collective memory into anti-hate law in the United States than in Germany.

The nature of the political system also affects the involvement of different actors in public discourses. America's political parties are not addressed in the Constitution and are less coherent in their message, in part because of the system of primary elections. By contrast, political parties in Germany are recognized by the Basic Law for the Federal Republic of Germany (the German constitution). Candidates for elective office are determined by party committees, and renominations depend on the loyalty with which representatives act toward their party while in office. Similarly, the American general public plays a greater role vis-à-vis the executive branch owing to popular elections of the president and, for the courts, to the jury systems and the popular election of most judges and prosecutors. These differences in all three branches of government suggest that American political and legal spheres are more porous, resulting in easier access to political and legal decisionmaking but also to more drastic variation from place to place within the United States (we return to this issue in the next chapter).

Finally, differences in the political sphere are complemented by distinct legitimatory ideas of political culture.[11] American constitutional democracy considers its primary aim the protection of civil rights and the limitation of government power, in line with the Federalist Papers. Such liberal democracy offers formal procedures, preferably court procedures, for the management of conflicts that emerge in the use of individual liberties. In clear contrast, the German model of consensus democracy, based on ideas of the enlightenment philosopher Immanuel Kant, aims at the consideration of all interests, formulated in general laws and concretized by experts. The outcome of state decisionmaking is not meant to reflect the sum total of articulated interests; rather, it is a model that is meant to be agreeable to all reasonable citizens apart from their individual interests. These differences inspire a stronger individual rights focus of American ideas about discrimination and hate crime laws compared with a more collective approach in Germany.

In short, despite globalizing pressures, we have to consider nation-specific exposure to global scripts and nation-specific institutions within which carrier groups form and affect memories and policymaking alike. Only then can we understand how collective memories, already colored by national contexts, contribute to the formation of policy responses to hate and hate-inspired violence. We readily acknowledge that a comparison of two countries does not allow for a crucial test of hypotheses. But, similar to our extended case studies of selected atrocities, our in-depth comparison contributes to theory. The following account of the creation of collective memory in Germany and the United States can be generalized to a comparison of countries in which criminal liability for atrocities was assigned with ones in which this rarely occurred, especially not at the command level; but also as comparisons of civil society with neo-corporate countries; of countries with low and high international dependency; or of winner-of-war and loser-of-war countries. These and other dimensions overlap, creating relatively unique cases, cautioning us against generalizing too hastily.

Hate Crime Law and Its Implementation

The legislation of hate crime statutes in the United States, most thoroughly analyzed in the award-winning work by the prominent American sociologists Valerie Jenness and Ryken Grattet (2001), is a relatively new phenomenon. It began in 1981 in the states of Oregon and Washington. By 1988 eighteen states had passed statutes, by 1990 twenty-eight, and by 1999 forty-one. In 1990 the federal government passed the Hate Crime Statistics Act and in 1994 the Hate Crime Sentencing Enhancement Act. Different from Germany, hate crime law in this country is not associated with law that seeks to protect the state from extremist anticonstitutional activities.[12]

The Hate Crime Sentencing Enhancement Act was passed by the U.S. Congress in 1994 and signed into law by President Clinton during that same year. Modeled after sentencing enhancement laws passed by the majority of states, it allows federal judges to impose penalty enhancements of "no less than three offense levels" above the penalty for the parallel crime.[13] This applies to all cases in which hate can be established at trial as the motive beyond reasonable doubt. As in most state-level laws, U.S. law identifies status provisions that speak to dimensions of social differentiation: race, color, religion, national origin, ethnicity, gender, disability, and sexual orientation.

American law thus avoids explicitly seeking the protection of particular groups that have suffered from victimization in the past, instead offering protection to all individuals no matter on which side of these lines of differentiation they fall (for example, women and men, blacks and whites). In contrast to German law, American law also avoids making reference to historic events that would provide reason for protection (for example, slavery or lynching), in line with the lack of references to national terror in the major symbols of cultural trauma reviewed in chapter 6 (for example, memorial days, monuments).

Yet the list of a specific set of dimensions in the law does allow civil society groups to see that their interests are recognized in the legislative process. It forges a compromise between the individual rights focus of American doctrine and the avoidance of national evil in collective memory, on one hand, and the work of civil society groups representing interests of minorities, on the other.[14] This interpretation is in line with work by Valerie Jenness, who concludes that interest group activity was important for the group's inclusion in hate crimes legislation, particularly early in the legislative process.[15]

In short, the absence of references to domestic evil in American collective memory and the activity of civil society groups and minority representation are both reflected in American hate crime law. Yet, consistent with American collective memory, events of foreign evil and hate are mobilized by groups in legislative processes (see the quotation of Kevin Berrill, director of the National Gay and Lesbian Task Force, in chapter 7 and Senator Orrin Hatch's comments quoted in the following chapter).

Groups strengthen their position, though, by supporting the memory of historic victimization abroad with statistical and individual accounts of more recent atrocities in the United States. For instance, the Anti-Defamation League recorded an increase in anti-Semitism between 1979 and the mid-1990s. This allowed the group to depict anti-Semitism as a serious social problem and suggests that data collection efforts were feasible. Subsequently, Senator Paul Simon at Senate hearings on the Hate Crime Statistics Act suggested that "if Mr. Schwartz over here with the [Anti-Defamation League] can collect data on this kind of problem, we ought to be able to do it in the Department of Justice. I think it is an important service that is needed in the nation" (cited in Jenness and Grattet 2001, 53). The National Gay and Lesbian Task Force and the Southern Poverty Law Center undertook similar efforts. These self-collected data, in conjunction with narratives and media coverage of particularly shocking acts of bigotry, helped legitimize and give credibility to the anti–hate crime movement.[16]

In sum, social movements in America created a general discourse on the vulnerability of particular social groups, which ultimately spawned the interest in hate crimes in the political sector. They did so by producing and presenting collective memories and cultural trauma, supporting them with references to the Holocaust, statistical data, and accounts of well-publicized gruesome crimes. Legislatures, open to the mobilization of such groups, ultimately debated and formally institutionalized the concept of hate crime. Yet reference to horrors of American history were equally absent, as they are missing from the most visible symbols of collective memory. Again, the listing of a range of dimensions of social organization in the law, allowing civil society groups to recognize themselves without granting group-specific rights, constitutes a compromise between the avoidance of national horrors in collective memory and an individual rights focus of American law on one hand and the groups' mobilization on the other.

Our account supports the notion that the shape of American hate crime law can be understood only by considering the complex interaction among several partly contradictory forces. These include the purification of collective memories that erases past national evil but highlights foreign atrocities, a legal and political culture focused on individual rights, and active civil society groups in the context of porous political institutions. These factors allow for groups' grievances to affect legislation even when these same groups have only partially affected collective political memory at the highest level of the American state.

Law Enforcement in the United States

The individualizing conception of victims of hate in American law is further institutionalized in the organization of hate crime law enforcement. While the number of prosecutors' offices with specialized hate crime units has risen, until recently only some larger offices, such as that in Los Angeles County, had units specializing in the prosecution of hate-motivated offenses. Others, such as the Trial Division of the New York County District Attorney's Office, work closely with their city police's Bias Crimes Units to investigate these crimes, and some districts have a liaison between police and prosecutors (American Prosecutors Research Institute 2000, 21). Yet, and more likely, prosecutors who normally handle property crimes will prosecute bias crimes involving vandalism; bias assaults are handled by violent crimes units, ethnic intimidation by civil rights units, and so on.

Despite the rarity of specialized offices, and despite the law's focus on individual as opposed to group rights, civil society groups that worked on legislation become active again at the enforcement level. Their engagement is encouraged in suggestions formulated by the American Prosecutors Research Institute (2000, 15), which advises that prosecutors work with other "critical agencies and groups" when responding to hate crime.[17] Groups listed by the institute include community groups such as interfaith coalitions and churches, community health and mental health centers, victims' rights organizations, tenant resident associations, and minority or community media and newspapers (American Prosecutors Research Institute 2000, 19).

The training of prosecutors on hate crime issues is often facilitated by groups who are carriers of hate-related collective memories: as the attorney for one interest group told us, "We seek to train and inform law enforcement about the issue of hate crime and how we might improve law enforcement practices." Correspondingly, a prosecutor we interviewed reported having attended a meeting facilitated and funded by the Simon Wiesenthal Center. In addition to their participation in training sessions, individual prosecutors report about information materials sent to them by traumatized groups. While the "state," as represented by the Department of Justice and other agencies, also plays a role in training, only one of our American interviewees had attended a conference administered by the Justice Department; the rest of the meetings were facilitated by interest or advocacy groups.

The localized organization of hate crime law enforcement and the strong role of local victim-group mobilization appear to color prosecutors' cognitions and attitudes. One prosecutor who attended training sessions facilitated by gay and lesbian organizations frequently referred to hate crime in the context of crimes against homosexuals.[18] Others contacted by race-based groups focused on race-based hate crimes in their interview responses.[19] What prosecutors see as typical hate crimes appears to vary with their group-initiated exposure to issues of hate.

In short, our qualitative materials support our theoretical expectations. First, international scripts do not seem to noticeably affect law and law enforcement in the hegemonic United States. Second, in line with quantitative research on the implementation of hate crime law as an outcome of social movement activity, its enforcement in the United States is strongly affected by activities of civil society groups in the context of porous institutions.[20] Third, specific groups' collective memories, through organization at the local level, inspire local law enforcement practice even if they do not affect collective political memory at the national level. Fourth, to the extent that federal law, in combination with an individual rights–focused political culture, constrains law enforcement organization and action, police and prosecutors are also informed by the institutionalization of collective memory at the national level. Our exploration thus suggests patterns in which collective memories, crystallized differently at various levels of society, differentially affect law and law enforcement. This argument becomes more convincing when we compare the American experience with that of one other country. Again we select Germany, whose collective memory we have used to illustrate the particularity of American memories (see chapter 6).

Hate Crime Law in Germany

In Germany, legal concern with hate first appears in the quasi-constitution (Grundgesetz, or Basic Law) of 1949, in immediate response to the Nazi regime and the Holocaust. This document was drafted by a group of elder statespersons, several of whom had themselves been victimized by the Nazi state. Article 3 of the Basic Law, part of a series of articles guaranteeing basic human rights, states in section 3 that no one may be discriminated against or favored because of that person's sex, parentage, race, language, homeland and origin, faith, or religious or political opinions. The Basic Law imposes limits on civil rights if these rights are used to endanger human rights or basic principles of democracy. For example, Article 9-3 of the Basic Law limits the right to free association of groups whose goals or activities offend against criminal law or are directed against the constitutional order or against the idea of reconciliation and respect between peoples (Völkerverständigung). Furthermore, according to Article 21-2, political parties that seek to harm or abolish the democratic order of the Federal Republic of Germany can be outlawed. The constitutional limitation of civil rights reflects the memory of the Weimar Republic among members of the Constitutional Council. They interpreted the demise of Weimar and the victory of Nazism at least partly as the consequence of a democratic order that was defenseless against the abuses of rights by its enemies.[21] The Constitutional Council's answer was the creation of a wehrhafte Demokratie, a democracy with the means of self-defense, even if self-defense implied the limitation of civil rights in particular situations. The Basic Law further links threats against the democratic order with those against minorities and international peace. Finally, according to Article 25, general rules of international law are part of federal law. They supersede federal law and immediately constitute rights and duties for residents of the Federal Republic. Clearly, the collective memory of the members of the Parliamentary Council, in combination with constraints set by the occupying powers, colored the Basic Law's central provisions regarding individual rights and the state's remedies against extremism and hate.

The Basic Law's restrictions of civil liberties are specified in path-dependent decisions on provisions of the German Criminal Code (Strafgesetzbuch) passed during the 1960s, 1970s, and 1980s. These provisions impose penalties (typically of up to three years' imprisonment or fines) for extremist activities. The following are from the 1985 Strafgesetzbuch:

> Paragraph 86 criminalizes membership in parties or associations that are directed against the democratic constitutional order or against the idea of international understanding (Völkerverständigung) or

activities that are directed at the dissemination of propaganda seeking to continue the efforts of any National Socialist association.

Paragraph 86a prohibits the dissemination of symbols of political parties proclaimed unconstitutional under paragraph 86. Such symbols may include flags, medals, pieces of uniforms, slogans, and forms of greetings.

Paragraph 130 criminalizes inciting hatred against sections of the population; calling for violent or arbitrary measures against them; and insulting them, maliciously exposing them to contempt, or slandering them (Volksverhetzung).

Paragraph 131 provides for a prison term of up to one year for producing, disseminating, exhibiting, or making available to persons below the age of eighteen writings that incite race hatred.

Finally, paragraph 194 determines that insult or slander, if directed against a person who was persecuted during the Nazi regime or against the name or memory of a deceased person who lost his or her life as a victim of the Nazi regime, can be prosecuted without petition by the victim (as opposed to insult and slander generally). This paragraph is mostly directed against spreading the "Auschwitz lie," that is, public denial of the existence of extermination camps during the Nazi era.

In short, German legal protections against hate are posed in general terms. Individual groups such as women, gays, Jews, Gypsies, or immigrants are not spelled out. While the Basic Law focuses on individual rights along abstract dimensions of social organization such as sex, parentage, race, language, or homeland and origin, the norms of the Criminal Code are even more general. They do not list such specific dimensions but seek to protect the constitutional order and minorities generally. They are more specific, however, as they refer to chapters of hate and broad categories of victims in German collective memory. They seek to protect "international understanding" (Völkerverständigung; paragraph 86), "sections of the population" (paragraph 130), against "race hatred" (paragraph 131), and those persecuted and killed by the Nazi regime (paragraph 194). These protections are further linked with the memory of the Holocaust (paragraph 130) and Nazism (paragraphs 86 and 130) and with lessons drawn for the protection of the democratic order (paragraph 86). Such framing clearly reflects basic features of German collective memory and cultural trauma of hate as outlined earlier.

Law Enforcement in Germany

Institutionalization of collective memory as law may not reach beyond symbolic significance if law is not enforced. The enforcement level also brings new social forces as well as old administrative trajectories to bear. We thus briefly examine the consequences of policing history and collective memory as reflected in legislation for later path-dependent institutionalization at the level of law enforcement.

Administrative trajectories reach back to special police forces for the protection of the state that have a long history in Europe generally, dating back to the era of absolute monarchies.[22] In Germany they originate in antidemocratic tools of the German Confederation (Deutsche Bund) of 1815, specifically the Central Investigatory Commission (Centralunter suchungskommission). Such agencies survived through several mutations into the Weimar Republic until the Nazi regime turned them into centralized, streamlined tools (that is, information-gathering and executive powers merged) that were no longer subject to court supervision.[23] Despite post-Nazism mistrust against agencies of state protection, the Allies, in a 1947 note to the Parliamentary Council, requested the "creation of central agencies for the collection of intelligence regarding 'subversive' elements" (quoted in Römelt 1977, 210). This initiative resulted in the Law on the Collaboration between the Federal Government and the States on Issues of the Protection of the Constitution of September 27, 1950. It thereby created a new system that adapted the old model of state protection to conditions in the new democratic state. Offices for the Protection of the Constitution at federal and state levels now collect data on extremist political activities and publish annual reports. These agencies are structurally separated from law enforcement, where special units within prosecutors' offices focus on cases of political extremism.[24] In line with constitutional norms and the criminal code, intelligence gathering and prosecution also include issues of hate and cases of hate crime. They closely reflect the concerns expressed in German hate crime laws, especially their embeddedness in the context of state protection. In the words of one prosecutor in an "extremism unit" (Extremismusdezernat), "It is true that cases of xenophobic violence, also racial violence and political extremism, attract particular attention in the public and also here in the prosecutor's office and all law enforcement authorities. This is expressed in the reporting duty [to the Ministry of Justice]. All major violent offenses will be treated . . . in the homicide unit—because xenophobic violence constitutes malicious intent, which implies mandatory life imprisonment, the highest penalty. . . . Or, apart from homicides, offenses with this [hate] background are handled in a special unit."

Organizational specialization is repeated at the level of the police, where "state protection units" (Staatsschutz) deal with cases of political extremism and hate-related offenses, from violent offenses to the spraying of xenophobic graffiti. Interviews with prosecutors indicate that collaboration between police and prosecutors is particularly close in these specialized units.

In addition to organizational differentiation, the state also provides training for those who work in specialized units. Interviewees reported that their prosecutors' offices offered regular seminars on activities of the radical Right. Such seminars are supplemented by internal memos on court decisions regarding extremism and hate cases and by regular articles in practitioner journals.[25]

Prosecutors are also aware that the sentencing stage of the criminal justice process provides for opportunities to consider hate motives.

> There is much discretion in the sentencing decision. . . . Paragraphs 46 and 47 [regarding the purposes of punishment] of the Criminal Code (Strafgesetzbuch) highlight the offender's motives and goals, the state of mind that speaks from the offense. The effects of the offense, the reputation of the Federal Republic in domestic and foreign media—all of these are legitimate considerations. . . . It is due to the Nazi past that the code includes provisions against inciting hatred against peoples, engagement in anticonstitutional organizations—there is nothing comparable in other countries. Downloading juvenile Nazi propaganda from U.S. Internet sites to distribute them here is illegal. The federal legislature has introduced these provisions into the Code in light of our past, also because foreign countries keep an eye on us.[26]

The reference to foreign countries indicates awareness of international concern among prosecutors. This is in line with increased international attention to the enforcement of hate crime laws following reunification and a wave of antiforeigner violence in the early 1990s. Nongovernmental organizations[27] and foreign politicians[28] alike express concern while also reporting initiatives by the German government, such as increasing enforcement staff and cracking down on extremists.

The recent history of law enforcement in Germany suggests the relevance of several factors highlighted in our theoretical model. First, cultural trauma associated with German history inspires intensified law enforcement. Second, the state, embedded in a web of international affiliations, is the prime carrier through which collective memories of hate are made relevant in law enforcement. Third, renewed international human rights concerns and post–Cold War initiatives affect law enforcement. Finally, administrative trajectories and the legacies of collective memories, partly mediated through law, are reflected in the organization of law enforcement and, through socialization, in the mindsets of its agents.

Conclusions: Correspondence Between Collective Memory and Hate Crime Law

Our comparative material for the United States and Germany illustrates how collective memory and cultural trauma, and their activation for political, legal, and moral purposes, differ across these two countries. We remember our findings in chapter 6 regarding the nation-specific nature of collective memories: In terms of substance, the United States focuses on domestic achievements, liberation from domestic evil, American military contributions to liberation from foreign evil, and the military generally. This contrasts with German collective memory, which stresses domestic evil itself and liberation by foreign powers but lacks commemorations of the military. In terms of the logic of commemoration, the United States tends to avoid reference to collectivities or groups that suffered from domestic evil. In addition, evil is commemorated in isolation from the nation's sociopolitical and historical context. In German collective memory, evil is very much tied to the memory of failing state structures. It embraces specific groups, particularly the victims of the Holocaust and among these especially the Jewish victims. It is likely that this focus is at least partly a result of international attention directed at Germany and its intense exposure to global scripts. We have now added new insights by showing how such divergent national memories of hate have become institutionalized in law and in law enforcement at the levels of law texts, organization, training of personnel, and cognitions and attitudes of enforcement agents. American and German memories, in interaction with nation-specific institutional contexts and exposure to global scripts, have thus taken organizational shape.

The effects of collective memory thus resemble those of other cultural phenomena such as religious orientations that, in interaction with additional social forces, have shaped laws and institutions of the state.[29] Cultural trauma, a specific form of collective memory, in distinction from the Protestant ethic, never a "lightweight coat that could be thrown off at any time" (Richard Baxter, quoted in Weber 2009, 123), became itself partially independent of its carriers. Even if the institutions of law and law enforcement do not form an iron cage, they do channel social action. Our account thus supports the idea of cultural and institutional path dependency of collective memory that Jeffrey Olick has explored and that is entailed in the work of Edward Shils.[30] Here we extend the argument into the spheres of law and formally organized institutions. Crucially in this context, we show that collective memories—themselves partially created through legal processes—matter. They inspire the social control of hatred and of the violence it sometimes promotes, here through legal regulation and its enforcement. American initiatives and follow-through are highly dependent, in an international comparative perspective, on immediate initiatives by interest groups. There is reason to believe that a less developed American memory of domestic atrocities and the nation's self-perception as a glorious liberator contribute to this situation. A closer look at a large number of American jurisdictions in the following chapter should shed additional light on this issue.

Chapter 9

Commemorating Injustice and Implementing Hate Crime Law Across Jurisdictions in the United States

T HE PREVIOUS chapter has shown that collective memories are indeed consequential for lawmaking and law enforcement. When making decisions about whether to pursue prosecutions, many German state attorneys have had one eye on the past. Collective memories are not determinative, but they do guide and constrain German law enforcers. Compared with the German case, the story about American law and law enforcement is less clear cut. Some patterns can be detected, and we have shown how the Holocaust crept into discussions of hate crime law in the early legislative debates, but in the end, in our estimation, American collective memory, like its law enforcement agencies, is porous and geographically variable. This chapter probes more deeply into the American case. We stick with the issue of hate crime law, but our substantive and methodological focuses shift notably. First, whereas the previous chapter is heavily weighted toward legislative decisions to demonstrate what we have labeled "applied commemoration," here we focus on law enforcement agencies. Second, in this chapter we propose some ways in which collective memory might be used for a quantitative analysis. Still, and with these differences in mind, we are primarily interested in a straightforward question that also underscores the previous chapter: To what extent do collective memories really matter in legal intervention against hate-motivated violence?

In the U.S. context, two answers seem equally plausible. We might say that collective memory makes for a nice academic theme; but whether and how memories are constructed is pretty benign and inconsequential. For instance, we could commemorate John F. Kennedy or Martin Luther King Jr. by naming schools after them, and in doing so we might evoke and memorialize icons and ideals of the civil rights era. But in the end, these

150

schools will teach math, science, and history, just as schools named after Catholic saints or civil war generals or those simply given a number, like P.S. 46. Similarly, we might commemorate the Holocaust through memorials that are designed to send strong symbolic messages. As the Holocaust scholar Oren Baruch Stier once stated, "We need [these symbols] as a way to relate to the events of the past."[1] But residents of cities with and without Holocaust memorials would probably agree about the inherent evil and reprehensible nature of the Holocaust. Commemorations and memorials might be symbolic, but they are only symbolic.

Nonetheless, we might argue that collective memories and the tangible structures that depict them are indeed consequential, or as the sociologists Larry Griffin and Kenneth Bollen (2009, 594) suggest, "memory matters." Griffin and Bollen make a persuasive case that collective memories of the civil rights movement influenced racial attitudes, although whether they influenced behavior remains an open question. From this perspective we might also argue that symbolic depictions of collective memories, for instance through memorials or even street naming, can tell us something about a local culture that has implications for law.

Perhaps it is not merely coincidence that South Carolina, which until July of 2000 flew the confederate flag high above its statehouse and thereafter moved it to a confederate soldier memorial, is one of five states without a hate crime law, while neighboring North Carolina created a hate crime law nearly two decades ago. We might also find it curious that precisely when Alabama removed the phrase "Heart of Dixie" from its license plate, it also began to comply with federal hate crime law.[2] These selective examples hardly make for convincing evidence, but they do align with an argument put forth earlier in this book: Collective memories are consequential for law, and their depiction in tangible structures tells us much about a local culture. Against this backdrop an intriguing thesis emerges: a map of memorials can simultaneously be interpreted as a map of meaning, which in turn serves as a roadmap to understanding differences in legislation and law enforcement.

This is fine conjecture, but clearly an evidentiary basis for such a claim is in order. With this in mind, we continue with the case of hate crime law, this time focusing exclusively on the United States and looking specifically at the practices and policies of law enforcement agencies.

Backdrop: Hate Crime Law and Its Implementation in the United States

As noted in the previous chapter, hate crime law represents a fairly recent legal initiative for responding to crime and violence motivated by bigotry in the United States. While laws designed to combat hatred and political extremism certainly predate the twentieth century, the term *hate crime* only recently entered the American legal lexicon.[3] The states of Washington and Oregon implemented these laws in the early 1980s, and legislation swept across the nation thereafter. At present, forty-five states and the District of Columbia have some form of hate or bias crime legislation on the books.[4]

However, if hate crime legislation is nearly a constant, the implementation and enforcement of these laws is tremendously variable by comparison. For example, some policing agencies have specific procedures for investigating hate crimes, while others have no policies at all. Many policing agencies regularly comply with federal law on the collection of hate crime data, while others entirely abstain. Hate crime prosecutions appear to be quite frequent in some states (for example, Maryland) but uncommon in others (for example, Louisiana).[5] And police in some counties report dozens of hate crimes each year, while other counties report none.

To better illustrate this variation, let us briefly consider a selective but revealing comparison. In 2007 the police in Washington, D.C. (population 588,000), reported forty-one hate crime incidents, while police in the city of Bangor, Maine (population 31,000), reported only seven. There is nothing particularly striking about this difference. Washington has a larger and more heterogeneous population with a higher crime rate, and thus we would surely expect more hate crime to be reported there. This unsurprising comparison becomes more intriguing when we note that, in the same year, no hate crimes were reported in the entire state of Mississippi (population 2.8 million). Is there really no hate crime in Mississippi, and by comparison much more in Bangor? Perhaps. But these differences more likely reflect variation in law enforcement agencies' commitment to hate crime policing. To the extent that the latter explanation carries weight, a rather interesting question emerges: Why is there such vast variation in law enforcement responses to hate crime within the United States?

Over the past few years researchers have approached this question from many angles, but what appears absent from this body of work is a sustained discussion of how history and culture come together to inform the implementation and enforcement of these laws. We see this as an instructive area of inquiry for advancing our ideas about the role of collective memory, although we are hardly the first to view hate crime law and its implementation as being intricately linked with legacies of injustice. Valerie Jenness and her colleagues, for instance, have shown that hate crime legislation is in some sense a legacy of earlier civil rights legislation.[6] That line of work suggests a fairly direct lineage between the content of civil rights laws and later hate crime laws.

Our approach differs in that we direct greater attention to the commemoration of past injustices, their symbolic meaning, and the way this meaning might relate to law enforcement practices. Following Jenness, we give due attention to the legacy of the civil rights movement, but we also bring in the collective memory of other events. For example, the emergence of an anti–hate crime movement and the subsequent diffusion of hate crime laws across the country coincide, perhaps not by chance, with a reinvigorated discourse about the Holocaust during the same period. To that end, images of the Holocaust were invoked as an analogical device during congressional testimony about hate crime statutes. As just one illustration, Senator Orrin Hatch, accompanied by the movie director Steven Spielberg, made the following remarks before the Senate Judiciary Committee: "To Jewish Americans, who have witnessed and suffered persecution, . . . vandalism and burning of synagogues, of the Torah, and of places of business—the defacing of cemeteries and synagogues with swastikas and Nazi slogans are horrible reminders of the intimidation and persecution of the Nazi regime and of the 'blood-libel' . . . It is well worth remembering the true lesson of 'Schindler's List'" (testimony before the Senate Judiciary Committee on the Hate Crime Statistics Act, June 28, 1994).

In some ways the senator's testimony is a microcosm of our larger argument that collective memories both motivate and help justify legal action. In this case, it is interesting and perhaps instructive that Hatch's reference to the Holocaust comes about one year after the United States Holocaust Memorial Museum was dedicated near the National Mall. Notice also the analogical comparison between Nazi persecution and contemporary hate crimes and an apparent assumption that the law can partly remedy the problem. We see an implicit connection here among historical persecution, contemporary memorials, and lawmaking. It is this constellation of factors that we empirically address in this chapter. In short, if we know something about the collective memory of a place, can we better predict the behavior of its law enforcement agencies?

What Commemoration Tells Us, and Why It Matters

Although the central question of this chapter is fairly simple, the rationale behind it requires some elaboration. Underlying our argument is Emile Durkheim's notion that law enforcement and sanctioning, at least to some extent, are replete with meaning and mirror a wider public discourse. As one reputable scholar of punishment, David Garland (1990, 214), states in his discussion of Durkheim's legacy, "Political decisions are always taken against a background of mores and sensibilities which, normally at least, will set limits to what will be tolerated by the public or implemented by the penal system's personnel." We might then suggest that implementing or enforcing hate crime law expresses disdain for bigotry and reinforces the community's collective conscience.

But this logic confronts a dilemma when we move from theory to analysis: How might we identify jurisdictions where hate crime law is viewed as legitimate or, in the parlance of Durkheimian sociology, where hate-motivated behavior poses an affront to the collective conscience? Emotions and attitudes, after all, are typically unobservable. Research suggesting a link between culture and law thus runs a risk of producing a circular argument. In other words, the temptation exists to infer a cultural norm from the social practice itself, which renders the argument tautological.[7] How then can we identify a normative environment conducive to the implementation of hate crime law?

Geographers and sociologists focusing on commemoration and place naming give us some leverage on this issue. The overarching argument among scholars of various disciplines is that memorials, place names, and street names are anything but idiosyncratic. As the Israeli geographer Maoz Azaryahu (1996, 320, 311) states, "Commemorative monuments, street names, and memorial plaques . . . merge the past and its myths with the landscape"; they transform an urban environment into a political setting. What is being commemorated, it seems, says much about who is calling for the commemoration. To briefly illustrate this point, consider the Karl-Marx-Allee in East Berlin. In 1949 this stretch was named Frankfurter Allee. It was renamed Stalinallee when the Soviets took control of East Berlin after World War II and then took its current name in 1961 during the widespread "de-Stalinization" period.[8] The geographic area remained constant, but the symbolic meaning of this space varied with the political culture, as reflected in the changing street name. Similar arguments have been made about place naming in the United States.[9] With respect to places that commemorate John F. Kennedy and Martin Luther King Jr., Roger Stump (1988, 215; our emphasis) implies that "places named for Kennedy and King represent more than simple memorials. They are public symbols of community values, attitudes and beliefs, revealing the character of both the figure commemorated *and the community that has honored him.*"

Sociologists, although drawing on a different theoretical corpus, share this general sentiment. In an influential article on collective memory in the U.S. Capitol, for instance, Barry Schwartz astutely observes that while objects of commemoration are typically found in the past, the issues motivating and shaping their selection always reflect concerns of the present.[10] Schwartz finds that before the Civil War, when national unity was tenuous and Congress was divided on key questions about the structure of government, memorials tended to fall back on the common denominators of our founding fathers and heroes. Once the nation's unity was more secure following the Civil War, more recent events as well as bureaucratic and political leaders were also commemorated. The symbolic commemoration of the past to a large extent reflects contemporary culture. In this vein, and with reference to the Holocaust, Jeffrey Alexander (2002, 53) suggests that "objectification can point to the sturdier embodiment of the values [the memorials] have created, and even the experiences they imply." The memorials indicate a deep institutionalization of the moral lesson of the Holocaust and its continuing significance; they crystallize collective sentiments.

Taken together, Durkheimian scholarship and more recent interpretive work on commemoration make three related assumptions. First, objects of collective memory carry symbolic weight and reflect facets of culture and unity. They represent a moral conscience. Second, legacies of the past enable and constrain government decisionmaking. The past penetrates the social and political spheres, frequently begetting recognition and demands for justice.[11] Third, tangible symbols of collective memory vary across social contexts. That is, commemorations of traumatic pasts not only vary over time and across nations, which has been the predominant focus of extant collective memory research, but also are particular to geographic areas within countries in a given time. Commemorations of former president John F. Kennedy, for example, are rare in the South, likely because his name is associated with the process of school desegregation that was opposed by many white Southerners.[12]

We suggest that symbolic commemorations of hate-laden events and gross injustices, such as the Holocaust, are indicative of a social climate that is highly attuned to the consequences of hatred. As neo-institutionalists might say, such commemorations are indicative of a normative legal environment that we presume would hasten the implementation of hate crime laws at the local level. To this end, we systematically test whether law enforcement agencies are more apt to create departmental hate crime policies, comply with hate crime law, and prosecute hate crimes where collective memories of bigotry are symbolically commemorated.

Commemorations of traumatic pasts, however, can take many forms or depict a variety of images. Here, we specifically focus on symbolic commemoration of the civil rights movement and the Holocaust. Commemoration of the civil rights movement and Holocaust differ in obvious and meaningful ways. The former involves domestic reflection, while the latter entails memory of atrocities committed in a foreign country. Commemorations of the civil rights movement entail memories of injustice by the U.S. government, such as turning a blind eye to lynching during the heyday of this practice, while Holocaust memory often emphasizes America's role in putting an end to the genocide. The Holocaust has been constructed as a universal symbol of evil with immense rhetorical power, while memory of lynching and civil rights abuses is more conflicted and arguably lacks the conscious reflection needed to affect legal action. Some historians even argue that American reflection on past injustice, slavery for instance, is a case of "active forgetting," a story of reconciled conflict over unresolved legacies.[13] With respect to the civil rights movement, Jacquelyn Hall (2005, 1233) adds that "the dominant narrative of the civil rights movement . . . distorts and suppresses as much as it reveals." In addition, the civil rights movement is intimately tied to contemporary race relations, which are characterized by a fair degree of pessimism about government intervention to prevent discrimination.[14]

The implication is that collective memories of domestic inequity, particularly in matters involving race relations, are more difficult to mobilize and connect with the concept of hate crime law. We see some evidence of this in testimonials before Congress in support of pending federal hate crime law. It is not surprising that the Holocaust, as the ultimate symbol of hatred, was invoked by members of Congress and leaders of advocacy organizations. Yet comparable references to the civil rights movement in congressional testimony appeared to be infrequent, in line with Francesca Polletta's findings about the relative rarity of Martin Luther King Jr.'s name being invoked for purposes of legislative action.[15] Accordingly, we test whether the implementation of hate crime law is more strongly associated with commemoration of the Holocaust than with commemoration of the civil rights movement.

We attempt to measure collective memories of past atrocity and injustice as expressed in two types of commemoration: the establishment of Holocaust centers (including memorials and museums) and the naming of streets or schools in honor of Martin Luther King Jr. The power of each of these indicators can easily be illustrated.

A Quantitative Assessment

In an oft-quoted line from Shakespeare's most famous of plays, Juliet rhetorically asks Romeo, "What's in a name"? Clearly, a lot. As the prominent cultural geographer Wilbur Zelinsky (1970, 746) once wrote with respect to personal names, "[The] choice of personal names comes closer to fulfilling the stated criteria for an ideal cultural measure than any other known item." Comparable arguments have been made for business, place, and street names. The late historian Harold Isaacs (1975, 73) noted that "the name of a country, of an individual, or a group, carries in it all the cargo of the past. The name . . . can often take us to where the heart can be found, leading us deep into history, the relationships, and the emotions that lie at the center of any such affair."[16] Sociologists have heeded these insights to construct innovative measures of culture. For instance, in a novel and, we think, successful attempt to measure the cultural South as distinct from the simple borders of the geographic South, John Shelton Reed (1976) looks at businesses with the words *Southern* or *Dixie* in their names. The two are by no means coterminous. *Dixie* is disproportionately found in the eastern portion of the Cotton South and captures much of the so-called Black Belt of the Deep South. According to Reed, *Dixie* has more to do with attitude than latitude and provides a cultural measure to separate the New South from the Old.

In this spirit, we argue that Martin Luther King Jr. street and school naming says something about local areas. Street naming is about how collective memories and representations of people or eras are constructed and commemorated through geographic contexts.[17] In his work on memorializing Martin Luther King through commemorative school naming, Stump (1988, 211) suggests that "trends in naming of places in King's honor appear to reflect his particular status as a national leader, and varying support for his ideals in different parts of the country." Or as former mayor Jim Marshall of Macon, Georgia, once stated, "Macon's Martin Luther King Jr., Boulevard leads to the heart of Macon—a fitting tribute to a man whose courage and lessons changed the hearts of many Americans."[18]

Martin Luther King is clearly not the only prominent civil rights leader, and the naming of schools and streets is not the only commemorative form. However, King's name more than any other is associated with the civil rights movement. The U.S. government chose his name and birthday to honor this period of American history, thus institutionally associating the memory of Martin Luther King with the memory of civil rights and the injustices this movement sought to overcome. Many civil rights museums and numerous schools are named in his memory as well. Hence, while his name is not the only reminder of this contentious era, it is the apotheosis of the civil rights movement and by all accounts the most prominent and widely institutionalized symbol of this era in American society.[19]

Our measure of commemoration of the Holocaust is more straightforward and probably requires less background. We identify this type of commemoration by the presence of a Holocaust center, museum, or memorial in the jurisdiction served by the law enforcement agency.[20] Again, the assumption is that these memorials convey a more general sentiment and raise awareness about issues of hatred and bigotry. As the website for the Boston Holocaust Memorial states, "This important Memorial causes us all to pause and think about the corrosive impact of prejudice, hatred, and bigotry, and the importance of speaking out against them."[21]

To empirically assess whether these measures are correlated with local law enforcement's response to hate crime, we use data from two samples. The first is a sample of large municipal policing agencies taken from the Law Enforcement Management Statistics Survey of Law Enforcement Agencies (U.S. Department of Justice, Bureau of Justice Statistics 2000).[22] Although the survey includes information on thousands of law enforcement agencies, we confine our analysis to municipal police departments with one hundred or more full-time officers.[23]

The second data source is a survey administered by Ryan King to a sample of district attorney's offices in the United States. This survey includes information on nearly four hundred offices in states with hate crime laws on the books and includes information on the presence of office hate crime policies and the number of hate or bias crime charges or indictments made by the office during the year 2003.[24]

What, then, is the association between our indicators of collective memory and hate crime law enforcement? We first consider compliance with federal hate crime law. This variable captures whether the police department complied with the provisions of the Hate Crime Statistics Act (HCSA). The act requires the U.S. attorney general to collect information on the prevalence of hate crime in the United States, although compliance remains highly variable.[25] For instance, in the year 2000, which is the year used in this analysis, nearly all law enforcement in counties along the western seaboard of the United States, like those in New England on the East Coast, complied with the HCSA and reported one or more hate crimes. However, compliance was sparse in the former Black Belt states of the South. Significant intrastate variation is also apparent. We suggest that one factor contributing to compliance is collective memory.

Figure 9.1 plots the percentage of police departments in the sample that complied with the HCSA against the presence or absence of each type of commemoration. The figure provides initial, if cautious, support for our argument. Looking first at the first two bars in the figure, which compare cities with and without streets or schools named for Martin Luther King, we see only a slight difference in compliance—a difference that is not statistically significant. Almost 82 percent of departments in cities with King commemorations complied with the HCSA compared with about 77 percent elsewhere. However, the results for Holocaust memorials, represented by the second pair of bars, are strikingly different. Nine out of ten policing agencies in cities with such memorials complied, which is well above the 77 percent in cities without Holocaust memorials.

Figure 9.1   Coincidence of Hate Crime Statistics Act Compliance and Commemoration, by Type of Commemoration

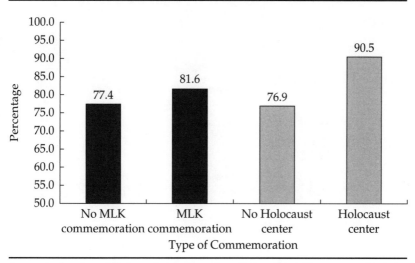

Source: Authors' compilation of data from Law Enforcement Management Statistics Survey (U.S. Department of Justice, Bureau of Justice Statistics 2001), Hate Crimes Statistics (U.S. Department of Justice, Federal Bureau of Investigation 2000), and authors' information on presence of Martin Luther King Jr. (MLK) schools and streets and Holocaust centers or memorials.

As a second measure of hate crime law implementation, we examine whether the city's police department created a policy or a hate crime unit to respond to these types of crime.[26] Figure 9.2 provides an initial look at this comparison, and the results are comparable to those reported in the previous figure. We find no statistically significant difference between cities with and without Martin Luther King commemorations; here, in fact, the relationship is slightly opposed to our expectations. Yet the data show a significant and substantial difference for cities with Holocaust memorials relative to those without (95.2 versus 82.6 percent).

Our final two measures pertain to district attorney's offices rather than police departments. One way that prosecutors can implement hate crime law at the local level is by creating office policies or designating specific personnel to this type of crime.[27] The results of this comparison, shown in figure 9.3, suggest significant differences for each type of commemoration. Only about 10 percent of district attorney's offices in places without Martin Luther King or Holocaust commemorations, as defined earlier, had implemented an office policy as of 2003. By comparison, nearly 28 percent of offices in districts with King commemorations and

Figure 9.2   Coincidence of Hate Crime Policies in Police Departments and Commemoration, by Type of Commemoration

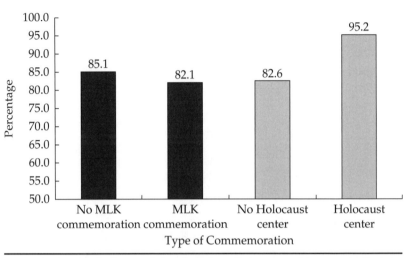

Source: Authors' compilation of data from Law Enforcement Management Statistics Survey (U.S. Department of Justice, Bureau of Justice Statistics 2001), Hate Crimes Statistics (U.S. Department of Justice, Federal Bureau of Investigaiton 2000), and authors' information on presence of Martin Luther King Jr. (MLK) schools and streets and Holocaust centers or memorials.

Figure 9.3   Coincidence of Hate Crime Policies in District Attorney's Offices and Commemoration, by Type of Commemoration

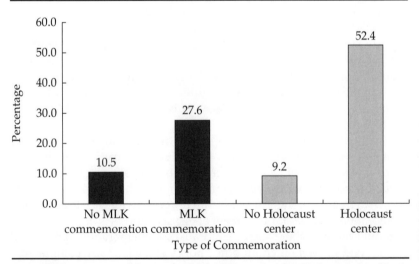

Source: Authors' survey of district attorney's offices and authors' information on Martin Luther King Jr. (MLK) schools and streets and Holocaust centers and memorials.

Figure 9.4   Coincidence of Hate Crime Prosecutions and Commemoration, by Type of Commemoration

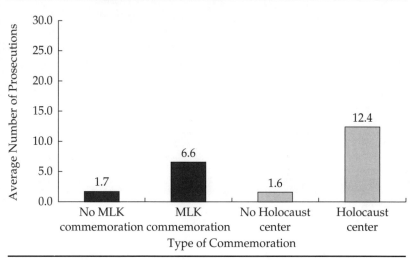

Source: Authors' survey of district attorney's offices and authors' information on Martin Luther King Jr. (MLK) schools and streets and Holocaust centers and memorials.

more than 52 percent of those in districts with Holocaust commemorations had hate crime policies or designated personnel.

Finally, we compare the number of hate crime prosecutions in districts with and without each type of commemoration (figure 9.4). In districts without commemorations, fewer than two cases of hate crime, on average, were prosecuted. Districts with commemorations of Martin Luther King average more than six hate crime prosecutions, and those with Holocaust commemorations more than a dozen.

All in all, there is at least a prima facie case to be made that local law enforcement responses to hate crime are associated with these specific depictions of collective memory. In some cases the differences on our outcome variables are quite remarkable, particularly for Holocaust commemorations. Nevertheless, we acknowledge that several factors could explain these correlations. The bar graphs might look considerably different if we accounted for some simple demographic factors such as the proportionate number of blacks or Jews. Perhaps places with larger Jewish populations are more likely to have Holocaust centers, although they might also provide more opportunity for hate crimes against Jews to be perpetrated, which could in turn elevate compliance. We might also point to the political environment. One could argue that liberal

Table 9.1   Regression Models

	Compliance	Police Department Policy	District Attorney's Office Policy	Prosecutions
Martin Luther King commemoration	.57*	−.13	.03	−.10
Holocaust commemoration	.95*	.51*	.89*	−.21
N	490	475	385	380

Sources: LEMAS survey and the authors' survey of district attorney's offices.
Note: Logistic regression was used for the compliance and district attorney's office policy models, an ordered logit estimator was used for the ordinal variable measuring police department policy, and a negative binomial estimator was used for the analysis of prosecutions. Models control for variables described in note 28, although these coefficients are not shown in the table.
*p<.05, one-tailed test

strongholds are more apt to commemorate episodes of injustice and also more likely to comply with legislation concerning civil rights.

Fortunately, we can statistically control for these and other potentially confounding variables in a regression model, which is shown in table 9.1.[28] Some of the bivariate correlations change appreciably when other covariates are taken into account. For instance, the association between naming streets or schools after Martin Luther King and compliance with the HCSA is now statistically significant ($b = .57$). Interestingly, this association was not significant in figure 9.1, but a suppressed effect emerged once we controlled for the proportion of African Americans in the city. The coefficient likely becomes significant because the percent black in the city is positively correlated with Martin Luther King street and school naming but negatively correlated with hate crime law compliance.[29] When we control for black population size, the commemoration of King emerges as a significant predictor of compliance. However, these commemorations are no longer significantly correlated with any other outcome variable. Taken together, it seems that commemorations of Martin Luther King are generally uncorrelated with local implementation and enforcement of hate crime law, a finding that we return to later.

The results in table 9.1 show that Holocaust memorials remain significantly associated with implementation in three of the four models, even when we control for other demographic factors, including an estimate of Jewish population size. The only measure for which the association is no longer significant is the number of prosecutions. It seems that commemorations of the Holocaust are associated with symbolic measures, such as instituting policies and complying with federal law, but such commemorations are not predictive of actual enforcement as measured by the number of prosecutions. Making sense of the latter finding requires some speculation, although two explanations seem likely. First, there may be some disjuncture here between law on the books and law in action. Establishing a policy or complying with a mandate is not predicated on a quantum of proof, whereas actually prosecuting a hate crime case requires proving the requisite mens rea, which can be difficult in these types of cases, even for district attorneys sensitive to hate crimes. Second, and related, law enforcement officials may create office policies as a show of compliance with a norm, although enforcing the policy may be a secondary concern either because it is not feasible (for example, not enough evidence in a potential hate crime case) or because doing so would interrupt the efficiency of the organization.[30]

Implications

In the end, what might we say about the consequences of local collective memories for the creation, implementation, and enforcement of law directed against hate-inspired actions? For one, collective memories are hardly divorced from lawmaking, as shown in chapter 8. We might indeed say that American hate crime legislation—or its equivalent in Germany—is intricately tied to collective memory. As suggested in the previous chapter, in this context legislation can even be thought of as a type of applied commemoration. We also point out in chapter 8 that American law enforcement, both police and prosecutors, is considerably more varied than German law enforcement in its thoughts and practices concerning American hate crime law. These laws are often disregarded in some locales while seemingly enforced vigorously in others. The present chapter shows that compliance and other forms of implementation are associated with commemorations of past injustice and atrocity, although clearly the type of commemoration matters.

We suggest that the distinction between collective memories of domestic bigotry and those of foreign hatred is significant, largely because memory of domestic wrongdoing is often conflicted and depoliticized and lacks consensus.[31] In some respects this notion builds on a century of sociological thought. In *The Division of Labor in Society*, Durkheim (1984, 58) argues that sentiments that bring about punishment draw their strength from the fact that they are "universally respected" and "not contested." Durkheim's insights find some additional credibility in this analysis. Commemoration of civil rights abuses and the Holocaust clearly differ in meaningful ways, the latter safely classified as what Jeffrey Alexander might call "sacred evil" (2004a, 222). The latter also was much more strongly correlated with our measures of implementation and enforcement of hate crime law.

In addition, we acknowledge that our measures of Martin Luther King commemorations were useful but nonetheless somewhat crude. By measuring these events quantitatively we lose some of the meaningful nuance that surrounds such commemorations. As just one illustration of contentious politics involved in commemoration, the street named in honor of Martin Luther King in Brent, Alabama, leads to a garbage dump. This placement subsequently generated political conflict and incited local African American leaders to petition for a change.[32] In such cases the commemoration seems ceremonial rather than the result of a unified consensus. Where this is the case, depictions of collective memory offer little guidance.

Finally, is it likely that local law enforcement responses to hate crime will have an impact on prejudice and intergroup conflict? We can unfortunately offer no definitive answer to this question. This important question is unlikely to be answered owing to the tremendous variability in hate crime reporting and other methodological problems.[33] Research on related themes, such as hate speech policies on college campuses, gives us some reason for optimism. Jon Gould, for instance, argues that the adoption of hate speech policies, although rarely enforced, has nonetheless influenced behavior on college campuses by creating a richer "culture of civility"(34). Others, however, have offered less sanguine predictions.[34] We cannot speak to this debate empirically, but we can say with a fair degree of confidence that collective memories, themselves partly shaped by legal institutions, are an important factor in determining whether laws directed against hate-inspired acts are created and whether they ultimately remain dormant or become an active force against violence.

And here a long line of arguments closes. We began our debate with thoughts about the merits of legal intervention against perpetrators against human rights and with ideas about the crucial intermediary role collective memory plays when trials contribute to ending cycles of violence. President Roosevelt and Justice Jackson had large-scale atrocities and aggressive warfare in mind when they hoped that Nuremberg would cement the horrors committed by Nazi Germany in the minds of the public. Similarly, scholars such as the political scientist Kathryn Sikkink insist that transitional justice interventions improve human rights records and strengthen democracy at the end of periods of dictatorship and civil war. We argue that Roosevelt and Jackson may well be right with their expectations, and we add that the sedimentation of past evil in collective memories for which they hoped is likely to be one crucial mechanism through which transitional justice produces its benefits. Several pieces of empirical evidence support such hopes and expectations, as illustrated for recent German history and policymaking against hate. For the United States, however, we find a mixed picture. The country does not cement memories of domestic evil to thereby prevent future violence, partly by avoiding legal consequences or directing them only against low-level perpetrators. The consequences are problematic, as we have seen. In the realm of hate-motivated violence in civil society we find relatively weak effects of memories of domestic evil against hate-inspired violence. However, we again find at least differentiated support for that part of our causal chain that leads from memories to intervention: Collective memories, when activated by carrier groups through cultivation of historical consciousness and the use of bridging metaphors, provoke legal interventions against such violence. This effect, in line with our expectation, is stronger where memories of foreign atrocities, pursued by criminal courts against high-ranking perpetrators, are at stake.

═ Chapter 10 ═

Conclusion: Atrocities, Law, and Collective Memory in the United States and Beyond

OUR JOURNEY through American memories of atrocities has yielded insights of scholarly and practical value. First, and at a very general level, our work corroborates what prior scholarship has long suggested: the structure of American memories of atrocities, domestic and foreign, are a crucial component of American culture and social life. Collective amnesia, which is always selective amnesia, is undoubtedly part of that structure as well. Second, law contributes to shaping this structure of memory. Trials against a few low-ranking perpetrators in domestic cases and prosecutions against high-ranking figures in foreign cases have left their traces in the minds of Americans. Third, once established, collective memories have consequences. Where high-ranking actors often have impunity, as in the United States, it is likely that caution against premature military intervention and excesses is reduced in international relations. Domestically, memories affect ways in which new laws against hate-motivated violence are shaped and enforced, at least in those jurisdictions where civil society groups press their case. In general, while law contributes to collective memories and the creation of norms, the latter in turn influences subsequent lawmaking and law enforcement. The cycle then continues—a phenomenon referred to as the recursivity of law.[1]

In this brief concluding chapter we reflect on some of our findings. However, the main purpose of this chapter is to locate our insights in a wider field, to ask what broader lessons we can take away from our examination. After all, while our case studies are few and deal with quite specific instances, legal cases against perpetrators of atrocities can be of many kinds and vary along several dimensions. Some of these we introduced at the outset (see table 1.1). Cases may be processed in different types of courts: domestic (for example, trials against Dirty War generals in Argentina), foreign (the Eichmann court in Jerusalem, Israel), or inter-

166

national (the International Military Tribunal in Nuremberg, Germany). These courts may be located in the country of which perpetrators are citizens (the Pol Pot trials in Cambodia) or abroad (the Balkan cases at the International Criminal Tribunal for the former Yugoslavia (ICTY) in The Hague, Netherlands).

Cases further differ in terms of the political context in which courts are sited and trials are held. We have argued that interventions in the context of regime continuity (for example, the United States) and regime change (such as in Germany) likely have different consequences. In addition, the nature of cases tried in court and of the convictions achieved differs across contexts and types of courts. Cases may address low-level, frontline perpetrators (for example, in the United States) or those at higher levels who bear ultimate responsibility (the former Yugoslavia, Iraq, or Argentina). They may involve individuals or collective actors, and they may hold responsible domestic or foreign perpetrators. These diverse contextual features of courts and cases are almost certainly consequential, and they are interrelated. Regime continuity, for example, more likely results in trials that implicate lower ranking personnel, as we have found for the United States; and the probability of intervention by international courts, especially when holding command-level officials accountable, is higher when smaller and weaker countries, as opposed to powerful ones, are accused of grave violations of humanitarian and human rights law.

Furthermore, depending on the nature of the political context, types of courts, and characteristics of cases, outcomes and impacts are also likely to differ. They too will vary along a number of dimensions, including the intensity of collective memory created by trials and the structure or shape of such memory that entails such specifics as the types of violent acts and characteristics of their perpetrators and victims. The characteristics of courts and cases, mediated by collective memory, are also likely to affect the chances of recurrence of grave human rights violations and the specific contours of future control mechanisms.

The larger field we consider is sketched out in table 10.1, which addresses two dimensions. One axis represents regime status; that is, did political institutions in place before the trial continue to dominate the state afterward, or was there significant regime change? The other axis breaks down the type of trial into three general categories: Was any criminal trial held at all in response to an atrocity, and if so, did domestic courts respond or were there foreign or international trials? We also mark those cases in which only low-level, frontline agents were prosecuted and high-level actors were spared.

Table 10.1 is not meant to be exhaustive; the approximately two dozen examples are primarily illustrative, and about half of them are discussed

Table 10.1   Regime Status and Type of Trial

	Type of Trial		
	None	Domestic Court	Foreign or International Court
Regime status			
Continuity	Slavery in the United States	*My Lai*	Balkans (early phase)
	Atrocities against Native Americans	*Haditha*	Sudan, Darfur
		Abu Ghraib	
	U.S. Internment of Japanese (World War II)		
	Stalinist purges		
	German genocide against Herero		
Change	Post-Communist Russia	Frankfurt Auschwitz trial	International Military Tribunal Nuremberg
	Armenian genocide	Iraq trials after Hussein's rule	Subsequent Nuremberg trials
		Argentina after Dirty War	Eichmann trial, Jerusalem
		Chile after Pinochet	Tokyo trial
			Rwanda trial
			Balkans (later phase)

Source: Authors' compilation.
Note: Entries in bold italic = trials in which only low-level, frontline agents were prosecuted. "Herero" refers to the German genocide against the Herero and Namaqua peoples in today's Namibia from 1904 to 1907. "Frankfurt Auschwitz trial" refers to the trials from 1963 to 1965 of staff of the Auschwitz concentration and extermination camp. "Sudan, Darfur" refers to prosecutions of President Omar al-Bashir of Sudan and others before the International Criminal Court.

in earlier chapters. The key point is that the table demarcates important dimensions of trials that are likely to have an impact on collective memory, even if indirectly. A few provisional conclusions reach beyond the specific empirical cases discussed in the preceding chapters. For one, table 10.1 indicates that cases followed by regime continuity are less likely to result in criminal trials than those involving regime change, a point we return to shortly. In addition, among cases with regime continuity in which trials did occur, low-level perpetrators appear concentrated in one particular cell: regime continuity combined with a domestic trial. Of the cases we selected, only the Frankfurt Auschwitz trial was preceded by regime change and held in a domestic court and involved the prosecution of relatively low-level perpetrators. In the German Nazi case, of course, many high-level perpetrators had previously been killed, committed suicide, escaped to foreign lands, or been tried by international courts and tribunals. Yet many mid-level perpetrators and some who had held high party and government offices continued living within German society without facing legal consequences. All trials held by international courts, before and after regime change, are at least also directed against high-level perpetrators with considerable command responsibility. The same might be said about the one example of a foreign trial of Nazi perpetrators, the trial against Adolf Eichmann before the Jerusalem court.

What, then, are the consequences of different types of responses for collective memory and cultural trauma? Before we address variations within the law–collective memory nexus, we first speak to the more fundamental distinction between cases in which atrocities resulted in trials and those with little or no legal recourse. Consider just the twentieth century, a period in which human rights laws were established and one that had already inherited the foundations of humanitarian law. Cases resulting in no trials include the slaughter in Namibia of some twenty-four thousand to seventy-five thousand members of the Herero tribe by German colonizers in 1904–1907.[2] While the Holocaust is vividly remembered in contemporary Germany, the genocide against the Herero in the former colony of South West Africa, committed just about three decades earlier, is barely known to any German today. Thus remembering is not simply in the nature of the German people. Although regime transitions typically facilitate commemoration, in the case of the Herero genocide memory did not set in even after the regime transition that followed just a decade later. It is likely instead that the lack of legal response in the Herero case, as opposed to the holding of trials against the Nazi perpetrators, contributes to this mnemonic difference.

Consider further the massive violation of human rights throughout the history of the Soviet Union, with its peak during the Stalinist regime, when tens of millions vanished in the Siberian camps. The perpetrators were never tried, and the atrocities are much less engraved in today's Russian collective memory than we might expect. Survey research in post-Soviet Russia shows that the Great Purge under Stalin is best remembered by those who lived through it. For later cohorts, researchers find evidence of a gradual loss of knowledge, a collective forgetting. Even glasnost, the policy of openness and transparency introduced by President Mikhail Gorbachev, was rather benign in this instance: "Neither distant family memories nor very recent revelations could provide the younger cohorts the same degree of knowledge possessed by older Russians" (Schuman and Corning 2000, 940).

We might also consider the case of the Armenian genocide perpetrated during World War I by the rulers and military of the Ottoman Empire, the predecessor of modern-day Turkey. Almost a million Armenians were slaughtered and thousands of women raped. Hundreds of thousands of victims endured grueling death marches from their homes into the desert, where they perished (a method of genocide similar to that used by the German colonizers against the Herero). This genocide did not at all go unnoticed abroad. Unlike the Holocaust, which reached public attention primarily after the war, the Armenian genocide drew media attention as it unfolded; 145 *New York Times* articles were published in 1915 alone. "On October 7, 1915, a *Times* headline blared, '800,000 ARMENIANS COUNTED DESTROYED'" (quoted in Power 2003, 9). Yet despite this attention abroad, in the absence of trials, atrocities like the Armenian genocide are unlikely to settle in the collective memory or take the shape of cultural trauma in the country of the perpetrators. Instead, they fall victim to collective amnesia.

Gary Bass (2000, 303), whose influential work on war crimes is briefly discussed in chapter 1, contrasts the Turkish case with that of Nazi Germany in his influential book *Stay the Hand of Vengeance.* "As the Constantinople prosecutions were collapsing, the British Foreign Office worried that the evidence of the court's files was disappearing. To this day, the Turkish government . . . goes to considerable lengths to deny the persecution of the Armenians. One cannot imagine Germany doing anything remotely like this, and Nuremberg is part of the reason."

We must be cautious not to attribute the nature of collective memory entirely to the presence or absence of criminal trials. A lack of court intervention correlates with other factors that would likely contribute to the collective forgetting of atrocities. For instance, in the Soviet Union, after Stalin's death and the demise of Stalinist doctrine in 1956, the Communist Party continued to rule the country with an iron fist. While the new rulers under Nikita Khrushchev sought to leave Stalinism behind, trials against its leading figures might have endangered the transition away from Stalinism or perhaps risked opening the dominant Communist Party to scrutiny from domestic or foreign audiences. Neither of these options was in the interest of Stalin's successors. Even the more recent end of the Soviet Union, which again was not accompanied by trials against perpetrators of grave human rights violations during decades of Communist rule, saw a continuity of personnel. For example, former president and now prime minister Vladimir Putin, himself a past member of the Communist Party, built his career in the much-feared secret service of the Soviet Union (the infamous KGB). Personnel continuity, even in the face of regime change, is a good foundation neither for the execution of trials nor for the cultiva-

tion of collective memories of past atrocities, be it through court intervention or other mechanisms.

In short, while the lack of legal response coincides with other factors
that contribute to the forgetting of grave violations of humanitarian and
human rights law, there is at least some indication that atrocities, when
not openly processed in courts of law, are more likely to result in a collective amnesia. It seems that such amnesia is one reason why criminal
trials accompanying regime change can mitigate later human rights violations.[3] However, the latter claim still remains subject to further empirical examination.

We now turn back to those cases in which courts did intervene. As
noted earlier in this chapter, legal intervention varies with respect to the
types and locations of courts, the political and social contexts in which
trials unfold, and the specific features of the cases in question. Where
along this complex set of dimensions do we find the cases examined in
our empirical chapters? What have we left out? What does the previous
literature say about the spaces in the field of inquiry that we did not
cover? What broader lessons might we draw?

Consider regime continuity versus regime change. As this volume
examines primarily American memories, we have largely dealt with conditions of regime continuity. For domestic cases, regime continuity is less
likely to result in trials, as the history of slavery and the near annihilation
of the Native American population show. No major trials were held
against the slave traders, the slaveholders, or those who committed atrocities against Native Americans. Indeed, in some cases law enabled these
episodes. We should caution, though, that these cruelties were perpetrated
at a time when legal responses to such outrages were practically unknown.
We can speak with greater confidence, however, about more recent occurrences. Where courts intervened in the post–World War II era, as in the
cases of My Lai, Haditha, and Abu Ghraib, they tended to address low-
ranking perpetrators. Higher ranks, those with substantial command
responsibility and political actors, are rarely charged and convicted.
Furthermore, for the frontline perpetrators who face charges, chances are
high that these charges will be dropped or their sentences commuted.
Where courts convict, the offenders' ranks tend to be even lower. This fun-
nel effect involves what appears to the public as the selection of low-level
scapegoats. Associated with it is a decoupling that exculpates those of
higher rank and entire organizations. This perception challenges the legitimacy of the legal process, as observed in both the My Lai and the Haditha
cases. To this end, even when courts sentence defendants to prison terms,
those sentences have a good chance of being commuted.

This pattern of selectively penalizing low-level perpetrators also has
consequences for collective memory. The My Lai massacre, which was

initially expected to leave an indelible mark on American identity, is not even mentioned in the majority of high school textbooks of subsequent decades. Most young people appear to be unaware of this atrocity. The intensity of memory is low—even if it might have been yet weaker in the complete absence of a trial. In addition, the structure of the memory, where it is preserved, reflects the narrative constructed in the court of law more closely than the journalistic and commission accounts; it is the low-level perpetrator who is remembered, not those of higher ranks who placed young soldiers in a situation in which "forward panics," with all their gruesome consequences, are likely to occur.[4] The lower number of killings charged (or the even lower number for which convictions were attained) is more likely to be referenced than the higher number cited in the journalistic and military commission reports. Furthermore, that part of the massacre for which evidence was most likely to carry weight in court is highlighted in textbooks and the media, not the spontaneous atrocities that were "just" backed up by high-quality journalistic and commission investigations. In addition, the cover-up by the army is barely mentioned. It may not be surprising, then, that the military continues to be among the most highly regarded institutions and the one in which Americans take most pride.

American memories, of course, also entail atrocities committed by non-Americans. The classic case is the Holocaust, the prime example of what Jeffrey Alexander calls "sacred evil" (2004a, 222). Such an evil is sacred because it cannot be surpassed, and the memory of it must not be profaned by comparing it to less horrendous occurrences. The Shoah indeed is nonetheless referred to when foreign atrocities and injustices are discussed, for example, in legislative debates and hearings on the issue of hate crime law. Moreover, the commemoration of the Holocaust is clearly associated with the enforcement of hate crime law in America, as documented in the previous chapter. What does this role of the Shoah tell us about the weight of legal proceedings? We can only speculate about the answer, but a few consequences seem likely. Obviously the Holocaust was unique in the way this genocide was methodically planned and executed. It is without precedent in human history, and that distinction alone would contribute to engraving it in a nation's collective memory.

Yet let us not forget that the Shoah was engraved in memory only with delay and not everywhere around the globe to the same degree.[5] Add to the uniqueness of the Shoah the fact that it was American soldiers and the American people who made great sacrifices to halt the murder and suffering. In light of the tendency of peoples and nations to celebrate their heroic deeds, this fact should further contribute to engraving the Holocaust in the American mind. The government's inaction in seeking to disrupt the annihilation, for example, its failure to bomb the known railway lines into the extermination camps, is barely present in the collective memory.

In addition to the role Americans played in ending the Holocaust through warfare, there is much reason to believe that the multitude of trials following the end of the Nazi regime contributed to solidifying the memories of the Holocaust in the American mind. This is even true for the International Military Tribunal, the primary focus of which was not the Holocaust but rather the conduct of aggressive war and war crimes. Yet the gruesome film depicting the state of the liberated camps was still shown at the trial, and references to the Holocaust were made repeatedly. In addition, the subsequent Nuremberg trials did address the Holocaust directly. Film depictions of these trials, most famously the 1963 Hollywood production *Judgment in Nuremberg*, played an additional role—even while this film strayed from the literal truth by dramatizing and merging events from distinct trials into one. It is at least likely that the intensity and structure of American memories of the Holocaust were affected by the trials and the ways in which these were reported and dramatized in the United States.

The horrors of the Balkan wars, the atrocities committed in their course, and the role President Slobodan Milosevic played in the unfolding of those crimes, of course, all pale when compared with the magnitude of the Holocaust. Yet here too unimaginable atrocities were committed; war crimes, crimes against humanity, and genocide were perpetrated. Also here, high-ranking leaders up to the level of the presidency were held legally responsible in an international court. This history may be too recent to determine how strong a mark it will leave on the American historical memory. Initial indications suggest, however, that here—as in the German case—the memory of a cruel leader and his followers will prevail. It is important to remember that such a collective memory was not a foregone conclusion. As shown in chapter 5, the depictions of Milosevic portrayed by diplomatic sources were quite different, and we cannot forget that Milosevic was presented quite differently when sharing the negotiation table in Dayton, Ohio, with Western leaders, including President Bill Clinton.

The symbolic force of law thus appears to influence American historical memories. We have not here examined the effect of the ICTY trials on the collective memory of Serbs, Milosevic's own people, or on the cultural trauma of the victims, most noteworthy the Bosnian Muslims. Other research suggests that international trials tend to create resentment, at least in those segments of the perpetrator group that—after long periods of exposure to their leaders' propaganda machine and motivated by lingering ideological or tribal loyalties—are most likely to continue to identify with them. Recent survey research shows that even the place of residency matters. Serbs in Belgrade, for example, insist that war criminals be tried in their places of origin; Serbs in Sarajevo and Vukovar—places hard hit by the war—instead believe that war criminals should be tried in places where they committed their crimes. They share this sentiment with other groups in the same locales.[6] In light of such data, an international court, and one in a distant land at that, is probably not the ideal setting for achieving legitimacy and influencing collective memories. Yet conducting trials in the country of the perpetrators, especially shortly after transitions, may present considerable practical challenges. Exceptions are situations of total defeat followed by regime change, as in Nuremberg or Tokyo. More data are needed before conclusions can be drawn. After all, when one takes a longer historical view, the legal pursuit of grave humanitarian law and human rights violations is a fairly recent invention.[7]

While the ICTY trials constitute rather recent history, half a century has passed since most of the Holocaust trials were held, and hence there has been much more time to observe the consequences. For this reason we turn our discussion back to the Shoah one more time. Trials following the Holocaust were indeed numerous, including an early post–World War II trial against participants in the "euthanasia" program at the Hadamar state sanatorium for the mentally ill; early U.S. Army war crimes trials held at the former Dachau concentration camp against 1,676 "lesser war criminals;" the International Military Tribunal and the subsequent American-held Nuremberg trials, including the famous lawyers' and doctors' trials; a British trial against offenders of the medical experimentations at the Ravensbrück concentration camp; a Soviet trial against offenders from the Sachsenhausen concentration camp near Berlin; and subsequent proceedings in both West and East Germany. All of this has been thoroughly researched, most recently documented in an edited volume published in association with the U.S. Holocaust Memorial Museum.[8]

Historians of post-Nazi Germany, many of whom are cited in this volume, are generally critical of the abstention from prosecution in too many cases.[9] They also challenge the ways in which trials were conducted, and they consider the punishments meted out to have been far too lenient, especially—but not exclusively—in the case of domestic trials. These historians cite diverse reasons for inadequacies in punishment, including the Allies' postwar policy goals, especially the delegitimization of the Nazi regime and attempts at the democratization of the German public (hence the focus on a relatively small number of Nazi leaders and the classification of many perpetrators as auxiliaries).[10]

In those trials in which top-level actors are selectively prosecuted by the international courts, one goal in selecting leaders as culprits is to delegitimize the regime over which they had presided. In the German case, this was simultaneously accompanied by the goal of decoupling the large majority of Germans from the attribution of guilt and transforming them into a democratic people. The pressure to follow this strategy grew with the beginning signs of the imminent Cold War between the U.S.-led West and the USSR-dominated East. Such selective prosecution made it easier for Germans to attribute guilt to the leaders of the Nazi state and to absolve themselves. Thus regime status is not the only crucial contextual factor for criminal trials. Other strategic, political, and geopolitical factors are also critical. They affect the type of trials likely to take place and their consequences.

One account, provided by the Canadian Holocaust historian Michael Marrus on the doctors' trial, one of the subsequent Nuremberg trials, is especially instructive.[11] Marrus argues that U.S. war crimes policy resulted in a fundamental distortion of the history of medical crimes committed under Nazism. The focus on leading perpetrators made doctors appear as members of a criminal conspiracy rather than as individuals sharing a firmly rooted common ideology. Attention was shifted away from the medical origins of medical crimes, and the affinity between medical ideas and Nazi ideology was missed. Furthermore, because of the nature of law, the trial focused on the war period alone and considered only non-German victims. This resulted in an almost exclusive focus on the gruesome and absurd medical experiments conducted in concentration camps while missing the systematic sterilization campaign that began soon after the Nazi takeover of Germany and produced four hundred thousand sterilizations of German women by 1945. Given the law's focus, the horror and degree of euthanasia programs was also underestimated.

While critical of the contours of collective memory fostered by the doctors' trial, Marrus nonetheless argues that the trial contributed to creating memories of atrocities and engraving them in the collective mind. These memories certainly serve to thoroughly delegitimize the Nazi regime and its worst outrages—even if they neglect other evil acts committed at the time. Marrus's position is supported by many historians, even in the face of cautionary notes. For example, while trials do tell history, the history of trials may, in reverse, be rewritten in light of changing political objectives or new definitions of past atrocities. One powerful example for this argument is the memory of the International Military Tribunal, which had not focused on the Judeocide, despite later beliefs to the contrary.[12] This belief emerged only when the Shoah became established as cultural trauma. Obviously this is a note on the presentist nature of the historical memory of trials, something Maurice Halbwachs (1992) might have anticipated. Memories of trials are subject to the same sociopolitical pressures as the history to whose construction they contribute.

Table 10.2 replicates the dimensions presented at the outset of this chapter, mapping regime status against the type of trial. But here we apply our

Table 10.2   Intensity of Collective Memory, by Regime Status and Type of Trial

	Type of Trial		
	None	Domestic Court	Foreign or International Court
Regime status			

Continuity	*Slavery in America*
	Atrocities against
	  Native Americans
	U.S. internment of
	  Japanese (World
	  War II)
	Stalinist purges
	German genocide
	  against Herero
		My Lai
		Haditha
		Abu Ghraib
			Balkans (early
			  phase)
			Sudan, Darfur

Change	Post-Communist
	  Russia
	Armenian
	  genocide[a]
		Frankfurt
		  Auschwitz trial
		Iraq trials after
		  Hussein's rule
		Argentina after
		  Dirty War
		Chile after
		  Pinochet
			International
			  Military
			  Tribunal,
			  Nuremberg
			Subsequent
			  Nuremberg trials
			Eichmann trial,
			  Jerusalem
			Tokyo trial
			Rwanda trial
			Balkans (later
			  phase)

Source: Authors' compilation.
Note: Entries in bold and italics = intense and unified acknowledgment or memory; entries in italics = struggle over acknowledgment or memory; normal font = weak memories. "Herero" refers to the German genocide against the Herero and Namaqua peoples in today's Namibia from 1904 to 1907. "Frankfurt Auschwitz trial" refers to the trials from 1963 to 1965 of staff of the Auschwitz concentration and extermination camp. "Sudan, Darfur" refers to prosecutions of President Omar al-Bashir of Sudan and others before the International Criminal Court.
[a]Trials attempted but aborted.

typology to the intensity of collective memories. Using our two dimensions to predict the intensity of memory is admittedly more complex and perhaps more prone to error because collective memories for several of these cases have not been fully studied and in some cases remain in flux.

A first glance at table 10.2 again suggests a fairly clear pattern. Cases that did not result in criminal trials, with or without regime continuity, show weak or contested memories. This is most clearly illustrated by the USSR in the post-Stalinist era and in the case of the German genocide against the Herero during the initial regime stability of the German Empire and after subsequent regime changes alike. The same holds for the case of the United States. Some readers might challenge our marking of those dark chapters of American history that did not result in trials as not having culminated in a unified and acknowledged collective memory. Yet we feel justified when making this assertion in light of several insights gained from prior scholarship and cited in earlier chapters. The atrocities against Native Americans are a firm component of contemporary history textbooks. Barely any American would doubt them. The slaughter of Native Americans is also no longer casually shown in Hollywood productions, as was the case into the 1950s. However, the National Museum of the American Indian on the Washington Mall makes few noticeable references to the suffering of Native American peoples. No national memorial day commemorates the eradication of the original American population, nothing akin to the day commemorating the German Reichspogromnacht (table 6.1).

Even for the case of slavery, the national mall in Washington seeks to uphold the sanitized view of American history. It does so despite the acknowledgement of slavery elsewhere, especially in a new genre of black history museums in America's inner cities with predominantly African American populations.[13] We have also found that the commemoration of Martin Luther King Jr., the great civil rights leader, is only weakly associated with the enforcement of hate crime law when compared with the rhetorical power of Holocaust memorials, alerting us to the ritualized and ceremonial ways in which he is remembered. Again, our point is not that slavery is absent in American collective memory but that the issue of culpability and its continuing significance remains sharply debated.[14] In short, it is not deeply entrenched in the American historical consciousness (as demonstrated in chapter 7).

We also see that regime continuity in combination with domestic trials—typically associated with a focus on low-level perpetrators—is not associated with strong collective memories. We have diagnosed the weak representation of My Lai in history textbooks, and there is no reason to expect a different outcome for Haditha or Abu Ghraib. Here the consequences of shaky collective memories are also on full display. There is much reason to speculate that they affect Americans' extraordinary pride in their military; strong public and congressional support for presidents who engage in warfare; and the expressed willingness of soldiers to break international and military law, at least under extreme situations.[15] Regime continuity in combination with international trials, however, is typically associated with the prosecution of high-level perpetrators. It is also often accompanied by deep division between segments of the population that represent the perpetrator and victim groups, such as Serbs and Bosnian Muslims in the Balkans or Arabs and black African tribal groups in the Sudan. It is no wonder that intense struggles emerge on how atrocities ought to be remembered under these circumstances.

Finally, cases of atrocities that are followed by regime change and are tried in domestic or in international courts leave intense collective memories of past grave violations of humanitarian and human rights law. This is easiest to explain in cases in which trials were also accompanied by truth commissions, as was nearly always the case in South America.[16] This pattern may also be easy to explain where trials were many and of diverse kinds and where they were a reaction to the greatest imaginable atrocities, as was the case in post-Nazi Germany. But the Balkan case, like the Rwandan genocide, also indicates that trials instill a sense of outrage in the victims' collective memory of the perpetrators.

The collective memory function may indeed play a major role in explaining why court intervention in the wake of atrocities is associated with improved democracy and human rights records.[17] Empirically, closing this loop is admittedly quite difficult. Nevertheless, we see tremendous continuity between our results—including the typologies in tables 10.1 and 10.2—and recent work focusing on human rights violations and the rule of law after criminal trials or tribunals. We have argued, for instance, that trials matter for collective memory but very little in cases of domestic trials and regime continuity, where low-level culprits tend to be selected for prosecution. We also think that trials have greater impact in the context of regime change, be they domestic, international, or foreign trials. This typology for the association between collective memory and trials nicely maps onto prior research on the aftermath of major human rights trials.

We have already noted that Kathryn Sikkink and her colleagues, not unlike Gary Bass in his work, find that trials matter because they reduce subsequent human rights violations (in line with our position that trials matter for collective memory). Focusing on domestic trials in transitional countries, Sikkink and colleagues find this to be highly consistent in South America (in line with our point about the greater impact of trials in the context of regime change). We suspect that collective memory or cultural trauma fills at least part of the black box—that is, the mechanisms that allow for a peaceful transition—in explanatory schemas that lead from judicial intervention to improvements in human rights, the rule of law, and democratic functioning (see figure 1.1). They do so even if trials soften the depiction of atrocities owing to the law's institutional logic, such as the tendency to focus on particular individuals instead of institutions and collectivities. Our analyses indicate that this transmission function of collective memory works especially well when leaders with high-level command responsibility are held criminally responsible for past atrocities.

What does this mean for Americans, on whose collective memory we have focused, and for their country? The United States is still the most powerful nation in the world. Its leaders command the largest and most potent military force. Its actions have serious consequences across the globe. It is a democracy, and collective memories held by Americans matter for what its leaders decide. In light of our findings, one condition is crucial for the sake of peaceful conflict resolutions, or at least for interventions that cost fewer lives, including lives of civilians: that actors in high-level command positions face legal responsibility when soldiers under their command (or hired guns under their administration) engage in war crimes, torture, or other crimes against humanity. Instead, however, impunity has prevailed in the past, with problematic consequences. This book also indicates, unfortunately, that threats of criminal liability are unlikely to originate from within the American government. If our hate crime enforcement work provides any guidance, then civil society groups, most likely ones that in some way identify with the victims of violence, would have to mobilize to overcome the impunity of those responsible at higher ranks. Such engagement would honor the memory of Maurice Halbwachs and his insight that interested actors need to get engaged to shape memory. Clearly, Americans should be able to learn from our findings about American memories and the law. Doing so would, we believe, advance the common good of the United States as well as global peace and stability.

Appendix A

History Textbooks Used in My Lai Content Analysis

Appleby, Joyce, Alan Brinkley, Albert S. Broussard, James M. McPherson, Donald A. Ritchie, and National Geographic Society. 2005. *The American Republic Since 1877.* Teacher ed. New York: Glencoe/McGraw-Hill.

Appleby, Joyce, Alan Brinkley, James M. McPherson, and National Geographic Society. 2003. *The American Journey.* Teacher's ed. New York: Glencoe/McGraw-Hill.

Appleby, Joyce, James M. McPherson, Alan Brinkley, and National Geographic Society. 1998. *The American Journey.* Student ed. New York: Glencoe/McGraw-Hill.

Ayers, Edward L., Robert D. Schulzinger, Jesus F. de la Teja, and Deborah Gray White. 2007. *American Anthem.* Teacher's ed. Austin, Tex.: Holt, Rinehart and Winston.

Bailey, Thomas A., ed. 1973. *The American Spirit: United States History as Seen by Contemporaries.* Vol. 2. Lexington, Mass.: Heath.

Bailey, Thomas A., and David M. Kennedy. 1983. *The American Pageant: A History of the Republic.* 7th ed. Lexington, Mass.: Heath.

Bailey, Thomas A., David M. Kennedy, and Lizabeth Cohen. 1998. *The American Pageant.* 11th ed. Boston: Houghton Mifflin.

Bartlett, Irving, Edwin Fenton, David Fowler, and Seymour Mandelbaum. 1975. *A New History of the United States: An Inquiry Approach.* New York: Holt, Rinehart and Winston.

Bauer, Nancy W. 1979. *The American Way.* Annotated teacher's ed. New York: Holt, Rinehart and Winston.

Berkin, Carol, and Leonard Wood. 1987. *Land of Promise: A History of the United States.* 2nd ed. Glenview, Ill.: Scott Foresman.

Blum, John M., William S. McFeely, Edmund S. Morgan, Arthur M. Schlesinger Jr., Kenneth M. Stampp, and C. Vann Woodward. 1989. *The National Experience: A History of the United States.* 7th ed. San Diego: Harcourt Brace Jovanovich.

Blum, John M., Edmund S. Morgan, Willie Lee Rose, Arthur M. Schlesinger Jr., Kenneth M. Stampp, and C. Vann Woodward. 1977. *The National Experience: A History of the United States Since 1865.* 4th ed. New York: Harcourt Brace Jovanovich.

Boorstin, Daniel J., and Brooks Mather Kelley. 1983. *A History of the United States.* Edited by Ruth Frankel Boorstin. Annotated teacher's ed. Lexington, Mass.: Ginn.

Boorstin, Daniel J., Brooks Mather Kelley, and Ruth Frankel Boorstin. 1992. *A History of the United States.* Needham, Mass.: Prentice Hall.

———. 2002. *A History of the United States.* Annotated teacher's ed. Needham, Mass.: Prentice Hall.

Borden, Morton, Otis L. Graham, Jr., Roderick W. Nash, and Richard E. Oglesby. 1970. *The American Profile.* Lexington, Mass.: Heath.

Boyer, Paul. 1998. *Boyer's The American Nation.* Annotated teacher's ed. Orlando, Fla.: Holt, Rinehart and Winston.

———. 2001. *Boyer's The American Nation.* Annotated teacher's ed. Austin, Tex.: Holt, Rinehart and Winston.

Bragdon, Henry W., Samuel P. McCutchen, and Charles W. Cole. 1973. *History of a Free People.* New York: Macmillan.

Bragdon, Henry W., Samuel P. McCutchen, and Donald A. Ritchie. 1992. *History of a Free Nation.* Teacher's ed. Lake Forest, Ill.: Glencoe/Macmillan/McGraw-Hill.

Brandwein, Paul, Nancy W. Bauer, and Susan R. Roop. 1980. *The United States: Living in Our World.* Teacher's ed. New York: Harcourt Brace Jovanovich.

Branson, Margaret. 1986. *America's Heritage.* Lexington, Mass.: Ginn.

Branson, Margaret Stimmann. 1975. *Land of Challenge.* Teacher guide. Lexington, Mass.: Ginn.

Brown, Richard C., and Herbert J. Bass. 1986. *One Flag, One Land: From Reconstruction to the Present.* Annotated teacher's ed. Morristown, N.J.: Silver Burdett.

Bulliet, Richard W., Pamela Kyle Crossley, Daniel R. Headrick, Steven W. Hirsch, Lyman L. Johnson, and David Northrup. 2009. *The Earth and Its Peoples: A Global History.* Brief 4th ed. Princeton, N.J.: Houghton Mifflin.

Burns, Robert E., Lee R. Boyer, James R. Felton, Philip Gleason, John J. Lyon, James E. O'Neill, and Charles J. Tull. 1973. *Episodes in American History: An Inquiry Approach.* Lexington, Mass.: Ginn.

Carnes, Mark C., and John Garraty. 2003. *The American Nation: A History of the United States.* 11th ed. New York: Longman.

Cayton, Andrew. 2000. *America: Pathways to the Present.* Teacher's ed. Needham, Mass.: Prentice Hall.

Cayton, Andrew, Elisabeth Israels Perry, and Allan M. Winkler. 1995. *America: Pathways to the Present.* Teacher's ed. Needham, Mass.: Prentice Hall.

Chapin, June R., Raymond J. McHugh, and Richard E. Gross. 1971. *Quest for Liberty: Investigating United States History.* Teacher's manual. San Francisco: Field Educational Publications.

Conlin, Joseph R. 1985. *Our Land, Our Time: A History of the United States.* Annotated teacher's ed. San Diego: Coronado Publishers.

Current, Richard N., Alexander DeConde, and Harris L. Dante. 1974. *United States History: Search for Freedom.* Glenview, Ill.: Scott Foresman.

Current, Richard N., T. Harry Williams, Frank Freidel, and Alan Brinkley. 1983. *American History: A Survey.* Vol. 2, *Since 1865.* 6th ed. New York: Knopf.

Danzer, Gerald, J. Jorge Klor de Alva, Larry S. Krieger, Louis E. Wilson, and Nancy Woloch. 1998. *The Americans.* Evanston, Ill.: McDougal Littell/Houghton Mifflin.

———. 2003. *The Americans.* Teacher's ed. Evanston, Ill.: McDougal Littell.

Davidson, James. 2000. *The American Nation.* Teacher's ed. Upper Saddle River, N.J.: Prentice Hall.

Davidson, James West, and John E. Batchelor. 1986. *The American Nation.* Annotated teacher's ed. Englewood Cliffs, N.J.: Prentice Hall.

Davidson, James West, and Mark H. Lytle. 1988. *The United States: A History of the Republic.* 4th ed. Annotated teacher's ed. Englewood Cliffs, N.J.: Prentice Hall.

———. 1990. *The United States: A History of the Republic.* 5th ed. Englewood Cliffs, N.J.: Prentice Hall.

Davidson, James West, and Michael B. Stoff. 1995. *The American Nation.* Englewood Cliffs, N.J.: Prentice Hall.

Dempsey, Joseph H., Herbert J. Bass, George A. Billias, and Emma Jones Lapsansky. 1979. *Our American Heritage.* Teacher's ed. Morristown, N.J.: Silver Burdett.

Divine, Robert A., T. H. Breen, George M. Fredrickson, and R. Hal Williams. 1999. *America, Past and Present.* 5th ed. New York: Longman.

Divine, Robert A., T. H. Breen, George M. Fredrickson, R. Hal Williams, Ariela J. Gross, and H. W. Brands. 2005. *America, Past and Present.* 7th ed. New York: Pearson Longman.

Drewry, Henry N., Thomas H. O'Connor, and Frank Freidel. 1984. *America Is.* 3rd ed. Columbus, Ohio: C. E. Merrill.

Eibling, Harold H., Carlton Jackson, and Vito Perrone. 1973. *Challenge and Change: United States History, the Second Century.* River Forest, Ill.: Laidlaw Bros.

Faragher, John Mack, Mary Jo Buhle, Daniel Czitrom, and Susan H. Armitage. 1994. *Out of Many: A History of the American People.* Combined ed. Englewood Cliffs, N.J.: Prentice Hall.

Garcia, Jesus, Donna M. Ogle, C. Frederick Risinger, and Joyce Stevos. 2005. *Creating America: A History of the United States, 1877 to the 21st Century.* Evanston, Ill.: McDougal Littell.

Garraty, John, and Mark C. Carnes. 2001. *A Short History of the American Nation.* 8th ed. New York: Longman.

Garraty, John A., Aaron Singer, and Michael J. Gallagher. 1982. *American History.* New York: Harcourt Brace Jovanovich.

Graff, Henry F. 1985. *America, the Glorious Republic.* Boston: Houghton Mifflin.

———. 1977. *The Free and the Brave.* Annotated teacher's ed. Chicago: Rand McNally.

Graff, Henry F., and John A. Krout. 1970. *The Adventure of the American People.* 2nd ed: Annotated teacher's ed. Chicago: Rand McNally.

Green, Robert P., Jr., Laura L. Becker, and Robert E. Coviello. 1986. *The American Tradition: A History of the United States.* Annotated teacher's ed. Columbus, Ohio: Merrill.

Hart, Diane, and David Baker. 1987. *Spirit of Liberty: An American History.* Annotated teacher's ed. Menlo Park, Calif.: Addison-Wesley.

Jordan, Winthrop D., Miriam Goldbatt, and John S. Bowles. 1985. *The Americans: The History of a People and a Nation.* Evanston, Ill.: McDougal Littell.

Kagan, Donald, Steven Ozment, and Frank M. Turner. 2001. *The Western Heritage.* 7th ed. Upper Saddle River, N.J.: Prentice Hall.

Kennedy, David M., Lizabeth Cohen, and Thomas A. Bailey. 2002. *The American Pageant: A History of the Republic.* 12th ed. Boston: Houghton Mifflin.

King, David C., and Charlotte C. Anderson. 1976. *Windows on Our World: The United States.* Edited by Lee Anderson. Annotated teacher's ed. Boston: Houghton Mifflin.

King, David C., Norman McRae, and Jaye Zola. 1995. *The United States and Its People.* Menlo Park, Calif.: Addison-Wesley.

Kolevzon, Edward R. 1978. *The Afro-Asian World: A Cultural Understanding.* Boston: Allyn and Bacon.

Kownslar, Allan O., and William R. Felder. 1972. *Inquiring About American History: Studies in History and Political Science.* New York: Holt, Rinehart and Winston.

Kownslar, Allan O., and Donald B. Frizzle. 1970. *Discovering American History.* New York: Holt, Rinehart and Winston.

LaRaus, Roger, Harry P. Morris, and Robert Sobel. 1990. *Challenge of Freedom.* 3rd ed. Mission Hills, Calif.: Glencoe.

Leinwand, Gerald. 1975. *The Pageant of American History.* Boston: Allyn and Bacon.

Linden, Glenn M., Dean C. Brink, and Richard H. Huntington. 1986. *Legacy of Freedom: A History of the United States.* Teacher's ed. River Forest, Ill.: Laidlaw Brothers.

Lippe, Paul. 1972. *The World in Our Day.* New ed. New York: Oxford Book Company.

Madgic, Robert F., Stanley S. Seaberg, Fred H. Stopsky, and Robin W. Winks. 1971. *The American Experience: A Study of Themes and Issues in American History.* Menlo Park, Calif.: Addison-Wesley.

Maier, Pauline. 1986. *The American People: A History.* Annotated teacher's ed. Lexington, Mass.: Heath.

May, Ernest. 1985. *A Proud Nation.* Teacher's ed. Evanston, Ill.: McDougal Littell.

Myers, Peter J. 1999. *United States History.* Upper Saddle River, N.J.: Globe Fearon.

Nash, Gary. 2004. *American Odyssey: The 20th Century and Beyond.* Teacher's ed. New York: Glencoe.

———. 1994. *American Odyssey: The United States in the Twentieth Century.* Teacher's ed., multimedia ed. New York: Glencoe/McGraw-Hill.

Nash, Gary B., and Julie Roy Jeffrey. 2001. *The American People: Creating a Nation and a Society.* Vol. 2, *From 1865.* 5th ed. New York: Longman.

Norton, Mary Beth, David M. Katzman, Paul D. Escott, Howard P. Chudacoff, Thomas G. Paterson, William M. Tuttle Jr., and William J. Brophy. 1988. *A People and a Nation: A History of the United States.* 2nd ed. Boston: Houghton Mifflin.

Peck, Ira, Steven Jantzen, and Daniel Rosen. 1987. *American Adventures.* 2nd ed. Austin, Tex.: Steck-Vaughn.

Ralston, Leonard F., and Harold H. Negley. 1973. *The Search for Freedom: Basic American History.* Philadelphia: Lippincott.

Rawls, James J., and Philip Weeks. 1985. *Land of Liberty: A United States History.* New York: Holt, Rinehart and Winston.

Reich, Jerome R., Arvarh E. Strickland, and Edward L. Biller. 1971. *Building the United States.* New ed. New York: Harcourt Brace Jovanovich.

———. 1971. *Teacher's Manual and Resource Guide for Use with "Building the United States."* New ed. New York: Harcourt Brace Jovanovich.

Risjord, Norman K., and Terry L. Haywoode. 1978. *People and Our Country.* New York: Holt, Rinehart and Winston.

———. 1982. *People and Our Country.* New York: Holt, Rinehart and Winston.

Ritchie, Donald A. 1999. *American History: The Modern Era Since 1865.* Teacher's ed. New York: Glencoe/McGraw-Hill.

———. 1985. *Heritage of Freedom: History of the United States.* New York: Macmillan.

Roden, Philip, Robynn L. Greer, Bruce Kraig, and Betty M. Bivins. 1984. *Life and Liberty: An American History.* Glenview, Ill.: Scott Foresman.

Sandler, Martin W., Edwin C. Rozwenc, and Edward C. Martin. 1971. *The People Make a Nation.* Boston: Allyn and Bacon.

Schwartz, Melvin, and John R. O'Connor. 1981. *The New "Exploring American History."* New York: Globe.

Schwartz, Sidney, and John R. O'Connor. 1979. *The New "Exploring Our Nation's History."* New York: Globe.

Sellers, Charles G., Henry Mayer, Edward L. Paynter, Alexander Saxton, Neil L. Shumsky, and Kent Smith. 1975. *As It Happened: A History of the United States.* Annotated teacher's ed. New York: Webster Division, McGraw-Hill.

Smith, Lew. 1977. *The American Dream.* Dallas, Tex.: Scott Foresman.

Sobel, Robert, Roger LaRaus, Linda Ann De Leon, and Harry P. Morris. 1982. *The Challenge of Freedom.* Teacher's ed. River Forest, Ill.: Laidlaw Bros.

Stuckey, Sterling, and Linda Kerrigan Salvucci. 2003. *Call to Freedom: 1865 to the Present.* Annotated teacher's ed. Austin, Tex.: Holt, Rinehart and Winston.

Todd, Lewis Paul, and Merle Curti. 1982. *Rise of the American Nation.* Liberty ed. New York: Harcourt Brace Jovanovich.

———. 1986. *Triumph of the American Nation.* Annotated teacher's ed. Orlando, Fla.: Harcourt Brace Jovanovich.

Unger, Irwin, and H. Mark Johnson. 1975. *Land of Progress: Teacher's Guide.* Annotated ed. Lexington, Mass.: Ginn.

Ver Steeg, Clarence L. 1985. *American Spirit: A History of the United States.* Boston: Allyn and Bacon.

Ver Steeg, Clarence L., and Richard Hofstadter. 1977. *A People and a Nation.* New York: Harper and Row.

Weinstein, Allen, and David Rubel. 2002. *The Story of America: Freedom and Crisis from Settlement to Superpower.* New York: DK Publishing.

Weinstein, Allen, and R. Jackson Wilson. 1978. *Freedom and Crisis: An American History.* Vol. 2, *Since 1860.* 2nd ed. New York: Random House.

Wickens, James F. 1973. *Highlights of American History: Glimpses of the Past.* Vol. 2. Chicago: Rand McNally.

Wilder, Howard B., Robert P. Ludlum, and Harriett McCune Brown. 1970. *This Is America's Story.* Edited by Howard R. Anderson. 3rd ed. New York: Houghton Mifflin.

———. 1983. *This Is America's Story.* 5th ed. Boston: Houghton Mifflin.

Wilz, John. 1978. *The Search for Identity: Modern American History.* Philadelphia, Pa.: Lippincott.

Wood, Leonard C., Ralph H. Gabriel, and Edward L. Biller. 1979. *America: Its People and Values.* 2nd ed. New York: Harcourt Brace Jovanovich.

Wood, Leonard, Philip A. Roden, Sandra S. Deines, William Siavelis, Mike Campbell, William C. Hardt, and Ray Miller. 1995. *American Voices: A History of the United States, 1865 to the Present.* Annotated teacher's ed. Glenview, Ill.: Scott Foresman.

═ Appendix B ═

Detailed Tables on Coverage of Milosevic

Table B.1   Sampled Articles, by Stage and Content

	Stage 1 (Three Years)	Stage 2 (Eight Years)	Stage 3 (Two Years)	Stage 4 (Five Years)	Total (Eighteen Years)
Number of articles	9 (3)	72 (9)	29 (14.5)	42 (8.4)	152 (8.44)
Front-page articles	2 (0.67)	16 (2)	7 (3.5)	5 (1)	30 (1.67)
Suffering mentioned	0 (0)	34 (4.25)	9 (4.5)	15 (3)	58 (3.22)
Injury	0 (0)	8 (1)	1 (0.5)	0 (0)	9 (0.5)
Rape	0 (0)	1 (0.125)	1(0.5)	0 (0)	2 (0.11)
Killing	0 (0)	33 (4.125)	5 (2.5)	15 (3)	53 (2.94)
Refugees	0 (0)	6 (0.75)	4 (2)	7 (1.4)	17 (0.94)

Source: Authors' compilation of information from *New York Times* articles about Slobodan Milosevic.

Note: Average number of articles per year in parentheses. Values under "suffering mentioned" do not add up to category totals because articles can mention more than one type of suffering.

Table B.2   Public Statements about Slobodan Milosevic, by Stage

	Stage 1 (Three Years)	Stage 2 (Eight Years)	Stage 3 (Two Years)	Stage 4 (Five Years)	Total (Eighteen Years)
Action by Milosevic	22 (7.33)	224 (28)	60 (30)	198 (39.6)	504 (28)
Journalist	12 (4)	98 (12.25)	19 (9.5)	78 (15.6)	207 (11.5)
Milosevic and representatives	3 (1)	25 (3.125)	12 (6)	73 (14.6)	113 (6.28)
Diplomats	0 (0)	30 (3.75)	1 (0.5)	1 (0.2)	32 (1.78)
Judicial (ICTY/Court)	0 (0)	1 (0.125)	0 (0)	21 (4.2)	22 (1.22)
Western governments	0 (0)	28 (3.5)	8 (4)	2 (0.4)	38 (2.11)
Other	7 (2.33)	42 (5.25)	20 (10)	23 (4.6)	92 (5.11)
Action at Milosevic	0 (0)	73 (9.125)	61 (30.5)	76 (15.2)	210 (11.67)
Journalist	0 (0)	21 (2.625)	24 (12)	56 (11.2)	101 (5.61)
Milosevic and representatives	0 (0)	0 (0)	0 (0)	0 (0)	0 (0)
Diplomats	0 (0)	6 (0.75)	0 (0)	0 (0)	6 (0.33)
Judicial (ICTY/Court)	0 (0)	1 (0.125)	1 (0.5)	9 (1.8)	11 (0.61)
Western governments	0 (0)	31 (3.875)	18 (9)	3 (0.6)	52 (2.89)
Other	0 (0)	14 (1.75)	18 (9)	8 (1.6)	40 (2.22)

Source: Authors' compilation of information from *New York Times* articles about Slobodan Milosevic.
Note: Average number of articles per year in parentheses. ICTY = International Criminal Tribunal for the former Yugoslavia.

═ Notes ═

Introduction

1. For instance, even British officials who initially questioned the Nuremberg tribunals conceded that the historical record would indeed be useful. Among the voices acknowledging the importance of the historical record was Ernest Pollock, Britain's solicitor general after World War I (Bass 2000, 302). On a related note, we might understand Roosevelt's and his allies' motivation and ultimately the Nuremberg tribunal itself as exemplifying Halbwachs's (1992) presentist perspective on the construction of collective memory. That is, the historical account of Nazi atrocities was articulated in a manner that suited the political interests of present-day actors.

2. By cycles of violence we mean reactions to acts of violence that themselves provoke future violent retaliation. This theme is prominently explored in the work of Minow (1998, 2002).

Chapter 1

1. A massive 2010 exhibit on the life and memory of Napoleon, displayed in the German Bundeskunsthalle (Federal Art Hall) in Bonn, shows impressively and—at times—gruesomely how the glorification of Napoleon in the early decades of the nineteenth century (even to some degree in occupied lands) gave way, as early as 1810, to a dark view and haunting memories of the suffering, destruction, and loss of human lives. The number of 2 million soldiers killed in the Napoleonic wars is cited and extrapolated in proportion to today's European population counts. Artwork and poetry by Francesco Goya, Heinrich Heine, and others reflect the misery, capture it symbolically, and pass it on to future generations (Kunst- und Ausstellungshalle der Bundesrepublik Deutschland 2010).

2. See Robin Wagner-Pacifici (2005, 147), who uses this story as a powerful illustration of the genealogy of surrenders.

3. See, by contrast, Jürgen Matthäus (2008) on the aborted attempts at trials against German leaders following World War I.

4. Bass (2000, 295).

5. See Cohen (2001) on states of denial.

6. Hayner (2001).

7. See T. Smith (2009); for details, see chap. 3 of this volume.

8. For skeptics, see, for example, Goldsmith and Krasner (2003); also Snyder and Vinjamuri (2003–2004) with more empirical evidence; see Pensky (2008) for a more differentiated approach. For proponents of intervention, see, for example, Teitel (2000); Sikkink and Walling (2007); Kim and Sikkink (2010); Sikkink (2011); for a related empirical study with similar findings, see Olsen, Payne, and Reiter (2010).

9. Goldsmith and Krasner (2003).

10. See Hagan (2003, 165).

11. Sikkink here refers to trials and other mechanisms in the rule-of-law tradition (see Sikkink 2011; Sikkink and Walling 2007; Kim and Sikkink 2010). It should be mentioned that Joseph Stalin was the first to suggest trials to prosecute Nazi perpetrators. But Stalin had the kind of deadly show trials in mind that his regime had applied to thousands of those accused of opposing his rule. Stalin's model was obviously not implemented at Nuremberg.

12. See Sikkink and Walling (2007); Kim and Sikkink (2010); Sikkink (2011); for a related empirical study with similar findings, see Olsen, Payne, and Reiter (2010). The relationship between trials and improved human rights outcomes identified here is not tautological, as the measures for democracy and human rights records concern the posttransition period (that is, after transitional justice had run its course), even if questions about causality remain.

13. See Bass (2000, 286–304).

14. In some cases the amount of information produced can be truly extraordinary. After Nuremberg, six freight cars were needed to haul the Schutzstaffel (SS) files alone. Justice Jackson reportedly told President Truman that the record assembled at Nuremberg exceeded 5 million pages (Bass 2000, 302).

15. Unlike Bass (2000), whose work we regard as authoritative on the topic of war crimes tribunals, we emphasize some of the unique aspects of trials that may affect their ability to "write the record of history," as many have claimed with Nuremberg. We elaborate on this later, but to name just a few: (1) Trials have rules of evidence to which historians are not beholden; (2) trials are dependent on the testimony of survivors; (3) who is conducting the trial (a domestic court? an international tribunal?) matters; and (4) who is charged matters. Finally, following Halbwachs, (5) some aspects of the truth are subjective and dependent on power struggles that occur after an event transpires.

16. See Greenberg and Dratel (2005) on the "torture papers" and Stewart (2006) on the promise of legal charges against the president.

17. On the doctors trial, see Marrus (2008); on other post-Nazism trials, further contributions to the volume in which this chapter appeared (Heberer and

Matthäus 2008) are also instructive; on the South African Truth and Reconciliation Commission, see Gibson (2004a, 2004b, 2006); on the role of law and memory more broadly, see Bass (2000, 304).

18. While we discuss the literature from which these insights are drawn in greater detail later in this chapter, some crucial publications should be mentioned here: The presentism thesis, developed by Halbwachs (1992), has been named such by Barry Schwartz (1982) and demonstrated in recent work by Gary Fine (2001). Jeffrey Olick (1999b) provides an outstanding illustration for the path dependency thesis for the commemoration of May 8, 1945, in Germany. Howard Schuman and Jacqueline Scott's (1989) work on group-specific and particularly cohort-specific memories of Americans has become a modern classic. Eviatar Zerubavel (2004, 2) uses the term "mnemonic battles" to refer to the conflicts between groups over collective memory; and Wagner-Pacifici and Schwartz (1991) and Schwartz and Schuman (2005), respectively, demonstrate for memories of the Vietnam War and of President Lincoln how collective memory is always in flux.

19. On the longer term history of atrocities and fatalities, see Rummel (1994).

20. Giesen (2004b).

21. See Savelsberg (2010, chaps. 1–2) on historic trends and their explanation.

22. See Levy (2010); see also Misztal (2010).

23. See Burawoy (1998).

Chapter 2

1. For reviews, see Thelen (1989), Zelizer (1995), and Olick and Robbins (1998).

2. The reader may be interested to know that the Nazi regime also greatly affected Mannheim's life. It did not extinguish it, as it did Halbwachs's; but Mannheim was forced to emigrate from Frankfurt, where he held a faculty position at the university, to the United Kingdom.

3. See Alexander et al. (2004).

4. These arguments are especially developed in Emile Durkheim's last great book, *The Elementary Forms of Religious Life* (2001).

5. For example, Loftus (1996).

6. See Funkenstein (1989).

7. See Coser (1992, 24).

8. This observation was first made by Mannheim (1952). Howard Schuman and Jacqueline Scott (1989) examine and confirm it empirically for Americans' memories of historical events.

9. See Harris (2002).

10. In the analyses that follow we recognize the textbook or media depictions of collective memory as sociological sites of memories, affected by the

institutional logics of American history textbook and media production. Yet such depictions are informed by social actors who, through their involvement in legal proceedings and aware of the constraints of legal rules, contributed material and recollections that became available to textbook writers and journalists. Feeding back to individual minds and memories, the depictions read in textbooks and mass media end up affecting the minds of their readers and get transformed into "collected memories" when survey researchers later ask some of the readers about their perceptions of American history. Even within the category of collective memory proper, we encounter complex and at times counterintuitive interactions between different levels of aggregation. The growing acknowledgment of the horrors of the Holocaust in the German national collective memory, for example, appears to have increased the tendency of German families to tell their family histories in ways that exculpate their grandfathers from evildoing (see Welzer, Moller, and Tschuggnall 2002); the pressure appears to be decreasing as time advances and as great-grandchildren contribute to family memory (Staas 2010 and other contributions to *Zeit Magazin*, no. 45 [November 4, 2010]).

11. First, both scholars challenged the empiricist conception of the past associated with David Hume, according to whom we, as enlightened subjects, have immediate access to the world and history. Halbwachs turned this notion on its head and suggested that historical information is in large part generated and determined by contemporary societal conditions and interests. Second, both Durkheim and Halbwachs go beyond Kantian a-priorism, which posits that humans understand the world through a set of universally given categories such as time, space, and notions of causality. Instead, presentists recognize that the categories through which we see the world are themselves societal creations. These constructions differ across time and social groups. See Durkheim (2001).

12. See Schwartz (1982); on ambiguities in Halbwachs, see Olick (1999a, 334–36).

13. See Fine (2001).

14. See Schwartz (1982, 2000).

15. See Olick (1999b) on the commemoration of May 8 and Olick and Levy (1997) on the memory of the Holocaust in Germany. See also, more recently, Jansen (2007) on the path dependency of the memory of historic figures.

16. See also Cunningham, Nugent, and Slodden (2010), which examines the durability of collective memory for the case of the 1979 Greensboro massacre. The authors show continuities but also a decrease in the polarization of competing narratives at the expense of elite institutional accounts.

17. We use this term in a manner quite similar to Alexander (2004a, 224).

18. The related notion of "genealogy" entails elements of both path dependency (the partial determination of later events by earlier ones) and bridging (the conscious borrowing from older scripts by current actors). It is masterfully illustrated by Robin Wagner-Pacifici (2005) in her work *The Art of Surrender*.

19. Halbwachs also links this argument with the insight that group-specific memories have consequences for present-day action. For instance, writing about legal cases, "the precise solution of which cannot be found within the codes or even within jurisprudence," Halbwachs (1992, 162, 163) stresses the weight of extrajudicial knowledge and memory: "We are transported from the present, from the realm of necessities and immediate influence, to a near or distant past. We no longer see the judge of today, but rather the man of the world . . . who remembers not only his conversation with his kin and friends of yesterday, of a month or several months ago, but also his whole life and experience, the ideas and judgments that he owes to family and friends, the traditions of the circles that he frequents and of the books that have taught him." Where such memories of judicial actors diverge, space for disagreement about the law is more likely. Here, of course, Halbwachs also demonstrates that his thought is more differentiated than he is at times credited for. His basic presentist argument is here modified by insights into effects of the past on the present.

20. See Schuman and Scott (1989). Larry Griffin (2004) specifies Schuman and Scott's findings for the civil rights movement by considering space; on cohorts and memory, see Larson and Lizardo (2007).

21. See Schuman and Corning (2006).

22. See Zerubavel (2004).

23. Yet see Diane Barthel's (1993) critique of romanticized images of the past, as communicated in staged agrarian communities such as Old Sturbridge Village or Williamsburg; see also Richard Handler and Eric Gable (1997) on limits of authenticity even as tour guides attempt to make Williamsburg more historically accurate and sensitive to African American experience. We thank Diane Barthel-Bouchier for alerting us to the literature on the heritage conservationist movement and the challenges it faced in doing "the right thing," that is, displaying what had been hidden.

24. See Robin Autry's (2010) work on a new brand of museums of African American history that display the cruelties of the slave trade and slavery in some black-dominated cities or city districts. Depictions here clash distinctly with those to be found in Washington, D.C., or other white-dominated places and institutions. On conditions of success in mnemonic struggles, for the case of the gay rights movement, see Armstrong and Crage (2006).

25. See Hubbard and Hasian (1998).

26. See Kubal (2009) for an in-depth study on the Columbus controversy.

27. See Schwartz and Schuman (2005).

28. Today, of course, is always tomorrow's yesterday. See, for instance, the sophisticated discussion of the "restlessness of events" in Wagner-Pacifici (2010).

29. More recently, however, a newly edited collection appeared, titled *Legal Institutions and Collective Memories* and edited by Susanne Karstedt (2009).

On the role of law in transitional justice situations see especially the contributions by Kim Lane Scheppele (chap. 10) on constitutional courts and Grażyna Skąpska (chap. 11) on property rights and collective memory in this volume.

30. See Durkheim (1984) in his *Division of Labor in Society;* for a recent interpretation, see Garland (1990).

31. See Collins's (1998, 22) arguments in *The Sociology of Philosophies.*

32. See Alexander's (2004a, 222) discussion of the cultural trauma of the Holocaust.

33. See the influential accounts by the anthropologist John Borneman (1997) and Carlos Nino (1996), the former legal adviser to the postdictatorship Argentinian president Raúl Alfonsin.

34. On transition situations, see Kritz (1995) and Teitel (2000). See also Gallant and Rhea (2010) for an optimistic assessment of effects of post-Nazism international justice intervention.

35. See the classic contributions by Max Weber (1976).

36. See Alexander (2004b, 16–17); Osiel (1997). Specifically on selectivities of Holocaust trials, see Douglas (2001). See also the fascinating work by Lynn Chancer (2005), who studies domestic high-profile crimes. She finds that legal reactions to such cases are well suited to mobilizing social movements but are limited tools toward the resolution of underlying social problems, owing to the either-or determinations of the legal system.

37. Carla Del Ponte (2006, 2008), the chief prosecutor of the International Criminal Tribunal for the former Yugoslavia and for Rwanda, adds to these concerns. She highlights the gaps in the judicial record even within the legal frame and notes, among other factors, the lack of an enforcement agency to allow for more thorough investigations, the lack of cooperation with states that have vested interests in the outcomes, and the destruction of documents and disappearing witnesses. In short, despite best efforts, the material gathered and permissible at trials is often a fraction of the historical record. Legal proceedings are at times a dubious ally to the production of historical knowledge.

38. See Alexander's (2004b) theoretical chapter in his volume on cultural trauma.

39. Galanter (1974, 97).

40. See, most recently, Carol A. Heimer and Arthur L. Stinchcombe's (2009) examination of how individual biographies are transformed to smoothly support legal narratives to the construction of which they are meant to contribute.

41. Some variation is to be expected, of course, depending on the types of legal institutions, for example their more particularistic or universalistic designs (see Arendt 1963 on the Eichmann court and Daniel Bell's 1980 critique of Arendt).

42. Levy and Sznaider (2004, 2005); also Levy (2010).

43. See Boyle (2002); Frank, Hironaka, and Schofer (2000).

44. See Fourcade and Savelsberg (2006).

45. See Hagan (2003); Meierhenrich (2006a).

46. Simultaneously, global standards often grow out of the universalization of local problems, and local practices may serve as models for solutions—as recently illustrated by Terence Halliday of the American Bar Foundation and Bruce Carruthers of Northwestern University in their work on the global spread of bankruptcy law; see Carruthers and Halliday (2006) and Halliday and Carruthers (2007).

47. See Kwon (2006).

48. See Kalberg (1994) for a contemporary explication of multifactorialism in Max Weber's historical-comparative method.

49. On this and the following, see especially Hayner (2001).

50. See Hayner (1994, 2001); Kritz (1995); Gibson (2004a, 2004b, 2006); Roche (2005); see also United States Institute of Peace (2006).

51. See Tanya Goodman (2009) on the crucial role of emotions in the South African Truth and Reconciliation Commission.

52. See Braithwaite (1989).

53. For further explorations of the South African Truth and Reconciliation Commission, see the contributions by Emilios Christodoulidis and Scott Veitch (2009), Heribert Adam (2009), and Gunnar Theissen (2009) in the edited volume by Karstedt (2009).

54. See Wilson (2001, 2003).

55. In addition to the superordination of collective over individual concerns, specific mechanisms of narrating the truth about past atrocities color the collective memory to which they contribute, as discussed by ethnographic researchers for several South African Truth and Reconciliation Commissions. The commission's Information Management System (Infocomm), for example, favors quantifiable forensic evidence: "In Infocomm's view the only knowledge that matters is that which can be counted and measured" (Wilson 2003, 375); see also Buur (2001).

56. For the exception of authoritarian states such as the People's Republic of China, see Trevaskes (2004).

57. See Gans (1979) on selectivities of media reporting generally and Wright, Cullen, and Blankenship (1995) on reporting about trials.

58. See Kahn (2000).

59. This strategy is supported by writers such as Deborah Lipstadt (1993).

60. See Heberer and Matthäus (2008).

61. See Minow (1998).

62. See Wagner-Pacifici and Schwartz (1991).

Chapter 3

1. *New York Times,* Niebuhr, and *Time* quotations are cited in Oliver (2006, 2–3).

2. Calley's sentence was subsequently commuted. He spent 3.5 years under house arrest.

3. Barry Schwartz and Howard Schuman (2005) show this in their masterful analysis of the changing images of Abraham Lincoln.

4. See Memorandum for Lieutenant General William R. Peers, 26 November 1969. The memorandum is included in the Peers Report, available at http://www.loc.gov/rr/frd/Military_Law/pdf/RDAR-Vol-I.pdf.

5. Memorandum for Lieutenant General William R. Peers, 26 November 1969.

6. Goldstein, Marshall, and Schwartz (1976, 314–16).

7. It was not until forty years after the massacre that William Calley made a public apology. Addressing members of a private club in his native Georgia he is quoted with these words: "There is not a day that goes by that I do not feel remorse for what happened that day in My Lai. I feel remorse for the Vietnamese who were killed, for their families, for the American soldiers involved and their families. I am very sorry" (quoted in London's *The Telegraph,* August 22, 2009).

8. See Collins (2008) for a recent and distinct depiction of My Lai as a "forward panic." For critiques and expansions of Collins's microsociological approach, see Cooney (2009) and Savelsberg (2010, chap. 5). For local memories and reconstructions in Vietnam, see Kwon (2006). These representations were not available in the United States in the 1970s and could thus not have affected the American collective memory of the trial. They are noteworthy as they inform us that the three narratives depicted here are not the only possible constructions of the massacre but are shaped by historical, national, and institutional contexts.

9. See Schwartz and Schuman (2005).

10. See Ravitch (2003, especially chap. 7, "The Mad, Mad, Mad World of Textbook Adoptions").

11. See Fitzgerald (1979).

12. See Loewen (1995).

13. We performed a search for the same keywords on the OCLC WorldCat FirstSearch database and compiled an additional list of articles and also of appropriate books. An Internet database search using Google Scholar yielded additional book and article sources. Finally, we performed a simple Internet search, using Google, for the same keywords, from which we gained one website as a valuable source.

14. Each book and article was also reviewed to gain additional sources.

15. For instance, the following appears in the *Rise of the American Nation*: "By the end of 1968 Americans had dropped more bombs on North Vietnam than they had used during all of World War II. . . . Vietnamese civilians bore the heaviest burden of suffering. Though air strikes were aimed at military targets, civilians were often the victims. By the end of 1967, civilian casualties were totaling between 100,000 and 150,000 a year. By 1968 at least 2 million of the 16 million people of South Vietnam were displaced and had become refugees" (Todd and Curti 1982, 433). *Our Land, Our Time* makes a brief and indirect reference to atrocities committed by American soldiers: "Many South Vietnamese were alienated by atrocities—some unintentional (such as the bombing of civilian targets), and some of the soldiers cracking under the pressure of a vicious war" (Conlin 1987, 766).

16. On delayed responses to the Nazi regime and the Holocaust, see Weil (1987), Giesen (2004a), and Alexander (2004a). The notion of latency, while applied in sociological work on collective trauma (for example, Giesen 2004a), was previously developed in psychoanalytic theories of trauma (see Caruth 1996).

17. In a few cases there are references to some of the more graphic details of the My Lai incident, but these are in the strong minority. For example, in *America: Pathways to the Present* there is a graphic quote from Private Meadlo, who states, "We huddled them up. We made them squat down. . . . I poured about four clips [about sixty-eight shots] into the group. . . . The mothers kept hugging their children. . . . Well, we kept right on firing" (quoted in Cayton 2000, 857).

18. As a representative illustration, consider the following passage from *A History of the United States* (Boorstin et al. 2002, 813): "Shortly after Tet, the American public was shocked to hear that United States troops had killed some 300 civilians, mostly women and children, in the little village of My Lai. The fact that the Viet Cong had murdered many hundreds of civilians during their month-long occupation of Huè was lost in the American distress over the atrocity committed by U.S. troops in My Lai." The next heading on the page is titled "The Fall of LBJ."

19. Articles in the *New York Times* could discuss multiple scripts per article, and hence multiple-response analysis was used for the *Times* sample.

20. Henderson was in charge of the 11th Brigade and was the highest ranking officer to be tried for the My Lai massacre.

21. On ways in which Rosa Parks and her arrest became the symbol of the Montgomery, Alabama, bus boycott and the civil rights movement more generally, despite the heroic contributions by many others, see Barry Schwartz (2009) and his arguments on the symbolic power of oneness.

22. For these values and more detailed analyses, see "National Pride in Comparative Perspective," by Tom W. Smith (2009), the director of the

Center for the Study of Politics and Society at the National Opinion Research Center, University of Chicago.

23.   On this and the following, see GSS News (2005, 2006, 4).

24.   See Ben Schott, "Who Do You Think We Are?" *New York Times*, February 25, 2007, sec. 4, 15.

25.   See Mental Health Advisory Team (MHAT) IV, Operation Iraqi Freedom 05-07 (2006).

26.   Minnesota Vietnam Veterans Memorial, available at: www.mvvm.org/.

27.   See Wagner-Pacifici and Schwartz (1991).

28.   In Connecticut, for example, state attorney general and 2010 Democratic U.S. Senate candidate Richard Blumenthal suggested, with growing intensity, that he served in Vietnam, while he was in fact never deployed there. He must have believed that such claims would win him votes—and he did win the election.

29.   See Winter (2006, 243, 281); see also Mosse (1990).

30.   This may have been one reason for the terrifying effect of the September 11, 2001, attacks and the killing of many American civilians in those attacks.

31.   See Caputo (1977).

32.   Collins cites Gibson (1986); Nick Turse and Debora Nelson, "Civilian Killings Went Unplanned," *Los Angeles Times*, August 6, 2006, A1, A8–9.

33.   See Kelman and Hamilton (2002, 210).

Chapter 4

1.   See Richard W. Stevenson, "Kerry Maintains Domestic Focus, Turning to Social Security and Medicare," *New York Times*, September 23, 2004, A24; and David E. Rosenbaum, "Nadar Asks for Antiwar Vote and Urges Iraq Pullout Date," *New York Times*, April 20, 2004, A16.

2.   See Schuman and Corning (2006).

3.   Alexander (2003), 67.

4.   Gordon (1997); McLean (2004); Benjamin (1968).

5.   We selected the leading national liberal and conservative newspapers and the news magazine that was most engaged in reporting about the Haditha incident.

6.   Repeats and articles from sections of the newspapers that list or summarize the contents of the paper, as well as those that mention the town of Haditha but not the incident, were excluded.

7.   The same means of excluding articles were applied to *Time* reports.

8.   Article can be found at http://www.time.com/time/nation/article/0,8599,1199792,00.html.

9. See Cooney (1994) on the social structure of evidence.

10. See also McCann and Silverstein (1998); McCann (2006).

11. See Collins (2001); Taylor (1995).

12. See Aminzade and McAdam (2001).

13. "The Haditha Marines: Why do you care?" available at: http://www. freerepublic.com/focus/f-bloggers/1857282/posts.

14. DefendOurMarines.com provides links to an extensive number of reports on the Haditha incident, investigation, and legal proceedings from various news sources. As mentioned in the text, it also contains links to photo-graphic and video evidence and transcripts of testimony from each of the pretrial hearings for the Haditha marines. The site also links to other sites dedicated to raising funds for each of the marines still facing trial as well as a section of "must reads" written about the Haditha marines by family members. Finally, it contains original commentary written for the site by Nathaniel Helms (a Vietnam veteran and writer), Jeffrey Dinsmore (a marine from the same unit as those accused of the killings), Don Dinsmore (the father of Jeffrey Dinsmore), and David Allender (a book editor) and links to commentary from other conservative blogs and news sources.

15. Statistically significant at the .01 level.

16. Gordon describes the ways in which the ghosts of her ancestors, African slaves in the United States, are present in her life. She describes the ghost as a "social figure" that acts as the evidence of haunting and prompts the researcher to dig deeper to better understand the role of history in social life.

17. See McLean (2004).

18. See Benjamin (1968).

19. See Kwon (2006).

20. See Aminzade and McAdam (2001).

Chapter 5

1. See Hagan (2003).

2. See Swidler (1986, 273).

3. In this respect the ICTY story resembles that of the International Military Tribunal or the international tribunals on Sierra Leone or Rwanda.

4. This part of the story is powerfully told in John Hagan's 2003 book *Justice in the Balkans: Prosecuting War Crimes in The Hague Tribunal* and in a series of recent journal articles (for example, Hagan and Levi 2005).

5. See Hagan (2003) and Hagan and Levi (2005) on the revival of legal responses; on Durkheimian arguments on punishment, see Garland (1990); and on its collective memory function, see Osiel (1997) and Savelsberg and King (2007).

6. See, for example, Kritz (1995).

7. On selectivities of media reporting, see Gans (1979); specifically for legal proceedings, see Wright, Cullen, and Blankenship (1995); on misrepresentations of legal proceedings, see Osiel (1997, 107).

8. See Paletz and Entman (1991); Powlick and Katz (1998).

9. See Auerbach and Bloch-Elkon (2005). The *Times* proved more conservative than the *Washington Post*, putting greater emphasis on security than on humanitarian principles. Yet both types of principles are represented in both papers.

10. Publications by historians, with their tradition of referencing complete bodies of literature on a specific case, document myriad studies. Here we mention only the collection referenced earlier (Heberer and Matthäus 2008) and two remarkable and relatively recent studies of the Auschwitz trial in Frankfurt from 1963 to 1965, Pendas (2006) and Wittmann (2005).

11. See Brustein (2003, 19).

12. We did not exclude press agency reports as we are primarily concerned with what gets presented to the American public, no matter the authorship.

13. For a more detailed breakdown of the articles, see table B.1 in appendix B. There we provide basic descriptive information on the number and nature of articles, distributed over the four periods, along with the number of front-page articles, the number of lengthy articles, and the types of suffering mentioned.

14. See table B.2 in appendix B for additional descriptive information.

15. See Wright, Cullen, and Blankenship (1995).

16. Some of the following are literal quotes. Elsewhere we paraphrase to increase coherence of the thematic strings of statements from the *Times*.

17. A final set of statements concern tactical moves of the court and procedural issues. They are less relevant to our argument, but we cite them here for completeness of the record: The Milosevic-led Serbian government refuses to cooperate, despite the Dayton agreement, according to Chief Prosecutor Richard Goldstone (January 28, 1996). In light of this, Goldstone mentions the possibility of economic sanctions in the case of the Milosevic-led Serb government's continuing refusal to cooperate (January 28, 1996). The war crimes tribunal issues an order freezing the assets of Milosevic (May 28, 1999). The content of these types of statements changes, of course, after the Yugoslav government extradites the former president to the ICTY: An ICTY official reads Milosevic his rights and his indictment charging him with crimes against humanity in Kosovo (January 20, 2001). Mr. Milosevic is given physical and mental examinations according to Mr. Jim Landale, a court spokesman (July 3, 2001). Simultaneously this spokesman characterizes Milosevic as cooperative at the detention center (July 3, 2001). Finally, citing Geoffrey Nice, a lead prosecutor, one article reports that Judge Richard May cut off Milosevic's microphone after he "assailed the court's legitimacy" (January 10, 2002).

18. Nancy Paterson actually never went to court—her role was in the cowriting of the indictment and in investigations. She is a "haunting" presence in various ways.

19. Elsewhere in the former Yugoslavia silencing is practiced. On covering and reframing as ways of managing the history of violence in Croatia, for example, see Rivera (2008). On collective silence in a different context, see Vinitzky-Seroussi and Teeger (2010).

20. See Schwartz and Schuman (2005) for an exploration of collective memories through survey research in the case of Abraham Lincoln.

21. See Fine (2001) on difficult reputations.

22. See Alexander (2004b); Osiel (1997); Savelsberg and King (2007).

23. See Landsman (2005, 6) on Roosevelt; the classical contributions by Durkheim (2001, 1984, 1973); and recent developments by neo-Durkheimians such as Garland (1990), Borneman (1997), Nino (1996); and P. Smith (2008).

24. See Hagan (2003).

25. Less reflected in media reporting is that diplomats use the pressure of the court already in earlier stages in the diplomatic game. In the words of Richard Holbrooke, one of the American chief diplomats involved in the Balkan conflict, "When it was established by the United Nations Security Council in 1993, the tribunal was widely viewed as little more than a public relations device. It got off to a slow start. . . . During our negotiations, the tribunal emerged as a valuable instrument of policy that allowed us, for example, to bar Karadzic and all other indicted war criminals from public office" (http://en.wikiquote.org/wiki/Richard_Holbrooke).

26. The remaining quotations in this chapter are also from Pendas (2006); pages are in parentheses.

Chapter 6

1. For instance, the National Civil Rights Museum in Memphis, Tennessee, includes a permanent exhibit titled *Unremitting Struggle,* which gives significant attention to the institution of slavery, particularly in comparison with what is highlighted on official websites. Another depicts the Jim Crow era and the black codes. In another example of contested memory, the Texas Board of Education became mired in controversy in 2010 when it broached the idea of changing the phrase "slave trade" to "Atlantic triangular trade" in social studies textbooks. See also Robin Autry's (2010) recent work on museums of African American history.

2. In terms of neo-institutional theory, Germany and the United States are differently exposed to global scripts. The course and the outcome of World War II, in combination with the Nazi dictatorship and the Holocaust, left Germany under the watchful eye of the world and with a special burden of proof that it is a worthy member of the international community. This

normative pressure is joined by Germany's higher level of international dependency, resulting, on the political side, from the country's membership in the European Union with its sets of rules including human rights standards. On the economic side, this dependency results from the German economy's dependence on foreign trade, with exports of $6,940 per capita in 2003, high compared with other large countries such as the United States ($2,554), Japan ($3,170), the United Kingdom ($4,480), and France ($4,959) in the same year.

3. See Lipset and Raab (1978).

4. See Hagan and Peterson (1995); Sampson and Wilson (1995).

5. See Tonry (1995) on the notion of "malign neglect."

6. See Manza and Uggen (2006).

7. See Peffley and Hurwitz (2007).

8. See chap. 2 and 3; see also Kelman and Hamilton (1989, 1–20).

9. See Beckett (1997) on public support for policies such as the "war on drugs" that have had differential effects on blacks and whites. Gallup polls indicate rather strong support for policies such as the death penalty (see their November 2010 report at http://www.gallup.com/poll/144284/Support-Death-Penalty-Cases-Murder.aspx) that have long been recognized for their discriminatory implications (see Peffley and Hurwitz 2007). With respect to the Iraq War, despite the knowledge of massive civilian losses, most Americans regard the surge in troops in 2007 as making the situation there better (as of July 2008; see: http://www.gallup.com/poll/1633/Iraq.aspx), although public opinion on this war has been somewhat fickle.

10. See Cohn-Sherbok (1992, 40–41).

11. See Thranhardt (1989).

12. Note that Flag Day is not an official national holiday according to the U.S. Office of Personnel and Management website.

13. See, for instance, a running list of reconstructed slave quarters at http://www.stratalum.org/extantquarters.html (we thank Diane Barthel for bringing this to our attention). Most of these are controlled by private groups, although a few are run by states or public educational institutions. It is worth emphasizing, however, that the interpretation of slavery in the United States has a noticeably different aura from what we see, for instance, in German memorials of World War II (for example, the Dachau concentration camp). As Richard Handler and Eric Gable (1997, 230) note in their astute exploration of "historical truth" at Colonial Williamsburg, there is a delicate balance of "richer, more powerful historiographical traditions" and more critical stories of slavery in the United States. Critical interpretations meet stiff resistance and must be negotiated with the more patriotic fervor that dominated for generations. A cursory comparison of websites for slave plantations (in the United States) and concentration

camp sites (in Germany) is also revealing. For instance, the website for the Evergreen Plantation in Louisiana features serene color photos, a reference to the popular book *Gone with the Wind,* and a link to French Creole architecture (http://www.nps.gov/history/nr/travel/louisiana/eve.htm). This differs markedly from, for instance, the Dachau website, which features only distant black and white, rather solemn photos, including the iconic gate with the text "ARBEIT MACHT FREI" (labor liberates). Such differences are a microcosm of more general differences in the collective memory of atrocity and injustice in the two nations.

14. This portion of our research was conducted in 2004. There have been some notable changes in memorials and museums since that time, such as the opening of the National Museum of the American Indian on the National Mall. However, the congressional websites that guided our inquiry have changed very little. Visiting the website of the German equivalent of the state department (Auswärtiges Amt) in 2010, after a change in the governing coalition and a shift in leadership, we find a redesigned website. Memorial sites are not listed as they were before. Yet a search with the term "memorial sites" (Gedenkstätten) provides a series of links, the vast majority of which are concerned with World War II, concentration camps, and the Holocaust (see: http://www.auswaertiges-amt.de/diplo/de/Infoservice/suche/Suchergebnis.jsp [July 2010]).

15. This exhibit continues to be featured on the website of the Deutscher Bundestag (see: http://www.bundestag.de/kulturundgeschichte/aus stellungen/wege/index.html [July 2010]). Since 2008 it is supplemented by a parallel exhibit in the Reichstags building, the home of the lower house of the German legislature (Bundestag). In addition, the Berlin Holocaust Memorial has since been dedicated, covering a vast area in the center of Berlin, adjacent to the area that houses the Parliament, the Chancellor's Office, and the Brandenburg Gate, one of the city's famous symbols (for the memorial's website see: http://www.holocaust-denkmal-berlin.de/)

16. Other categories include Cathedrals and Churches, the Smithsonian Institution, Government Buildings, Historic Area Houses, Parks and Gardens, and Day Trips from D.C.; see: http://www.senate.gov/pagelay out/visiting/one_item_and_teasers/monuments_img_coll.htm. The House website as of May 28, 2004 (http://www.house.gov/house/tour_dc.html) provides a similar selection under subheadings such as Memorials, Monuments, and Points of Interest; Outdoor Theaters; Plantations; Historical Mansions; Sports; Theatres; Tours. Most sites of historical interest are listed under the first and last headings. They include all but two of the sites listed on the Senate website, while adding the Ford's Theatre where President Lincoln was assassinated (and the Lincoln Museum), the United States Holocaust Memorial Museum, and government buildings and museums that are not centrally related to the history of the nation (art, postal, Smithsonian). Nongovernment websites, directed at tourists to the nation's capital, offer similar lists, at times adding sites such as Constitution

Gardens, the Family Tree of Life Statue (honoring the African American family), the A. Philips Randolph Statue (honoring the civil rights activist), and the National Law Enforcement Officers Memorial.

17. The state department, of course, represents Germany in the international community. The selection of memorials on its website thus provides a construction of national memory that documents to the world how contemporary Germany cultivates the memory of Nazism and its horrors, especially the Holocaust, thus distancing itself from the heritage of the terror regime while accepting responsibility, to be a legitimate member of the international community of states. Beyond those included in table 6.2 are the New Synagogue of Berlin; the "Topography of Terror," a memorial, then under development, on the site of the Gestapo, SS, and Reichs Security Main Office headquarters; the Association of the Sponsors and Friends of the former Jewish Orphanage in Pankow; and a link to memorial sites to Nazi history in Germany generally, including the sites of former concentration camps that have been maintained as museums and memorials (http://www.auswaertiges-amt.de/www/de/aussenpolitik/friedenspolitik/osze/as_konferenz/dokumente/links3_html).

18. An updated exhibit is shown today in the Deutsche Dom in Berlin. The link is provided by the website of the German parliament (Deutscher Bundestag), which offers a free catalogue to the public.

19. All translations from the exhibition catalogue, legal documents, and prosecutors' interviews are by the authors.

20. They include memorials at train stations from which victims of the Holocaust were deported; the site of a Jewish community center, where Jewish men and boys were detained to be transported to the camps but eventually freed thanks to protests by their wives and mothers; and the "stumbling stones" (Stolpersteine), selected cobblestones with inscriptions that note names of victims of the Holocaust and where they once lived.

21. These listings refer to the time that this research was undertaken (spring of 2004), and we acknowledge that some changes have occurred, or are about to. For instance, the National Museum of the American Indian recently opened, and an African American History and Culture Museum is scheduled to open (as part of the Smithsonian) in 2015. A key question for this research is whether the darker chapters of American Indian and African American history will occupy a central place in these museums. This remains to be seen and might inform future research on national collective memory.

22. Only below the surface of monuments and websites lie memories of American failures, for example, in Michael Berenbaum's (1993) *The World Must Know: The History of the Holocaust as Told in the United States Holocaust Memorial Museum*, where we find references to the refusal to accept more Jewish immigrants after the Evian conference, Roosevelt's failure to comment on the Nuremberg laws, aversion to allowing more Jews into the country in the late 1930s, the ill-fated *St. Louis* (ship with Jewish refugees

refused entry into American ports by U.S. authorities), the failure to bomb Auschwitz (the text gives the impression that this could have been done), and the State Department's concealment of information that Jews were being murdered (Berenbaum 1993, 3, 49, 34, 56–57, 144, 163). Here we also find references to other atrocities that are not subjects of the museum, such as the slave trade and mistreatment of Native Americans during the Western expansion.

23. See Welzer, Moller, and Tschuggnall (2002).

Chapter 7

1. See Bilder (2006) for a complete listing of such events and for a critical discussion.

2. As a point of clarification, we use the term *law* quite broadly here to include, for instance, legislation, resolutions in legislative bodies, law enforcement actions, or the repeal of legislation.

3. See Rosenblum (2002), Booth (2001), Hayner (2001), and Macklem (2005).

4. See Schudson (1997).

5. See Balfour (2003) on slavery reparations.

6. See also Geertz (1973).

7. This argument has been powerfully developed by Jeffrey Alexander (2002).

8. See Alexander (2002, 2004a, 2004b).

9. See also Levy and Sznaider (2004, 2005).

10. Some nongovernmental organizations and government actors may in fact have purposefully used such memory to advance and legitimize intervention.

11. See Novick (1999).

12. A part of the general framework of the agreement states, "The parties agree to cooperate fully with all entities, including those authorized by the United Nations Security Council, in implementing the peace settlement and *investigating and prosecuting war crimes and other violations of international humanitarian law*" (University of Minnesota Human Rights Library, accessed in 2007, our emphasis, available at: http://www1.umn.edu/humanrts/icty/dayton/daytonframework.html).

13. See Levy and Sznaider (2005).

14. Examples include the campaign by the Organization of African Unity in the early 1990s, Namibia's Herero people's call for reparations for a pre–World War II massacre committed by German colonial military forces, and the International Panel of Eminent Personalities to Investigate the 1994 Genocide in Rwanda and the surrounding events (see Torpey 2001, 340–41).

15. See Izumi (2005).

16. See Alexander (2002, 46); Yamamoto (2002).

17. Cited in Jenness and Grattet (2001, 55).

18. See Seixas (2004, 8).

19. Consistent with this claim, Jacquelyn Hall (2005, 1262) writes that "understanding how the past weighs on the present . . . can help cut through the miasma of evasion and confusion that cripples our creativity from the start. For many white Americans have moved through what the critical theorist Walter Benjamin termed 'this storm . . . we call progress' without coming to terms with the past."

20. We clarify two points here. First, the argument about reparations in this context is explanatory rather than normative. That is, the question is why reparations have rarely been debated in Congress rather than whether the debate should take place. Second, the post–Civil War constitutional amendments clearly spoke to the issue of slavery and equal rights. Yet as Du Bois has argued, these were rights written on paper but not realized in fact during Jim Crow. Moreover, the central issue here is specific redress for crimes of the past, or what W. J. Booth (2001) labels "memory-justice," as opposed to constitutional modifications.

21. We explore this in detail in chap. 8.

22. See Polletta (1998, 486).

23. See Hall (2005).

24. Polletta (1998, 490).

25. Weber (1976); for a contemporary interpretation of Weber's argument, see Kalberg (1994, 58–62).

26. See Alexander (2004b, 11–12).

27. See Galanter's (2002) discussion.

28. For related arguments in the realm of international human rights law, see Savelsberg (2010).

29. Torpey (2001, 339) alludes to a similar point. As he notes, "Ethnic and racial conceptions of groups are more likely to have visible, ongoing referents than class conceptions. That fact undermines the likelihood that class-related injustices will capture the imagination of the successors of those who suffered them and make them into the focus of a campaign for commemoration and reparations."

30. See Harris (2002, 2006).

31. On the deactivating consequences of the failure to pass memories on across generations, see Mario Luis Small's (2004) report on Villa Victoria, a Hispanic barrio in Boston.

32. We might also think of the Emmett Till case as a recent example of what Galanter (2002) terms "righting old wrongs." After forty-nine years the case was reopened by the U.S. Department of Justice in 2004 to determine whether the two acquitted defendants were accompanied by others during the commission of Till's murder. No indictments were issued.

Chapter 8

1. *Hate crime law* is an American neologism that does not have an exact equiv-
    alent in Germany. In this chapter we use the phrase somewhat liberally to
    include German and U.S. laws that aim to control expressions of bigotry
    and hatred. We include laws that prohibit expression outright (such as
    Holocaust denial in Germany) and laws that consider bigotry as a motiva-
    tion for a criminal offense (such as hate crime sentencing enhancements in
    the United States).

2. See the Bill of Rights of the U.S. Constitution, the Canadian Charter of
    Rights, and the Basic Law of the Federal Republic of Germany.

3. See *R. v. Keegstra*, [1990] 3 S.C.R. 697.

4. There are certainly some exceptions in the United States (for example,
    Chaplinky v. New Hampshire [1942]), but relative to those of other countries
    the U.S. courts have favored prohibitions only when they are likely to
    cause an immediate breach of the peace or when expressed in the course of
    other criminal conduct.

5. The literature on differences in the United States is extensive and shares a
    rather high degree of continuity. See, for instance, the work of Valerie
    Jenness and colleagues (Jenness 1999; Jenness and Broad 1997; Jenness and
    Grattet 2001), among others (McVeigh, Welch, and Bjarnason 2003; Martin
    1995, 1996; Boyd, Berk, and Hamner 1996).

6. See, for example, Boyle (2002); Meyer, Ramirez, and Soysal (1992); Frank,
    Hironaka, and Schofer (2000).

7. See Knoke and Pappi (1991).

8. See Passel, Capps, and Fix (2004).

9. See for a thorough discussion Brubaker (1992).

10. See Koopman and Statham (1999, esp. 682).

11. These differences have been masterfully explored by a leading German
    theorist of comparative analysis, Richard Münch (2000).

12. A brief note on our methodology is in order at this point. For hate crime
    law, we reviewed relevant law texts and related literature. For the organi-
    zation of hate crime law enforcement, we reviewed relevant literature. In
    addition, given the scarcity of literature on the enforcement of hate crime
    law in comparative perspective, we conducted a set of in-depth interviews
    with prosecuting attorneys who were likely to handle potential hate crime
    cases in both countries, supplemented by a review of media reports. We
    interviewed prosecutors in the states of Minnesota and Wisconsin (14) and
    in the German state of Lower Saxony (10) in 2002 and 2004. These attorneys
    would have been likely to prosecute or be involved in decisionmaking had
    the office encountered a potential hate crime or extremism case. They were
    identified by reviewing organizational charts of the respective prosecutors'

offices or by communication with the justice minister, the county attorney, an office liaison, or the head of the criminal division in the respective offices.

13. These are murder; nonnegligent manslaughter; forcible rape; aggravated assault; simple assault; intimidation; arson; and destruction, damage, and vandalism of property.

14. Multiple interest groups and social movement organizations played a role in the criminalization of hate crimes, including the Anti-Defamation League of B'nai B'rith, the National Institute Against Prejudice and Violence, the Center for Democratic Renewal, the Southern Poverty Law Center, the National Gay and Lesbian Task Force, and the National Victim Center (see Jenness and Grattet 2001, 32–39).

15. See Jenness (1999).

16. See Jenness and Broad (1997); Jenness (1999); Jacobs and Henry (1996).

17. The American Prosecutors Research Institute, now part of the National District Attorneys Association, is a "resource center for training, research, [and] technical assistance" for prosecutors (available at: http:/www/ ndaa.org/ndaa_mission.html, para. 2, accessed August 3, 2011).

18. One such prosecutor said, "If there are laws saying you can't harm others that are different, I value that law. People have been assaulted because of their sexual orientation."

19. This prosecutor's examples include one in which "a Hmong gang vandalized a Somali home." He also remarked, "We just do not see much [hate crime] because we are so white out here." He identified hate crime with race issues alone.

20. See McVeigh, Welch, and Bjarnason (2003).

21. See discussion on Bundestag exhibit in chap. 6; for an account by one of the Parliamentary Council's members, see Schmid (1979).

22. See Deflem (2002).

23. See Römelt (1977).

24. Annual Report of the Office for the Protection of the Constitution (2002).

25. See, for example, *Kriminalistik* 85(1): 38–43; *Kriminalistik* 84(4): 202–08; and *Juristische Rundschau,* February 2003, 72. Some uncertainty appears to exist, however, between the prosecution of hate crime for its own sake and its subordination to the goal of state protection. Former federal prosecutor Alexander von Stahl, for example, stated in the wake of an attack on a group of foreigners in which the offenders proclaimed the Hitler salute, that this was evidence of a desire to "re-establish a National Socialist dictatorship in Germany" (quoted in Marc Fisher, "Germany Targets Firebombers," *Montreal Gazette,* November 24, 1992, A1), and thus these attackers are "endangering the internal security of the German Federal Republic and seeking to liquidate, invalidate, or undermine the basis of [the] constitution" (Human Rights Watch 1995, 60). Von Stahl thus interprets a hate crime in the context of state security and constitutional protection concerns. More

extreme, another German prosecutor stated in a media interview that he would decline to get involved in cases in which foreigners were attacked unless there was a political motive (Human Rights Watch 1995, 59). Similar statements can be found in our prosecutor interviews, even though prosecutors also stressed the public interest in prosecuting hate crimes when offenses against the state are not involved: "In cases of extremism, xenophobia, racism . . . prosecution is always in the public interest" and thus required.

26. Yet prosecutors also argue the need to weigh principles of retribution and deterrence with due process and with the principle of rehabilitation, especially in the case of juvenile offenders, as numerous statements in our interviews indicate. They further like to stress a need to withstand "press sensationalism."

27. Human Rights Watch (1995, 53), for example, reports that the Federal Office for the Protection of the Constitution (Bundesamt für Verfassungsschutz) has enlarged its division to focus on right-wing and xenophobic violence and formed a special task force to pool information about right-wing and xenophobic crimes (Human Rights Watch/Helsinki, interview with Gerhard Siegele, Internal Security Division, Federal Ministry of the Interior, Bonn, June 30, 1994). Later in the same year, Human Rights Watch reported that the Federal Office of Criminal Investigation (Bundeskriminalamt) increased personnel assigned to its division on right-wing extremism, restructured its operations, and established a working group to assist the states in developing strategies to deal with right-wing violence (letter from the Federal Ministry of the Interior to Human Rights Watch, September 5, 1994).

28. U.S. Representative Joseph Kennedy, visiting Berlin, openly criticized the Kohl government, saying it did not appear to have any concrete plans to combat rightist extremism (Bill Schiller, "Cancer of Right-Wing Extremism Spreading in Germany," *Toronto Star*, December 6, 1992, H1). Only two days earlier Chancellor Helmut Kohl had "sought to reassure the international community that Germany was doing everything possible to curb right-wing extremism and halt the violence against foreigners" (Judy Dempsey, "Kohl Calms Foreign Concern: Diplomats Told of Efforts to Stop Racist Attacks," *Financial Times*, December 4, 1992, 2). The temporal coincidence between xenophobic violence and a state visit by Israeli prime minister Yitzhak Rabin further fueled international criticism. In response, German authorities engaged in an unprecedented crackdown on right-wing extremists. New political parties were banned, demonstration requests were denied, laws against disturbing the peace were tightened, the state police agencies (Landeskriminalämter) created new positions to deal with right-wing extremism, and police raids occurred with greater frequency (Aronowitz 1994; *Süddeutsche Zeitung*, November 30, 1992).

29. See the impressive comparative work by the Yale sociologist Philip Gorski (2003).

30. See Olick (1999b); Shils (1981).

Chapter 9

1. United States Holocaust Memorial Museum, "Holocaust Symbols: The Icons of Memory," available at: www.ushmm.org/research/center/presenta tions/features/details/2005-04-01/ (accessed September 19, 2010).

2. The phrase appeared on the 2001 plates but not the 2002 plates (http:// www.worldlicenceplates.com/usa/US_ALXX.html). In 2000 Alabama did not participate in the federal hate crime reporting program, and in 2001 the five participating law enforcement agencies in the state reported no incidents. In 2002 the number of participating agencies increased sixfold, and two incidents were reported.

3. Examples of earlier laws dealing with hate-inspired violence and intimidation include various group-libel statutes that punished those who made defamatory remarks against others because of their race or ethnicity (Levin 2001, 725) or state laws taking aim at the Ku Klux Klan in the 1920s (Walker 1994).

4. According to the Anti-Defamation League, which tracks and monitors hate crime laws across states, only Arkansas, Georgia, Indiana, South Carolina, and Wyoming do not have hate crime laws on the books. It is also noteworthy that state laws differ with respect to the types of crimes covered under the hate crime provisions. Similarly, the specific groups protected under law differ markedly from state to state. For instance, some statutes include sexual orientation as a protected category (for example, California) while others omit this classification (for example, Mississippi).

5. According to the 2001 National Survey of Prosecutors, 90 percent of Maryland counties prosecuted one or more hate crimes compared with 25 percent of counties in Louisiana. However, the survey contains no data on the number of prosecutions in each county, so we make this claim cautiously (but see King 2008 for additional descriptive information on hate crime prosecutions for a sample of counties).

6. See, for example, Jenness (1999); Jenness and Broad (1997).

7. We might point to Durkheim's ideas on law and the collective conscience as indicative of this problem. He suggests that law reflects the collective conscience of a society. And how do we know about the nature of the collective conscience? By looking at the law. This is clearly an oversimplified illustration, but it demonstrates the potential tautology inherent to this type of argument. Garland (1990, 229) suggests a similar problem of circularity when discussing Pieter Spierenburg's (1984) historical work on executions. Increased sensitivity among the public was an alleged reason for the decline in public executions, yet the decline in executions was also used as evidence of increasing sensitivity. This logic makes an argument difficult to falsify.

8. See Azaryahu (1986); also Azaryahu (1997).

9. See Stump (1988).

10. Schwartz (1982, 395).

11. See Vinitzky-Seroussi (2002).

12. See Alderman (2000).

13. See Blight (2001, 4).

14. See Bobo and Smith (1998).

15. See Polletta (1998).

16. We were introduced to Isaacs's quote while reading the work of John Shelton Reed (1976).

17. See the work of Derek Alderman (2000, 681) for a thorough elaboration of this idea.

18. Quoted in Alderman (2000, 675).

19. A few additional points about the use of school and street names are in order. In addition to being value-laden and established methods of commemoration, street and school naming are largely the domain of local jurisdictions and local governments as opposed to state policies, thus they permit comparisons within as well as across states. In addition, the numeric presence of Martin Luther King (MLK) streets and schools is vast enough to allow for a quantitative comparison of law enforcement responses to hate crime across jurisdictions with and without MLK streets. Still, we acknowledge the limitations of using this commemorative form. Using alternative commemorations such as Frederick Douglass memorials might be fruitful because, arguably, they would require a higher threshold of civil rights consciousness. Mindful of such limitations, we nonetheless see analytic utility in measuring commemoration of domestic civil rights struggles by MLK commemorations. On account of their visibility and meaning, MLK memorials serve as a useful commemorative form for testing the association between collective memory (through commemoration) and law enforcement outcomes. Also of importance is how we obtained these data. Our data on MLK street naming were taken from the 2001 *PhoneDisc PowerFinder*. *PowerFinder* is an electronic telephone directory with a database of residences and businesses, including their street addresses. This directory is essentially a U.S. phone book and hence a rich resource for finding information on street names at the city level. Within each state we searched for all MLK streets and then coded all cities accordingly (presence of MLK street coded "1" and absence coded "0"). Although most street names were titled "Martin Luther King," we used alternate possibilities as well, including "Dr. Martin Luther King (Jr.)," "Rev. Martin Luther King (Jr.), "MLK," and "ML King," and other permutations (for example, Rev. MLK). Data on school names were taken from the National Center for Education Statistics CCD Public School Data File.

20. We collected these data from the 2003 Directory of the Association of Holocaust Organizations (Shulman 2003), which maintains a log of all Holocaust organizations and centers in the United States and includes

information on location and date of establishment. Additional information was taken from the Global Directory of Holocaust Museums from the Israeli Science and Technology website (http://www.science.co.il/Holocaust-Museums.asp).

21. Boston Holocaust Memorial, "Towers of Memory and Hope Near the Freedom Trail," available at: http://www.boston-discovery-guide.com/boston-holocaust-memorial.html.

22. For additional information about the data and sampling procedures, see U.S. Department of Justice, Bureau of Justice Statistics (2001).

23. We do so for three reasons. First, municipal police jurisdictions are more confined than other law enforcement agencies (for example, sheriff's departments or state police); including state police, for instance, would be problematic because their jurisdiction may include the better part of an entire state, yet their work is largely confined to highways or rural areas. Second, municipal police departments largely have law enforcement responsibilities, whereas sheriff's departments are responsible for staffing local courts and jails or transporting suspects in custody. Third, restricting the analysis to large policing agencies ensures that the sample is not biased by small agencies that might have very little hate crime and where the focal independent variables, commemorations, are unlikely to be present. This leaves a sample of about 491 policing agencies.

24. For a complete description of the survey methodology, see King (2008, 1364–67).

25. We measure compliance with the provisions of the HCSA as a dichotomous variable where values of "1" indicate that the police department complied with the HCSA all four quarters in the year 2000. Since local law enforcement agencies submit quarterly hate crime reports to the Federal Bureau of Investigation as part of the Uniform Crime Reporting Program, it is plausible that a law enforcement agency could partially comply by submitting reports for one, two, or three quarters of the year, yet the overwhelming majority of police departments participated either for all four quarters or not at all. Approximately 92 percent of the large municipal departments in the sample participated either four quarters or not at all. Agencies not reporting all four quarters are coded "0" in the analysis.

26. Large policing agencies in the Law Enforcement Management Statistics Survey of Law Enforcement Agencies sample were probed about their actions toward hate crime, with response choices as follows: (1) The problem has not been officially addressed; (2) the department has policies or procedures for responding to this type of crime; (3) personnel are specifically designated for responding to hate crime; or (4) the agency has a specialized hate crime unit. For presentation in figure 9.2 we compare agencies that did not officially address the problem with those that created a policy or designated personnel—categories 2 through 4. We treat this as an ordinal variable in table 9.1.

27. Specifically, offices were coded as having a policy if they had a formal office policy on handling hate crime cases, one or more designated hate crime attorneys, or a designated hate crime unit.

28. Specifically, we control for the percent black in the city and the Jewish population per 1,000 in the county in which the city is located. The latter information is taken from the Glenmary Research Center's decennial survey of religious congregations (see Jones et al. 2000), although the data are not available at the city level. We thus use the county Jewish population as a proxy for the city population in models of police departments. Also taken into account are city population size (logged), region (South versus non-South), and the degree of political conservatism as measured by the percentage of the county voting for George W. Bush in the 2000 presidential election (the county figure is used as a proxy for city conservatism since city-level figures were unavailable). In addition, we control for the presence and/or breadth (or both) of the hate crime law (depending on the outcome) and, when modeling compliance, we control for general crime reporting as measured by the number of months the agency submitted general crime data as part of the Uniform Crime Reporting requirements in 2000.

29. See King (2007).

30. Sociological research in the neo-institutional tradition refers to this phenomenon as decoupling. See, for instance, the work of Lauren Edelman (for example, 1990, 1992) for a thorough account of how and why organizations develop symbolic shows of compliance with a norm (for example, policies), even if they are likely to remain merely symbolic.

31. For evidence, see Kammen (1991), Polletta (1998), and Balfour (2003).

32. See Alderman (2000).

33. See Franklin (2002).

34. On the former position, see Gould (2005, 175); on the latter, see Jacobs and Potter (1998).

Chapter 10

1. See Halliday and Carruthers (2007); Levy (2010).

2. See Steinmetz (2007).

3. See Sikkink and Walling (2007); Sikkink (2011).

4. See Collins (2008, 83–133).

5. See Novick (1999).

6. See Hagan and Kutnjak Ivković (2006).

7. See Savelsberg (2010) on conditions and timing of the emergence of human rights law.

8. See Heberer and Matthäus (2008).

9. See Heberer and Matthäus (2008).

10. Further reasons cited include the rising hostilities against the Soviet Union and the Cold War, West Germany's failure to incorporate war crimes and crimes against humanity into its criminal code (after the 1955 abolishment of Control Council Law 10), continuities in personnel between the justice systems of the Nazi state and the Federal Republic of Germany, and the population's empathy with military leaders.

11. See Marrus (2008).

12. See Bloxham (2008).

13. See Autry (2010).

14. See the Texas State Board of Education's attempt to rename the "slave trade" as the "Atlantic triangular trade" in its social studies curriculum, reported in chap. 6. From a very different political camp, the Harvard professor Henry Lewis Gates recently wrote a *New York Times* editorial ("Ending the Slavery Blame Game," April 22, 2010, available at: www.nytimes.com/2010/04/23/opinion/23gates.html [accessed January 10, 2011]) about the complicity of the slave-trading kingdoms of western and central Africa (that is, Africans were also complicit, not just Europeans and Americans). This article directly relates to reparations, which also remains a hotly contested issue (see our review of Balfour's work in chap. 7).

15. See Mental Health Advisory Team (MHAT) IV (2006).

16. As Kathryn Sikkink and Carrie Booth Walling (2007, 430) note, every country in the Americas that had a truth commission also had a domestic trial.

17. See Sikkink (2011); Kim and Sikkink (2010); also Olsen, Payne, and Reiter (2010).

References

Adam, Heribert. 2009. "Divided Memories: How Emerging Democracies Deal with the Crimes of Previous Regimes." In *Legal Institutions and Collective Memory*, edited by Susanne Karstedt, 79–100. Oxford: Hart.

Alderman, Derek H. 2000. "A Street Fit for a King: Naming Places and Commemoration in the American South." *The Professional Geographer* 52(4): 672–84.

Alexander, Jeffrey C. 2002. "On the Social Construction of Moral Universals: The 'Holocaust' from War Crime to Trauma Drama." *The European Journal of Social Theory* 5(1): 5–85.

———. 2003. *The Meanings of Social Life: A Cultural Sociology.* New York: Oxford University Press.

———. 2004a. "On the Social Construction of Moral Universals: The 'Holocaust' from War Crime to Trauma Drama." In *Cultural Trauma and Collective Identity*, edited by Jeffrey C. Alexander, Ron Eyerman, Bernhard Giesen, Neil J. Smelser, and Pjotr Sztompka, 196–263. Berkeley: University of California Press.

———. 2004b. "Toward a Theory of Cultural Trauma." In *Cultural Trauma and Collective Identity*, edited by Jeffrey C. Alexander, Ron Eyerman, Bernhard Giesen, Neil J. Smelser, and Pjotr Sztompka, 1–30. Berkeley: University of California Press.

Alexander, Jeffrey C., Ron Eyerman, Bernhard Giesen, Neil J. Smelser, and Pjotr Sztompka, eds. 2004. *Cultural Trauma and Collective Identity.* Berkeley: University of California Press.

Alterman, Eric. 1997. "Bosnian Camps: The Barbed Tale." *The Nation* 265(August 4): 17–20.

American Prosecutors Research Institute. 2000. *A Local Prosecutor's Guide for Responding to Hate Crimes.* Alexandria, Va.: American Prosecutors Research Institute.

Aminzade, Ron, and Doug McAdam. 2001. "Emotions and Contentious Politics." In *Silence and Voice in the Study of Contentious Politics*, edited by Ronald R. Aminzade, Jack A. Goldstone, Doug McAdam, Elizabeth J. Perry, William H. Sewell, Sidney Tarrow, and Charles Tilly, 14–50. Cambridge: Cambridge University Press.

Anleu, Sharyn Roach, and Kathy Mack. 2005. "Magistrates' Everyday Work and Emotional Labour." *The Journal of Law and Society* 32(4): 590–614.

Annual Report of the Office for the Protection of the Constitution. 2002. Available at: http://www.verfassungsschutz.de/en/publications/annual_reports/vsbericht2002_engl.html/vsb2002_engl.pdf (accessed October 1, 2004).

215

Arendt, Hannah. 1963. *Eichmann in Jerusalem: A Report on the Banality of Evil*. New York: Viking Press.

Armstrong, Elizabeth A., and Suzanna M. Crage. 2006. "Movements and Memory: The Making of the Stonewall Myth." *The American Sociological Review* 71(5): 724–51.

Aronowitz, Alexis A. 1994. "Germany's Xenophobic Violence: Criminal Justice and Social Responses." In *Hate Crime: International Perspectives on Causes and Control*, edited by Mark S. Hamm, 37–70. Cincinnati, Ohio: Anderson.

Auerbach, Yehudith, and Yaeli Bloch-Elkon. 2005. "Media Framing and Foreign Policy: The Elite Press vis-à-vis US Policy in Bosnia, 1992–1995." *The Journal of Peace Research* 42(1): 83–99.

Autry, Robin. 2010. "The Political Economy of Memory: The Standardization of Oppositional Histories at Black Museums." Unpublished paper. Wesleyan University.

Ayers, Edward L., Robert D. Schulzinger, Jesus F. de la Teja, and Deborah Gray White. 2007. *American Anthem*. Teacher's ed. Austin, Tex.: Holt, Rinehart and Winston.

Azaryahu, Maoz. 1986. "Street Names and Political Identity: The Case of East Berlin." *The Journal of Contemporary History* 21(4): 581–604.

———. 1996. "The Power of Commemorative Street Names." *Environment and Planning D: Society and Space* 14(3): 311–30.

———. 1997. "German Reunification and the Politics of Street Names: The Case of East Berlin." *Political Geography* 16(6): 479–93.

Bailey, Thomas A., ed. 1973. *The American Spirit: United States History as Seen by Contemporaries*. Vol. 2. Lexington, Mass.: D. C. Heath.

Bailey, Thomas A., and David M. Kennedy. 1983. *The American Pageant: A History of the Republic*. 7th ed. Lexington, Mass.: Heath.

Bailey, Thomas A., David M. Kennedy, and Lizabeth Cohen. 1998. *The American Pageant*. 11th ed. Boston: Houghton Mifflin.

Balfour, Lawrie. 2003. "Unreconstructed Democracy: W. E. B. DuBois and the Case for Reparations." *The American Political Science Review* 97(1): 33–44.

Barthel, Diane. 1993. "Back to Utopia: Staged Symbolic Communities." In *The Ethnic Quest for Community: Searching for Roots in the Lonely Crowd, Research in Community Sociology*, edited by Michael W. Hughely and Arthur Vidich, 3:97–112. New York: JAI Press.

Bass, Gary J. 2000. *Stay the Hand of Vengeance: The Politics of War Crimes Tribunals*. Princeton, N.J.: Princeton University Press.

Beckett, Katherine. 1997. *Making Crime Pay: Law and Order in Contemporary American Politics*. New York: Oxford University Press.

Bell, Daniel. 1980. "The Alphabet of Justice: On 'Eichmann in Jerusalem.' " In *The Winding Passage: Essays and Sociological Journeys, 1960–1980*, 303–13. Cambridge, Mass.: ABT Books.

Benjamin, Walter. 1968. *Illuminations, Essays, and Reflections*. Edited by Hannah Arendt. Translated by Harry Zahn. New York: Schecker.

Berenbaum, Michael. 1993. *The World Must Know: The History of the Holocaust as Told in the United States Holocaust Memorial Museum*. Boston: Little, Brown.

Bilder, Richard B. 2006. "The Role of Apology in International Law and Diplomacy." *The Virginia Journal of International Law* 46(3): 433–73.

Blight, David W. 2001. *Race and Reunion: The Civil War in American Memory.* Cambridge, Mass.: Harvard University Press.

Bloxham, Donald. 2008. "Milestones and Mythologies: The Impact of Nuremberg." In *Atrocities on Trial*, edited by Patricia Heberer and Jürgen Matthäus, 263–82. Lincoln: University of Nebraska Press.

Blum, John M. 1981. *The National Experience: A History of the United States.* New York: Harcourt Brace Jovanovich.

Blum, John M., Edmund S. Morgan, Willie Lee Rose, Arthur M. Schlesinger Jr., Kenneth M. Stampp, and C. Vann Woodward. 1977. *The National Experience: A History of the United States Since 1865.* 4th ed. New York: Harcourt Brace Jovanovich.

Bobo, Lawrence D., and Ryan A. Smith. 1998. "From Jim Crow Racism to Laissez-Faire Racism: The Transformation of Racial Attitudes." In *Beyond Pluralism: The Conception of Groups and Group Identities in America*, edited by Wendy F. Katkin, Ned Landsman, and Andrea Tyree, 182–220. Urbana: University of Illinois Press.

Boorstin, Daniel J., Brooks Mather Kelley, and Ruth Frankel Boorstin. 2002. *A History of the United States.* Annotated teacher's ed. Needham, Mass.: Prentice Hall.

Booth, W. J. 2001. "The Unforgotten: Memories of Justice." *The American Political Science Review* 95(4): 777–91.

Borneman, John. 1997. *Settling Accounts: Violence, Justice, and Accountability in Postsocialist Europe.* Princeton, N.J.: Princeton University Press.

Boyd, Elizabeth, Richard Berk, and Karl Hamner. 1996. "Motivated by Hatred or Prejudice: Categorization of Hate-Motivated Crimes in Two Police Divisions." *The Law and Society Review* 30(4): 819–50.

Boyle, Elizabeth Heger. 2002. *The Measure of Mothers' Love: Female Genital Cutting in Global Context.* Baltimore, Md.: Johns Hopkins University Press.

Braithwaite, John. 1989. *Crime, Shame, and Reintegration.* Cambridge: Cambridge University Press.

Brubaker, Rogers. 1992. *Citizenship and Nationhood in France and Germany.* Cambridge, Mass.: Harvard University Press.

Brustein, William I. 2003. *Roots of Hate: Anti-Semitism in Europe Before the Holocaust.* New York: Cambridge University Press.

Burawoy, Michael. 1998. "The Extended Case Method." *Sociological Theory* 16(1): 4–33.

Buur, Lars. 2001. "Institutionalizing Truth: Victims, Perpetrators, and Professionals in the Work of the South African Truth and Reconciliation Commission." Ph.D. diss., Aarhus University, Aarhus, Denmark.

Caputo, Philip. 1977. *A Rumor of War.* New York: Ballantine.

Carnes, Mark C., and John Garraty. 2003. *The American Nation: A History of the United States.* 11th ed. New York: Longman.

Carruthers, Bruce G., and Terence C. Halliday. 2006. "Negotiating Globalization: Global Scripts and Intermediation in the Construction of Asian Insolvency Regimes." *Law and Social Inquiry* 31(3): 521–84.

Caruth, Cathy. 1996. *Unclaimed Experience: Trauma, Narrative, and History.* Baltimore, Md.: Johns Hopkins University Press.

Cayton, Andrew. 2000. *America: Pathways to the Present.* Needham, Mass.: Prentice Hall.

Chancer, Lynn S. 2005. *High-Profile Crimes: When Legal Cases Become Social Causes.* Chicago: University of Chicago Press.

Christodoulidis, Emilios, and Scott Veitch. 2009. "Reflections on Law and Memory." In *Legal Institutions and Collective Memory,* edited by Susanne Karstedt, 63–78. Oxford: Hart.

Cohen, Stanley. 2001. *States of Denial: Knowing About Atrocities and Suffering.* Cambridge: Polity Press.

Cohn-Sherbok, Dan. 1992. *The Crucified Jew: Twenty Centuries of Christian Anti-Semitism.* New York: Harper Collins.

Collins, Randall. 1998. *The Sociology of Philosophies: A Global Theory of Intellectual Change.* Cambridge, Mass.: Harvard University Press.

———. 2001. "Social Movements and the Focus of Emotional Attention." In *Passionate Politics: Emotions and Social Movements,* edited by Jeff Goodwin, James M. Jasper, and Francesca Polletta, 27–44. Chicago: University of Chicago Press.

———. 2008. *Violence: A Micro-sociological Theory.* Princeton, N.J.: Princeton University Press.

Conlin, Joseph R. 1987. *Our Land, Our Time A History of the United States.* San Diego, Calif.: Coronado Publishers.

Cooney, Mark. 1994. "Evidence as Partisanship." *The Law and Society Review* 28(4): 833–58.

———. 2009. *Is Killing Wrong? A Study in Pure Sociology.* Charlottesville: University of Virginia Press.

Coser, Lewis A. 1992. "Maurice Halbwachs, 1877–1945." In *On Collective Memory,* edited by Lewis Coser, 1–34. Chicago: University of Chicago Press.

Cunningham, David, Colleen Nugent, and Caitlin Slodden. 2010. "The Durability of Collective Memory: Reconciling the 'Greensboro Massacre.' " *Social Forces* 88(4): 1517–42.

Current, Richard N., Alexander DeConde, and Harris L. Dante. 1974. *United States History: Search for Freedom.* Glenview, Ill.: Scott Foresman.

Dawson, Michael C. 1994. *Behind the Mule: Race and Class in African-American Politics.* Chicago: University of Chicago Press.

Deflem, Matthieu. 2002. *Policing World Society: Historical Foundations of International Police Cooperation.* Oxford: Oxford University Press.

Del Ponte, Carla. 2006. "Investigation and Prosecution of Large-Scale Crimes at the International Level: The Experience of the ICTY." Unpublished paper.

———. 2008. *Madame Prosecutor: Confrontations with Humanity's Worst Criminals and the Culture of Impunity.* Translated by Bruno Amato. Milan, Italy: Feltrinelli Editore.

Deutscher Bundestag. 1983. *Fragen an die Deutsche Geschichte: Ideen, Kräfte, Entscheidungen. Von 1800 bis zur Gegenwart.* Bonn: Presse und Informations-zentrum, Deutscher Bundestag.

Divine, Robert A., T. H. Breen, George Fredrickson, and R. Hal Williams. 2003. *America Past and Present.* Reading, Mass.: Addison-Wesley.

Douglas, Lawrence P. 2001. *Making Law and History in the Trials of the Holocaust.* New Haven, Conn.: Yale University Press.

Durkheim, Emile. 1973. *Moral Education.* New York: Free Press.

———. 1984. *The Division of Labor in Society.* Translated by W. D. Halls. New York: Free Press. First published 1893.

———. 2001. *The Elementary Forms of Religious Life.* Translated by Carol Cosman. Oxford: Oxford University Press. First published 1912.

Edelman, Lauren B. 1990. "Legal Environments and Organizational Governance: The Expansion of Due Process in the American Workplace." *The American Journal of Sociology* 95(6): 1401–40.

———. 1992. "Legal Ambiguity and Symbolic Structures: Organizational Mediation of Civil Rights Law." *The American Journal of Sociology* 97(6): 1531–76.

Edelman, Murray J. 1985. *The Symbolic Uses of Politics.* Chicago: University of Illinois Press.

Eyerman, Ron. 2001. *Cultural Trauma: Slavery and the Formation of African American Identity.* Cambridge: Cambridge University Press.

Feldman-Savelsberg, Pamela, Flavien Ndonko, and Song Yang. 2005. "Remembering the 'Troubles': Reproductive Insecurity and the Management of Memory in Cameroon." *Africa* 75(1): 10–29.

Fine, Gary A. 2001. *Difficult Reputations: Collective Memories of the Evil, Inept, and Controversial.* Chicago: University of Chicago Press.

Fitzgerald, Frances. 1979. *America Revised: History Schoolbooks in the Twentieth Century.* Boston: Little, Brown.

Fourcade, Marion, and Joachim J. Savelsberg. 2006. "Introduction: Global Processes, National Institutions, Local Bricolage: Shaping Law in an Era of Globalization." *Law and Social Inquiry* 31(3): 513–19.

Frank, David John, Ann Hironaka, and Evan Schofer. 2000. "The Nation-State and the Natural Environment over the Twentieth Century." *The American Sociological Review* 65(1): 96–116.

Franklin, Karen. 2002. "Good Intentions: The Enforcement of Hate Crime Penalty Enhancement Statutes." *The American Behavioral Scientist* 46(1): 154–72.

Funkenstein, Amos. 1989. "Collective Memory and Historical Consciousness." *History and Memory* 1(1): 5–26.

Galanter, Marc. 1974. "Why the Haves Come Out Ahead: Speculations on the Limits of Legal Change." *The Law and Society Review* 9(1): 95–160.

———. 2002. "Righting Old Wrongs." In *Breaking the Cycles of Hatred: Memory, Law, and Repair,* by Martha Minow, edited by Nancy L. Rosenblum, 107–31. Princeton, N.J.: Princeton University Press.

Gallant, Mary J., and Harry M. Rhea. 2010. "Collective Memory, International Law, and Restorative Social Processes After Conflagration: The Holocaust." *The International Criminal Justice Review* 20(3): 265–79.

Gamson, William A. 1992. "The Social Psychology of Collective Action." In *Frontiers in Social Movement Theory,* edited by Aldon Morris and Carol Mueller, 53–76. New Haven, Conn.: Yale University Press.

Gans, Herbert J. 1979. *Deciding What's News: A Study of CBS Evening News, NBC Nightly News, Newsweek, and Time.* New York: Pantheon Books.

Garland, David. 1990. *Punishment in Modern Society: A Study in Social Theory.* Chicago: University of Chicago Press.

Geertz, Clifford. 1973. "Ideology as a Cultural System." In *The Interpretation of Cultures*, by Clifford Geertz, 193–233. New York: Basic Books.

Gibson, James L. 2004a. *Overcoming Apartheid: Can Truth Reconcile a Divided Nation?* New York: Russell Sage Foundation.

———. 2004b. "Truth, Reconciliation, and the Creation of a Human Rights Culture in South Africa." *The Law and Society Review* 38(1): 5–40.

———. 2006. "Overcoming Apartheid: Can Truth Reconcile a Divided Nation?" *The Annals of the American Academy of Economic and Social Science* 603: 82–110.

Gibson, James William. 1986. *The Perfect War: Technowar in Vietnam*. Boston: Atlantic Monthly Press.

Giesen, Bernhard. 2004a. "The Trauma of Perpetrators: The Holocaust as the Traumatic Reference of German National Identity." In *Cultural Trauma and Collective Identity*, edited by Jeffrey C. Alexander, Ron Eyerman, Bernhard Giesen, Neil J. Smelser, and Pjotr Sztompka, 112–54. Berkeley: University of California Press.

———. 2004b. *Triumph and Trauma*. Boulder, Colo.: Paradigm.

Goldsmith, Jack, and Stephen D. Krasner. 2003. "The Limits of Idealism." *Daedalus* 132(47): 47–63.

Goldstein, Joseph, Burke Marshall, and Jack Schwartz. 1976. *The My Lai Massacre and Its Cover-up: Beyond the Reach of Law? The Peers Commission Report, with a Supplement and an Introductory Essay on the Limits of Law*. New York: Free Press.

Goodman, Tanya. 2009. *Staging Solidarity: Truth and Reconciliation in a New South Africa*. Boulder, Colo.: Paradigm.

Gordon, Avery F. 1997. *Ghostly Matters: Haunting and the Sociological Imagination*. Minneapolis: University of Minnesota Press.

Gorski, Philip S. 2003. *The Disciplinary Revolution: Calvinism and the Rise of the State in Early Modern Europe*. Chicago: University of Chicago Press.

Gould, Jon B. 2005. *Speak No Evil: The Triumph of Hate Speech Regulation*. Chicago: University of Chicago Press.

Greenberg, Karen J., and Joshua L. Dratel. 2005. *The Torture Papers: The Road to Abu Ghraib*. Cambridge: Cambridge University Press.

Griffin, Larry J. 2004. " 'Generations and Collective Memory' Revisited: Race, Region, and Memory of Civil Rights." *The American Sociological Review* 69(4): 544–57.

Griffin, Larry J., and Kenneth A. Bollen. 2009. "What Do These Memories Do? Civil Rights Remembrance and Racial Attitudes." *The American Sociological Review* 74(4): 594–614.

GSS News (General Social Survey–National Opinion Research Center). 2005. Newsletter. July, no. 19. Available at: http://www.norc.org/nr/rdonlyres/5321e64c-7ad6-42b2-8c64-56adbe478644/0/gssnews2005.pdf (accessed June 3, 2011).

———. 2006. Newsletter. July, no. 20. Available at: http://www.norc.uchicago.edu/NR/rdonlyres/882D2485-7115-440A-9C9B-B28C7BDF6BAA/0/GSSNEWS2006.pdf (accessed June 3, 2011).

Hagan, John. 2003. *Justice in the Balkans: Prosecuting War Crimes in The Hague Tribunal*. Chicago: University of Chicago Press.

Hagan, John, and Scott Greer. 2002. "Making War Criminal." *Criminology* 40(2): 231–64.

Hagan, John, and Saja Kutnjak Ivković. 2006. "War Crimes, Democracy, and the Rule of Law in Belgrade, the Former Yugoslavia, and Beyond." *The Annals of the American Academy of Political and Social Science* 605(1): 129–51.

Hagan, John, and Ron Levi. 2005. "Crimes of War and the Force of Law." *Social Forces* 83(4): 1499–534.

Hagan, John, and Ruth Peterson. 1995. "Criminal Inequality in America." In *Crime and Inequality,* edited by John Hagan and Ruth Peterson, 14–36. Palo Alto, Calif.: Stanford University Press.

Halbwachs, Maurice. 1992. *On Collective Memory.* Edited by Lewis Coser. Chicago: University of Chicago Press.

Hall, Jacquelyn Dowd. 2005. "The Long Civil Rights Movement and the Political Uses of the Past." *The Journal of American History* 91(4): 1233–63.

Halliday, Terence C., and Bruce G. Carruthers. 2007. "The Recursivity of Law: Global Norm Making and National Lawmaking in the Globalization of Corporate Insolvency Regimes." *The American Journal of Sociology* 112(4): 1135–1202.

Handler, Richard, and Eric Gable. 1997. *The New History in an Old Museum: Creating the Past in Colonial Williamsburg.* Durham, N.C.: Duke University Press.

Harris, Fredrick C. 2002. "Collective Memory, Collective Action, and Black Activism in the 1960s." In *Breaking the Cycles of Hatred: Memory, Law, and Repair,* by Martha Minow, edited by Nancy L. Rosenblum, 154–69. Princeton, N.J.: Princeton University Press.

———. 2006. "It Takes a Tragedy to Arouse Them: Collective Memory and Collective Action During the Civil Rights Movement." *Social Movement Studies* 5(1): 19–43.

Hayner, Priscilla B. 1994. "Fifteen Truth Commissions, 1974 to 1994: A Comparative Study." *The Human Rights Quarterly* 16(4): 597–655.

———. 2001. *Unspeakable Truths: Confronting State Terror and Atrocity.* London: Routledge.

Heberer, Patricia, and Jürgen Matthäus, eds. 2008. *Atrocities on Trial.* Lincoln: University of Nebraska Press.

Heimer, Carol A., and Arthur L. Stinchcombe. 2009. "Biographies: Legal Cases and Political Transitions." In *Legal Institutions and Collective Memories,* edited by Susanne Karstedt, 283–315. Oxford: Hart.

Hersh, Seymour M. 1970. *My Lai 4.* New York: Random House.

Hubbard, Bryan, and Marouf A. Hasian Jr. 1998. "The Generic Roots of the Enola Gay Controversy." *Political Communication* 15(4): 497–513.

Human Rights Watch. 1995. *Germany for the Germans: Xenophobia and Racist Violence in Germany.* New York: Human Rights Watch.

Isaacs, Harold R. 1975. *Idols of the Tribe: Group Identity and Political Change.* New York: Harper and Row.

Izumi, Masumi. 2005. "Prohibiting 'American Concentration Camps': Repeal of the Emergency Detention Act and the Public Historical Memory of the Japanese American Internment." *The Pacific Historical Review* 74(2): 165–93.

Jacobs, James B., and Jessica S. Henry. 1996. "The Social Construction of a Hate Crime Epidemic." *The Journal of Criminal Law and Criminology* 86(2): 366–91.

Jacobs, James, and Kimberly Potter. 1998. *Hate Crimes: Criminal Law and Identity Politics*. New York: Oxford University Press.

Jansen, Robert S. 2007. "Resurrection and Appropriation: Reputational Trajectories, Memory Work, and the Political Use of Historical Figures." *The American Journal of Sociology* 112(4): 953–1007.

Jenness, Valerie. 1999. "Managing Differences and Making Legislation: Social Movements and the Racialization, Sexualization, and Gendering of Federal Hate Crime Law in the U.S., 1985–1998." *Social Problems* 46(4): 548–71.

Jenness, Valerie, and Kendal Broad. 1997. *Hate Crimes: New Social Movements and the Politics of Violence*. Hawthorne, N.Y.: Aldine de Gruyter.

Jenness, Valerie, and Ryken Grattet. 2001. *Making Hate a Crime: From Social Movement to Law Enforcement*. New York: Russell Sage Foundation.

Jones, Dale E., Sherri Doty, Clifford Grammich, James E. Horsch, Richard Houseal, Mac Lynn, John P. Marcum, Kenneth M. Sanchagrin, and Richard H. Taylor. 2000. *Religious Congregations and Membership in the United States, 2000*. Nashville, Tenn.: Glenmary Research Center.

Kahn, Robert A. 2000. "Rebuttal Versus Unmasking: Legal Strategies in R. v. Zundel." *Patterns of Prejudice* 34(3): 3–15.

Kalberg, Steven. 1994. *Max Weber's Historical-Comparative Methodology*. Chicago: University of Chicago Press.

Kammen, Michael. 1991. *Mystic Chords of Memory: The Transformation of Tradition in American Culture*. New York: Knopf.

Karstedt, Susanne, ed. 2009. *Legal Institutions and Collective Memories*. Oxford: Hart.

Kelman, Herbert C., and V. Lee Hamilton. 1989. *Crimes of Obedience: Toward a Social Psychology of Authority and Responsibility*. New Haven, Conn.: Yale University Press.

———. 2002. "The My Lai Massacre: Crimes of Obedience and Sanctioned Massacres." In *Corporate and Governmental Deviance: Problems of Organizational Behavior in Contemporary Society*, edited by M. David Ermann and Richard J. Lundman, 195–221. Oxford: Oxford University Press.

Kim, Hunjoon, and Kathryn Sikkink. 2010. "Explaining the Deterrence Effect of Human Rights Prosecutions for Transitional Countries." *The International Studies Quarterly* 54(4): 939–63.

King, Ryan D. 2007. "The Context of Minority Group Threat: Race, Institutions, and Complying with Hate Crime Law." *The Law and Society Review* 41(1): 867–92.

———. 2008. "Conservatism, Institutionalism, and the Social Control of Intergroup Conflict." *The American Journal of Sociology* 113(5): 1351–93.

Knoke, David, and Franz Urban Pappi. 1991. "Organizational Action Sets in the U.S. and German Labor Policy Domains." *The American Sociological Review* 56(4): 509–23.

König, René, ed. 1967. *Handbuch der empirischen Sozialforschung*. Vol. 1. Stuttgart: Enke.

Koopman, Ruud, and Paul Statham. 1999. "Challenging the Liberal Nation State? Postnationalism, Multiculturalism, and the Collective Claims-Making of Migrants and Ethnic Minorities in Britain and Germany." *The American Journal of Sociology* 105(3): 652–96.

Kritz, Neil J., ed. 1995. *Transitional Justice: How Emerging Democracies Reckon with Former Regimes.* Foreword by Nelson Mandela. Washington, D.C.: United States Institute of Peace.

Kubal, Timothy. 2009. *Cultural Movements and Collective Memory: Christopher Columbus and the Rewriting of the National Origin Myth.* New York: Pellgrave.

Kunst- und Ausstellungshalle der Bundesrepublik Deutschland, Bonn. 2010. *Napoleon und Europa: Traum und Trauma.* Curated by Bénédicte Savoy with collaboration from Yann Potin. Munich: Prestel.

Kwon, Heonik. 2006. *After the Massacre: Commemoration and Consolation in Ha My and My Lai.* Berkeley: University of California Press.

Landsman, Stephan. 2005. *Crimes of the Holocaust: The Law Confronts Hard Cases.* Philadelphia: University of Pennsylvania Press.

Larson, Jeff A., and Omar Lizardo. 2007. "Generations, Identities, and the Collective Memory of Che Guevara." *The Sociological Forum* 22(4): 425–51.

Leinwand, Gerald. 1975. *The Pageant of American History.* Boston: Allyn and Bacon.

Levin, Brian. 2001. "Extremism and the Constitution: How America's Legal Evolution Affects the Response to Extremism." *The American Behavioral Scientist* 45(4): 714–54.

Levy, Daniel. 2010. "Recursive Cosmopolitization: Argentina and the Global Human Rights Regime." *The British Journal of Sociology* 61(3): 579–96.

Levy, Daniel, and Natan Sznaider. 2004. "The Institutionalization of Cosmopolitan Morality: The Holocaust and Human Rights." *The Journal of Human Rights* 3(2): 143–57.

———. 2005. *The Holocaust and Memory in the Global Age.* Philadelphia, Pa.: Temple University Press.

Lippe, Paul. 1972. *The World in Our Day.* New and enlarged edition. New York: Oxford Book Company.

Lipset, Seymour Martin, and Earl Raab. 1978. *The Politics of Unreason: Right-Wing Extremism in America, 1790–1977.* Chicago: University of Chicago Press.

Lipstadt, Deborah. 1993. *Denying the Holocaust: The Growing Assault on Truth and Memory.* New York: Free Press.

Loewen, James W. 1995. *Lies My Teacher Told Me: Everything Your American History Textbook Got Wrong.* New York: Touchstone.

Loftus, Elizabeth F. 1996. *Eyewitness Testimony.* Cambridge, Mass.: Harvard University Press.

Macklem, Patrick. 2005. "Rybná 9, Praha 1: Restitution and Memory in International Human Rights Law." *The European Journal of International Law* 16(1): 1–23.

Mannheim, Karl. 1952. "The Problem of Generations." In *Essays on the Sociology of Knowledge,* edited by Paul Kecskemeti, 276–320. London: Routledge.

Manza, Jeff, and Christopher Uggen. 2006. *Locked Out: Felon Disenfranchisement and American Democracy.* New York: Oxford University Press.

Marrus, Michael R. 2008. "The Nuremberg Doctors' Trial and the Limitations of Context." In *Atrocities on Trial,* edited by Patricia Heberer and Jürgen Matthäus, 103–22. Lincoln: University of Nebraska Press.

Martin, Susan. 1995. "A Cross-burning Is Not Just an Arson: Police Social Construction of Hate Crimes in Baltimore County." *Criminology* 33(3): 303–26.
———. 1996. "Investigating Hate Crimes: Case Characteristics and the Law Enforcement Response." *The Justice Quarterly* 13(3): 455–80.
Matthäus, Jürgen. 2008. "Lessons of Leipzig: Punishing German War Criminals After the First World War." In *Atrocities on Trial*, edited by Patricia Heberer and Jürgen Matthäus, 3–23. Lincoln: University of Nebraska Press.
McCann, Michael. 2006. "Law and Social Movements: Contemporary Perspectives." *The Annual Review of Law and Social Science* 2: 17–38.
McCann, Michael, and Helena Silverstein. 1998. "The 'Lure of Litigation' and Other Myths About Cause Lawyers." In *The Politics and Practice of Cause Lawyering*, edited by Austin Sarat and Stuart A. Scheingold, 261–92. New York: Oxford University Press.
McLean, Stuart. 2004. *The Event and Its Terrors: Ireland, Famine, Modernity*. Palo Alto, Calif.: Stanford University Press.
McVeigh, Rory, Michael R. Welch, and Thoroddur Bjarnason. 2003. "Hate Crime Reporting as Successful Social Movement Outcome." *The American Sociological Review* 68(6): 843–67.
Meierhenrich, Jens. 2006a. "Conspiracy in International Law." *The Annual Review of Law and Social Science* 2: 341–57.
———. 2006b. "A Question of Guilt." *Ratio Juris* 19(3): 314–42.
Mental Health Advisory Team (MHAT) IV, Operation Iraqi Freedom 05-07. 2006. *Final Report*. Office of the Surgeon, Multi-national Force–Iraq, and Office of the Surgeon General, United States Army Medical Command (November 17).
Meyer, John W., Francisco O. Ramirez, and Yasemin Nohoglu Soysal. 1992. "World Expansion of Mass Education, 1870–1980." *The Sociology of Education* 65(2): 128–49.
Minow, Martha. 1998. *Between Vengeance and Forgiveness: Facing History After Genocide and Mass Violence*. Boston: Beacon Press.
———. 2002. *Breaking the Cycles of Hatred: Memory, Law, and Repair*. Edited by Nancy L. Rosenblum. Princeton, N.J.: Princeton University Press.
Misztal, Barbara A. 2010. "Collective Memory in a Global Age: Learning How and What to Remember." *Current Sociology* 58(1): 24–44.
Mosse, George. 1990. *Fallen Soldiers: Reshaping the Memories of the World Wars*. New York: Oxford University Press.
Münch, Richard. 2000. "Politische Kultur, Demokratie und politische Regulierung: Deutschland und USA im Vergleich." In *Die Vermessung kultureller Unterschiede: USA und Deutschland im Vergleich*, edited by Jürgen Gerhards, 15–32. Opladen: Westdeutscher Verlag.
Nier, Charles Lewis. 1995. "Racial Hatred: A Comparative Analysis of the Hate Crime Laws of the United States and Germany." *The Dickinson Journal of International Law* 241(13): 241–79.
Nino, Carlos Santiago. 1996. *Radical Evil on Trial*. New Haven, Conn.: Yale University Press.
Novick, Peter. 1999. *The Holocaust in American Life*. Boston: Houghton Mifflin.
Olick, Jeffrey K. 1999a. "Collective Memory: The Two Cultures." *Sociological Theory* 17(3): 333–48.

———. 1999b. "Genre Memories and Memory Genres: A Dialogical Analysis of May 8, 1945, Commemorations in the Federal Republic of Germany." *The American Sociological Review* 64(3): 381–402.

———. 2005. *In the House of the Hangman: Agonies of German Defeat, 1943–1949.* Chicago: University of Chicago Press.

Olick, Jeffrey K., and Daniel Levy. 1997. "Collective Memory and Cultural Constraint." *The American Sociological Review* 62(6): 921–36.

Olick, Jeffrey K., and Joyce Robbins. 1998. "Social Memory Studies: From Collective Memory to the Historical Sociology of Mnemonic Practices." *The Annual Review of Sociology* 24: 105–40.

Oliver, Kendrick. 2006. *The My Lai Massacre in American History and Memory.* Manchester, U.K.: Manchester University Press.

Olsen, Tricia D., Leigh A. Payne, and Andrew G. Reiter. 2010. *Transnational Justice in Balance: Comparing Processes, Weighing Efficacy.* Washington, D.C.: United States Institute of Peace.

Osiel, Mark J. 1997. *Mass Atrocities, Collective Memory, and the Law.* New Brunswick, N.J.: Transaction Publishers.

Paletz, David L., and Robert M. Entman. 1991. *Media, Power, Politics.* New York: Free Press.

Passel, Jeffrey S., Randy Capps, and Michael Fix. 2004. "Undocumented Immigrants: Facts and Figures." Washington, D.C.: Urban Institute. Available at: http://www.urban.org/publications/1000587.html (accessed August 3, 2011).

Peffley, Mark, and John Hurwitz. 2007. "Persuasion and Resistance: Race and the Death Penalty in America." *The American Journal of Political Science* 51(4): 996–1012.

Pendas, Devin O. 2006. *The Frankfurt Auschwitz Trial, 1963–65: Genocide, History, and the Limits of Law.* Cambridge: Cambridge University Press.

Pensky, Max. 2008. "Amnesty on Trial: Impunity, Accountability, and the Norms of International Law." *Ethics and Global Politics* 1(1–2): 1–40.

Polletta, Francesca. 1998. "Legacies and Liabilities of an Insurgent Past: Remembering Martin Luther King, Jr., on the House and Senate Floor." *Social Science History* 22(4): 479–512.

Power, Samantha. 2003. *A Problem from Hell: America and the Age of Genocide.* New York: Perennial.

Powlick, Philip J., and Andrew Z. Katz. 1998. "Defining the American Public Opinion/Foreign Policy Nexus." *The Mershon International Studies Review* 42(1): 29–61.

Ravitch, Diane. 2003. *The Language Police: How Pressure Groups Restrict What Students Learn.* New York: Knopf.

Reed, John Shelton. 1976. "The Heart of Dixie: An Essay in Folk Geography." *Social Forces* 54(4): 925–39.

Rivera, Lauren A. 2008. "Managing 'Spoiled' National Identity: War, Tourism, and Memory in Croatia." *The American Sociological Review* 73(4): 613–34.

Roche, Declan. 2005. "Truth Commission Amnesties and the International Criminal Court." *The British Journal of Criminology* 45(4): 565–81.

Römelt, Günter. 1977. "Geschichte und heutiger Standort der Staatsschutzpolizei." *Kriminalistik* 1977(5): 207–12.

Rosenblum, Nancy L. 2002. "Memory, Law, and Repair." In *Breaking the Cycles of Hatred: Memory, Law, and Repair,* by Martha Minow, edited by Nancy L. Rosenblum, 1–13. Princeton, N.J.: Princeton University Press.

Rummel, Rudolph J. 1994. *Death by Government.* New Brunswick: Transaction Publishers.

Sampson, Robert J., and William J. Wilson. 1995. "Toward a Theory of Race, Crime, and Urban Inequality." In *Crime and Inequality,* edited by John Hagan and Ruth Peterson, 37–54. Palo Alto, Calif.: Stanford University Press.

Savelsberg, Joachim J. 2010. *Crime and Human Rights: Criminology of Genocide and Atrocities.* London: Sage.

Savelsberg, Joachim J., and Ryan D. King. 2005. "Institutionalizing Collective Memories of Hate: Law and Law Enforcement in Germany and the United States." *The American Journal of Sociology* 111(2): 579–616.

———. 2007. "Law and Collective Memory." *The Annual Review of Law and Social Science* 3:189–211.

Scheppele, Kim Lane. 2009. "Constitutional Interpretation After Regimes of Horror." In *Legal Institutions and Collective Memory,* edited by Susanne Karstedt, 233–58. Oxford: Hart.

Schmid, Carlo. 1979. *Erinnerungen.* Bern: Scherz.

Schudson, Michael. 1997. "Lives, Laws, and Language: Commemorative Versus Non-Commemorative Forms of Effective Public Memory." *The Communication Review* 2(1): 3–17.

Schuman, Howard, and Amy D. Corning. 2000. "Collective Knowledge of Public Events: The Soviet Era from the Great Purge to Glasnost." *The American Journal of Sociology* 105(4): 913–56.

———. 2006. "Comparing Iraq to Vietnam: Recognition, Recall, and the Nature of Cohort Effects." *The Public Opinion Quarterly* 70(1): 78–87.

Schuman, Howard, and Jacqueline Scott. 1989. "Generations and Collective Memories." *The American Sociological Review* 54(3): 359–81.

Schwartz, Barry. 1982. "The Social Context of Commemoration: A Study in Collective Memory." *Social Forces* 61(2): 374–402.

———. 2000. *Abraham Lincoln and the Forge of National Memory.* Chicago: University of Chicago Press.

———. 2009. "Collective Forgetting and the Symbolic Power of Oneness: The Strange Apotheosis of Rosa Parks." *The Social Psychology Quarterly* 72(2): 123–42.

Schwartz, Barry, and Howard Schuman. 2005. "History, Commemoration, and Belief: Abraham Lincoln in American Memory, 1945–2001." *The American Sociological Review* 70(2): 183–203.

Seixas, Peter, ed. 2004. *Theorizing Historical Consciousness.* Toronto: University of Toronto Press.

Shils, Edward. 1981. *Tradition.* Chicago: University of Chicago Press.

Shulman, William L. 2003. *Association of Holocaust Organizations Directory.* Bayside, N.Y.: Queensborough Community College, Holocaust Resource Center and Archives.

Sikkink, Kathryn. 2011. *The Justice Cascade.* New York: W. W. Norton.

Sikkink, Kathryn, and Carrie Booth Walling. 2007. "The Impact of Human Rights Trials in Latin America." *The Journal of Peace Research* 44(4): 427–45.

Skąpska, Grażyna. 2009. "Paying for Past Injustices and Creating New Ones: On Property Rights Restitution in Poland as an Element of Unfinished Transformation." In *Legal Institutions and Collective Memory*, edited by Susanne Karstedt, 259–81. Oxford: Hart.

Small, Mario Luis. 2004. *Villa Victoria: The Transformation of Social Capital in a Boston Barrio.* Chicago: University of Chicago Press.

Smelser, Neil J. 2004. "Psychological Trauma and Cultural Trauma." In *Cultural Trauma and Collective Identity,* edited by Jeffrey C. Alexander, Ron Eyerman, Bernhard Giesen, Neil J. Smelser, and Pjotr Sztompka, 31–59. Berkeley: University of California Press.

Smith, Philip. 2008. *Punishment and Culture.* Chicago: University of Chicago Press.

Smith, Tom W. 2009. "National Pride in Comparative Perspective." In *The International Social Survey Programme, 1984–2009: Charting the Globe,* edited by Max Haller, Roger Jowell, and Tom W. Smith, 197–221. New York: Routledge.

Snyder, Jack, and Leslie Vinjamuri. 2003–2004. "Trials and Errors: Principle and Pragmatism in Strategies of International Justice." *International Security* 28(3): 5–44.

Spierenburg, Pieter. 1984. *The Spectacle of Suffering: Executions and the Evolution of Repression.* Cambridge: Cambridge University Press.

Staas, Christian. 2010. "Was geht mich das noch an?" *ZEIT Magazin,* no. 36: 12–15.

Steinmetz, George. 2007. *The Devil's Handwriting: Precoloniality and the German Colonial State in Quingdao, Samoa, and Southwest Africa.* Chicago: University of Chicago Press.

Stewart, James G. 2006. "Rethinking Guantánamo: Unlawful Confinement as Applied in International Criminal Law." *The Journal of International Criminal Justice* 4(1): 12–30.

Stump, Roger W. 1988. "Toponymic Commemoration of National Figures: The Cases of Kennedy and King." *Names* 36(3–4): 203–16.

Süddeutsche Zeitung. 1992. "Seiters will weitere rechtsextremistische Vereine verbieten." November 30.

Swidler, Ann. 1986. "Culture in Action: Symbols and Strategies." *The American Sociological Review* 51(2): 273–86.

Taylor, Verta. 1995. "Watching for Vibes: Bringing Emotions into the Study of Feminist Organizations." In *Feminist Organizations: Harvest of the New Women's Movement,* edited by Myra Marx Ferree and Patricia Yancey Martin, 223–33. Philadelphia, Pa.: Temple University Press.

Teitel, Ruti G. 2000. *Transitional Justice.* Oxford: Oxford University Press.

Theissen, Gunnar. 2009. "Common Past, Divided Truth: The Truth and Reconciliation Commission in South African Public Opinion." In *Legal Institutions and Collective Memory,* edited by Susanne Karstedt, 101–134. Oxford: Hart.

Thelen, David. 1989. "Memory and American History." *The Journal of American History* 75(4): 1117–29.

Thranhardt, Dietrich. 1989. "Patterns of Organization Among Different Ethnic Minorities." *The New German Critique* 46:10–26.

Todd, Lewis Paul, and Merle Curti. 1982. *Rise of the American Nation*. New York: Harcourt Brace Jovanovich.

Tonry, Michael H. 1995. *Malign Neglect: Race, Crime, and Punishment in America*. New York: Oxford University Press.

Torpey, John. 2001. " 'Making Whole What Has Been Smashed': Reflections on Reparations." *The Journal of Modern History* 73(2): 333–58.

Trevaskes, Susan. 2004. "Propaganda Work in Chinese Courts: Public Trials and Sentencing Rallies as Sites of Expressive Punishment and Public Education in the People's Republic of China." *Punishment and Society* 6(1): 5–22.

Turk, Austin. 1982. *Political Criminality*. Thousand Oaks, Calif.: Sage.

United States Institute of Peace. 2006. *Truth Commissions Digital Collection*. Available at: http://www.usip.org/library/truth.htm (accessed July 19, 2006).

University of Minnesota Human Rights Library. 2010. "Summary of the Dayton Peace Agreement on Bosnia-Herzegovina." Available at: http://www1.umn. edu/humanrts/icty/dayton/daytonsum.html (accessed September 25, 2005).

U.S. Department of Justice, Bureau of Justice Statistics. 2001. *Law Enforcement Management Statistics: 2000 Sample Survey of Law Enforcement Agencies*. Ann Arbor, Mich.: Inter-university Consortium for Political and Social Research.

U.S. Department of Justice, Federal Bureau of Investigation. 2000. *Uniform Crime Reporting Program Data: Hate Crime Data, 2000* [Computer file]. ICPSR23783-v1. Ann Arbor, Mich.: Inter-University Consortium for Political and Social Research [distributor], 2008-11-14. doi:10.3886/ICPSR23783.

Vinitzky-Seroussi, Vered. 2002. "Commemorating a Difficult Past: Yitzhak Rabin's Memorials." *The American Sociological Review* 67(1): 30–51.

Vinitzky-Seroussi, Vered, and Chana Teeger. 2010. "Unpacking the Unspoken: Silence in Collective Memory and Forgetting." *Social Forces* 88(3): 1103–22.

Wagner-Pacifici, Robin. 2005. *The Art of Surrender: Decomposing Sovereignty at Conflict's End*. Chicago: University of Chicago Press.

———. 2010. "Theorizing the Restlessness of Events." *The American Journal of Sociology* 115(5): 1351–86.

Wagner-Pacifici, Robin, and Barry Schwartz. 1991. "The Vietnam Veterans' Memorial: Commemorating a Difficult Past." *The American Journal of Sociology* 97(2): 376–42.

Walker, Samuel. 1994. *Hate Speech: The History of an American Controversy*. Lincoln, Neb.: Bison Books.

Weber, Max. 1976. *Economy and Society*. Berkeley: University of California Press.

———. 2009. *The Protestant Ethic and the Spirit of Capitalism*. Translated and with an introduction by Stephen Kalberg. Oxford: Oxford University Press.

Weil, Frederick. 1987. "Cohorts, Regimes, and the Legitimation of Democracy: West Germany Since 1945." *The American Sociological Review* 52(3): 308–24.

Weinstein, Allen, and R. Jackson Wilson. 1978. *Freedom and Crisis: An American History*. Vol. 2, *Since 1860*. 2nd ed. New York: Random House.

Welzer, Harald, Sabine Moller, and Karoline Tschuggnall. 2002. *Opa war kein Nazi: Nationalsozialismus und Holocaust im Familiengedächtnis*. Frankfurt am Main: Fischer.

Wilson, Richard A. 2001. *The Politics of the Truth and Reconciliation Commission in South Africa: Legitimizing the Post-Apartheid State*. Cambridge: Cambridge University Press.

———. 2003. "Anthropological Studies of National Reconciliation Processes." *Anthropological Theory* 3(3): 367–87.

Winter, Jay. 2006. *Remembering War: The Great War Between Memory and History in the Twentieth Century.* New Haven, Conn.: Yale University Press.

Wittmann, Rebecca E. 2005. *Beyond Justice: The Auschwitz Trial.* Cambridge, Mass.: Harvard University Press.

Wright, John P., Francis T. Cullen, and Michael B. Blankenship. 1995. "The Social Construction of Corporate Violence: Media Coverage of the Imperial Food Products Fire." *Crime and Delinquency* 41(1): 20–36.

Wuterich, Frank. 2007. Interview by Scott Pelley, *60 Minutes*, CBS, August 29.

Yamamoto, E. K. 2002. "Reluctant Redress: The U.S. Kidnapping and Internment of Japanese Latin Americans." In *Breaking the Cycles of Hatred: Memory, Law, and Repair*, edited by Martha Minow, 132–39. Princeton, N.J.: Princeton University Press.

Zelinsky, Wilbur. 1970. "Cultural Variation in Personal Name Patterns in the Eastern United States." *The Annals of the Association of American Geographers* 60(4): 743–69.

Zelizer, Barbie. 1995. "Reading the Past Against the Grain: The Shape of Memory Studies." *Critical Studies in Mass Communication* 12(2): 214–39.

Zemans, Frances Kahn. 1983. "Legal Mobilization: The Neglected Role of Law in the Political System." *The American Political Science Review* 77(3): 690–703.

Zerubavel, Eviatar. 2004. *Time Maps: Collective Memory and the Social Shape of the Past.* Chicago: University of Chicago Press.

=== Index ===

Boldface numbers refer to figures and tables.

231